How Big is a BIG NUMBER?

Sara Miller McCune founded SAGE Publishing in 1965 to support the dissemination of usable knowledge and educate a global community. SAGE publishes more than 1000 journals and over 800 new books each year, spanning a wide range of subject areas. Our growing selection of library products includes archives, data, case studies and video. SAGE remains majority owned by our founder and after her lifetime will become owned by a charitable trust that secures the company's continued independence.

Los Angeles | London | New Delhi | Singapore | Washington DC | Melbourne

PAUL KILLEN & SARAH HINDHAUGH

How Big is a BIG NUMBER?

LEARNING TO TEACH MATHEMATICS IN THE PRIMARY SCHOOL

SAGE | LearningMatters

Learning Matters
An imprint of SAGE Publications Ltd
1 Oliver's Yard
55 City Road
London EC1Y 1SP

SAGE Publications Inc.
2455 Teller Road
Thousand Oaks, California 91320

SAGE Publications India Pvt Ltd
B 1/I 1 Mohan Cooperative Industrial Area
Mathura Road
New Delhi 110 044

SAGE Publications Asia-Pacific Pte Ltd
3 Church Street
#10-04 Samsung Hub
Singapore 049483

© Paul Killen and Sarah Hindhaugh 2018

First published 2018

Editor: Amy Thornton
Production controller: Chris Marke
Project management: Swales & Willis Ltd, Exeter, Devon
Marketing manager: Dilhara Attygalle
Cover design: Wendy Scott
Typeset by: C&M Digitals (P) Ltd, Chennai, India
Printed and bound in the UK

Library of Congress Control Number: 2017954851

British Library Cataloguing in Publication Data

A catalogue record for this book is available from the British Library

ISBN 978-1-5264-0413-8
ISBN 978-1-5264-0414-5 (pbk)

At SAGE we take sustainability seriously. Most of our products are printed in the UK using FSC papers and boards. When we print overseas we ensure sustainable papers are used as measured by the PREPS grading system. We undertake an annual audit to monitor our sustainability.

Contents

Acknowledgements

This book is dedicated to the many wonderful primary trainees we have met and taught over the past years at LJMU. We have learned so much from you and we hope you have learned something from us.

About the authors

After previously working in secondary schools, Further Education and Higher Education, **Paul Killen** is now Head of Primary Programmes at Liverpool John Moores University and over almost 20 years has taught primary and secondary mathematics education to a vast range of Initial Teacher Training (ITT) courses including PGCE, Undergraduate and School Direct. Paul was also Programme Leader for Teach First in Liverpool and for 7 years delivered mathematics at the Teach First Summer Institutes in Canterbury, Warwick and Leeds.

Sarah Hindhaugh began her career teaching in primary schools where she became a school mathematics coordinator and a lead mathematics teacher for Liverpool Education Authority. For the last 17 years she has been a Senior Lecturer in mathematics at Liverpool John Moores University where she manages the mathematics provision across all ITT routes including undergraduate and postgraduate courses.

INTRODUCTION

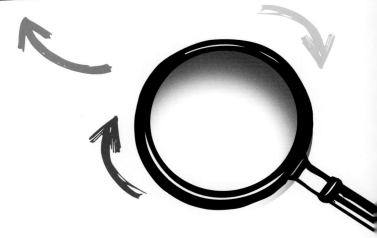

Introduction

We are passionate about mathematics. We love maths and we love teaching maths.

As such, it upsets us greatly to hear adults say, *I can't do maths* or *I hate maths*. It is even worse to hear children make such comments. We believe that through effective teaching, every child has the potential to achieve a high level of mathematical proficiency. We go further. Anyone with a negative mathematical outlook has been failed by their teachers.

Mastery of mathematics is an issue currently high on the education agenda. However, to be able to deliver mastery, teachers need to not only be confident in their curriculum subject knowledge, they must also have a deep understanding of the pedagogical knowledge that will allow any mathematical topic to be taught in the most effective way.

It is our belief that many of us were taught mathematics by being provided with a range of, what we call, 'rules and their recipes'. Very often, such rules were not explained or justified. We want all students and all children to fully understand what they are doing in mathematics and why they are doing it. A mastery approach in mathematics avoids teaching children rules and it presents all new work in the context of children's existing knowledge.

This book seeks to bring together these three elements of mastery, curriculum knowledge and pedagogy. We trust that by reading this book you will become more secure in your own mathematical understanding and will therefore become a more effective teacher. In the same way that children will deepen their understanding of mathematics by 'doing' it, you will develop your 'mastery of pedagogy' through teaching it.

It has been our pleasure to teach students how to teach mathematics for many years and it is they who have inspired us to write this book. We know that many of our students began their training lacking confidence in their own ability at mathematics. Yet time and again, we have seen them blossom into highly effective teachers with a desire to ensure all children achieve mathematical success.

Contained within each chapter of this book, we offer teaching ideas, as well as opportunities for you to reflect on various aspects of mathematical knowledge and pedagogy. We also include tasks for you to complete in each chapter. There are two types of task: the first type provides you with the opportunity to work through some specific examples related to each theme – in the appendix, we provide the solutions to these. However, this is not a mathematics textbook. Rather, we want you to think how each mathematical idea we discuss can be developed in the classroom to promote mastery. Thus, the second type of task we include is designed to offer ideas to stretch and challenge both you and the children in your class.

What maths can you see?

The key to mastering any mathematical topic and its corresponding skills is to be able to apply the new knowledge in a variety of different contexts. Equally, children need to be able to recognise the mathematics in various problems and situations. With this in mind, we will conclude each chapter with a photograph.

For the reader, this is an opportunity to think of the application of mathematics in a wide range of situations. Each image could also be used as a stimulating starter activity with a group of children. For each photograph, we simply invite you to identify, 'What maths can you see?' Sometimes the mathematics is obvious and links directly to elements covered in that chapter. However, sometimes the mathematics is less clear.

Each photograph has the potential to lead to a rich discussion about the mathematics that is all around us and to apply mathematical thinking to a real-life context. We believe that it is through such discussion that children will master different mathematical ideas. There is no right or wrong way to approach this. The teacher will lead this discussion through a series of open questions and children may see connections with aspects of mathematics that you do not. In the appendix to this book, we offer some guidance and possible avenues to explore in relation to each photograph.

We hope that you find this book interesting and that at least some of the ideas we provide will enable you to deliver stimulating mathematics lessons to all of the children you teach throughout your career.

MASTERS OF THE CLASSROOM

- Defining a 'master'
- Maths is a verb
- What does the National Curriculum say?
- Questions, questions
- Asian thinking
- Rounding up
- What maths can you see?

Masters of the classroom

Our book begins with consideration of what 'mastery in mathematics' actually is and what 'mastery' may look like in the classroom. We discuss key principles of mastery and how the teacher can develop mastery in their pupils.

Over the past few years, many educators, educational thinkers and politicians have promoted the use of the phrase 'mastery' in relation to mathematics. However, before talking about the value of any concept, we need to have at least some idea of what it is. Our, perhaps contentious, interpretation is that there are many commentators who use the term mastery, without knowing what it really is … but it does sound good!

Defining a 'master'

It may surprise you that we choose to begin this book on mathematics with a little English grammar. However, in order for you to gain an understanding of the term 'mastery', it is useful to consider our everyday use of the term, as the word 'master' can be a noun, an adjective or a verb. Exploring these different uses may give us some insight into what the phrase means in terms of teaching mathematics.

As a noun, 'master' could be used to describe such diverse things as:

- a person who owns a dog or other animal

- a person who captains a merchant ship

- a male teacher

- a young man.

These different uses of the word 'master' lead us to a number of other descriptions including: mastery; mastermind; masterclass; master of ceremonies; grandmaster; chess master; masterpiece; masterstroke; master of disguise; old Master; headmaster; bandmaster; station master; postmaster.

Equally, 'master' can be used as an adjective to describe many roles or objects, such as master chef, master baker, master bedroom, master's degree, master tape. When used as a verb, one may talk about 'mastering a skill' or even to 'mastermind a crime'.

The *Oxford English Dictionary* describes the verb 'to master' as, *gaining complete knowledge of, or skill in a subject, technique*, and the word 'mastery' as, *complete knowledge or command of a subject or skills.*

These definitions may lead you to ask, *What is a complete knowledge?*

Perhaps the greatest of all mathematical thinkers was Albert Einstein, who once said:

> *Only one who devotes himself to a cause with his whole strength and soul can be a true master. For this reason mastery demands all of a person.*

Wow! This sounds hard doesn't it? The term 'master' seems to imply being some sort of expert or genius – or even a wizard!

Given these varied perspectives on what mastery may be, it is worth considering how this can possibly apply to primary mathematics. Can a child actually be a master of mathematics? And if so, what would this look like?

It is our view that a child can indeed be a master of mathematics; the art of the mathematics teacher is to ensure that children are presented with the opportunities to enable this to happen.

Maths is a verb

It is possible to find a book that will show you where you should place your fingers on a guitar to play a D or an A minor chord. Alternatively, someone may show you where to place your fingers on a piano keyboard to play a C chord. Does that mean you can learn to play the guitar or piano by just reading about it? Similarly, we have watched many cookery programmes that show us how to bake bread or make a soufflé. Does that mean therefore that after watching these programmes we can bake a tasty loaf or know that our soufflé will rise? Like many things, the knowledge of what to do is important, but to become proficient at any of these activities, practice is required. The only way to become proficient at a musical instrument or at cooking is to keep practising. The more we engage with the activity, the better at it we become. It is the same with mathematics.

Mathematics has a body of knowledge that requires acquisition. However, that knowledge alone is insufficient for us to become proficient in it. We need to practise using this new knowledge. First, perhaps by relating it to existing knowledge. Then, this knowledge needs to be applied, in a variety of situations, moving from the familiar to the unfamiliar. In this sense, we see mathematics as a verb – a 'doing' word. Deep learning comes from *doing* mathematics. The Chinese philosopher Confucius famously said:

> *I hear and I forget. I see and I remember. I do and I understand.*

This sums up the way we would like children to learn mathematics.

Just do it

It may have been easy for Confucius to say we should get children to 'do' mathematics. But what does that mean? For some teachers, in days gone by, that may have meant finding a worksheet with enough questions to reduce the chance that a child could actually complete their work within the lesson. In such lessons, differentiation of work can become using the same questions with harder numbers.

Many American school textbooks have perhaps over a hundred questions on each topic. The evenly numbered questions have the answers at the back and are completed in the lesson. Only the Teacher's Guide has the answers to the odd numbers, so they become the homework.

Mastery moves completely away from this idea. Maths mastery is not about children completing the most questions, nor children completing similar questions with bigger numbers.

Reflection

Suppose you are planning to teach long multiplication. How would you know if each child in your class has learned long multiplication?

How many long multiplication questions would you expect children to do by themselves in order for you to be assured that they have understood the concept?

What does the National Curriculum say?

You may think that a good place to start considering any questions about maths mastery is the mathematics National Curriculum. Does it surprise you therefore that the words 'master', 'mastery' and 'mastering' do not appear anywhere in the mathematics content of the Primary National Curriculum? The words you do see in the mathematics National Curriculum include: fluency; conceptual understanding; mathematical reasoning; problem solving; enjoyment; curiosity and application. These are what we would like to define as some of the *principles of mastery*. It is perhaps by thinking of a child who can evidence some of these principles that we can move towards an image of mastery.

How to master maths

The primary mathematics curriculum is clear that children need to challenged by being offered

rich and sophisticated problems before any acceleration through new content.

You may be able to recall lessons from your own mathematics education where the teacher finished a topic before you had really understood it and then quickly moved on to something different. This is what we call *aquaplanic learning* as only the surface of each topic is considered. Children can 'aquaplane' from one topic to another, making no connections whatsoever between any of them. Such approaches result in learning not being secure and may lead to a child learning only what they cannot do. A mastery approach seeks to eliminate aquaplanic learning.

We see 'mastery' as a pedagogical approach to teaching and learning within mathematics. Any aspect of the mathematics curriculum can be developed to mastery level: by this, we mean that new learning is assimilated into each child's existing knowledge and understanding. Children need to be able to apply new knowledge in a wide variety of contexts to fully demonstrate deep understanding of each new topic. By this token, a child could indeed master a simple concept, such as knowing what a triangle is, or knowing that $1 + 3 = 4$, or a more complex area of mathematics such as long division.

A mastery approach ensures that we do not move children on to a new concept before they have a secure understanding of the one they are working on. When pupils do grasp concepts, a mastery pedagogy challenges children with tasks that help them to correctly use the appropriate vocabulary, to generalise their knowledge, to apply their knowledge in different contexts and to use the skills that they have acquired to solve new problems.

Maths mastery is developed through a rich range of varied activities. Maths mastery is promoted by discussion. Maths mastery involves helping children to gain the confidence to apply their knowledge. In short, maths mastery is high-quality teaching.

Questions, questions

For us, a key aspect of a mastery approach to teaching mathematics is high-quality questioning and discussion. Children must learn how to talk about mathematics and verbalise their thinking. We want them to make predictions, to justify answers, to think about mistakes. Children need to become confident and be willing to offer answers. Teachers, therefore, need to value each child's contribution. Any answer, right or wrong, can become a teaching and learning point. The way in which these opportunities are used by the teacher is vital. Securing learning is dependent upon skilful questioning, which is why we place such an emphasis on the quality of questions that teachers use. We have often seen students plan an excellent lesson on paper, but the delivery of that lesson was weak because the student had not thought sufficiently about the key questions that can help cement children's learning.

Essentially there are two different types of questions that a teacher can use. A *closed question* is one that has a single answer. For example:

- How many sides has a quadrilateral?

- What is the largest prime number below 20?

- What is the difference between 38 and 91?

- What is the area of a rectangle with sides 9 cm and 4 cm?

- If school starts at 8:50 am and finishes at 3:20 pm, how long is the school day?

- What is the next number in the sequence: 3, 7.5, 12 ... ?

Open questions allow the child to think more widely and demonstrate a broader, deeper understanding. Open questions have more than one correct answer. For example, each of the above closed questions can be changed into open questions as follows:

- Tell me the names of all the quadrilateral shapes you know.

- Give me any prime number less than 20.

- What two numbers have a difference of 53?

- Draw a rectangle with an area of 36 cm².

- If a school day is $6\frac{1}{2}$ half hours long, what could the school start and finish times be?

- Find the missing numbers in the sequence: 3, __ , 12, __.

Using open questions provides natural opportunities to extend mathematical discussion by asking children to explain their choices.

Task 1.1

Identify five different solutions to the open question:

- Find the missing numbers in the sequence: 3, __ , 12, __.

As a teacher, you need to be thinking about lines of questioning that:

1. Ensure children understand key vocabulary and encourage them to correctly use that vocabulary in their responses.

2. Allow children to reflect upon their answers. Rather than tell a child that their answer is right or wrong, get them to justify it, to explain their reasoning. Ask the class if anyone else agrees. Permitting children to think about their response may enable a child to self-diagnose any error they may have made.

3. Scaffold the learning in order to ensure that each child is clear about what is being asked. If necessary you should be able to 'repackage' the question to make it more accessible.

4. Extend the problem by asking the child to apply their thinking to a slightly different situation. Such questions may often begin with, *What if … ?*

Mastery Task

Here are four statements. Divide your class into groups and give one statement to each group. Children have to decide whether their statement is true, false or sometimes true. Children need to not only give an answer, but also justify that answer. For each statement, we have added some questions that give you a line of questioning to use which will help the children think more deeply about their responses. Do not feel the need to ask every question, as what you ask depends upon the children's responses.

Statement	Teacher questions
The product of three prime numbers is always odd.	• What does 'product' mean? • Give me a simple example where this is true. • Is there an example you can give me where it is false? • Can you tell if it is true without performing the calculation? • What if I only used two-digit numbers?
All numbers have an even number of factors.	• What is a factor? • What is the smallest number of factors a number may have? • What do we call numbers with only two factors? • What is the smallest/largest two-digit number that has only two factors? • Are there any numbers that have an odd number of factors? • What is a square number? Give me an example. • How many factors has your square number? Why?
The sum of three consecutive numbers is a multiple of three.	• What does 'consecutive' mean? • What numbers are multiples of 3? • How can you test if a number is a multiple of 3? • What if the numbers included two prime numbers such as 41, 42, 43? • Does it work for negative numbers? • Can you explain why it works?
The sum of the digits of any multiple of 9 will always equal 9.	• What does sum/multiple mean? • Give me some examples of multiples of 9. • What is the highest two-digit/smallest three-digit multiple of 9? • What is 9×51? • What if I multiply 9 by a three-digit number?

You can use this idea to deepen understanding in any topic you may teach.

Asian thinking

The 2014 National Curriculum mastery principles reflect those from Asian countries, which are known for their high performance in mathematics. Compared to children in England, children in these countries – including Singapore, China and Japan – by the time they reach Year 10 equivalent, are (on average) up to three years ahead (Pisa 2012).

The education system is quite different in these countries and the mindset is that all children can do well in mathematics. Mathematics teachers are specialists, rather than generalists, in their field. They are highly qualified with both deep subject and pedagogical knowledge. In particular, they have an excellent ability to question children about their mathematics in a way that encourages deep understanding, whilst identifying those who need immediate intervention. Children work through the curriculum at a similar pace, with practice and consolidation playing an important role. Differentiation is through intervention, resources and individual support.

Each lesson has a clear structure where children explore problems through enquiry, building in fluency and deep understanding of concepts at the same time. The aim is to master each topic through **Concrete**, **Pictorial** and **Abstract** (CPA) methods.

> **Concrete** – Involves the use of resources so that children can manipulate these to support their learning.

> **Pictorial** – Encourages the children to represent their work systematically as a picture to build confidence and enable a problem to be solved. We will explore this further in the next section.

> **Abstract** – Allows children, once they have the foundations of understanding, to solve problems more independently, building on the skills acquired using concrete and pictorial methods in an abstract context.

The CPA approach is sometimes interpreted as concrete in Early Years/Foundation Stage, pictorial in Key Stage 1 and abstract in Key Stage 2.

The design of the lessons naturally builds in opportunities to consolidate, explore and develop fluency of understanding: not only how to do the mathematics, but why. At the same time, in working towards mastery, children will minimise memorisation and simultaneously maximise transferability skills. In addition, trainee teachers in Asian countries benefit from developing their questioning skills, both through observing good practice and teaching their own lessons, whilst on placement in the schools.

Many schools in England have now adopted this Asian style of teaching within their lessons, using 'Singapore' or 'Shanghai' mathematics schemes. There are financial implications which schools need to consider in adopting these schemes, as the cost of buying new workbooks each year for every child and new resources for each class can be considerable. The emerging results show that many children have a much deeper grasp of the skills and concepts they are learning. However, for some children who do not make the required progress within the lesson, intervention strategies are required, sometimes at the expense of maintaining a broad and balanced curriculum.

Raising the bar

Asian teaching uses pictorial representation to solve problems. This is known as the 'bar method'. The purpose is to develop a visual picture representing the problem using blocks or 'bars' to enable children to solve the problem. Representing problems in this way develops both a deeper understanding, as well as an ability to explain the mathematical concepts being explored. Additionally, the 'picture' helps children to establish/record what they know after reading the question and what they need to find out, revealing which calculations are needed to solve the problem.

There are three types of bar method which can be used. The following section considers each of these and applies them to a variety of mathematical problems. Reading through these examples will allow you to become familiar with bar methods and see how they can be used to visually support mathematical learning.

Bar method 1: Part to whole

The following examples explore bars using a part to whole model for all four operations.

Addition

A farmer has 125 sheep. He buys 56 cows at market. How many animals does he own altogether?

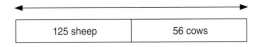

Since we know the two parts, the image helps reinforce that we need to find the whole:

$$125 + 56 = 181$$

Subtraction

264 children take part in a swimming gala; 121 are boys, how many girls take part?

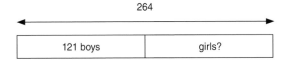

In this example, we know the whole is the total number of children so subtraction is used to calculate the missing part, the number of girls.

$$264 - 121 = 143$$

Multiplication

Laura takes six minutes to run a full circuit of a racing track. If she runs round four times how long will it take her in total?

If one lap takes six minutes that is one part. To solve the problem, we need to calculate four parts.

$$6 \times 4 = 24 \text{ minutes}$$

Division

Rob saves the same amount from his pocket money each week. After six weeks Rob has £30. How much did he save each week?

The whole is £30 and we know how many parts there are so we need to divide to find how much each part is worth.

$$£30 \div 6 = £5$$

Bar method 2: Comparison

The examples below show how written problems involving comparisons can be represented using the bar models.

Addition

23 men are on a bus. There are 16 more women than men. How many women are on the bus?

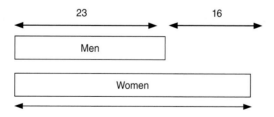

We can directly compare the number of men to women. To find the number of women we add:

$$23 + 16 = 39$$

Subtraction

Two schools went to watch a football match. School A took 276 children to the match and school B took 329 children. How many more children did school B take?

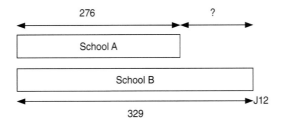

We compare the schools directly. To find how many more children went we subtract school A from school B to find the difference:

$$329 - 276 = 53$$

Multiplication

There are 15 blue flags on a strip of bunting. There are four times as many purple flags. How many purple flags are there?

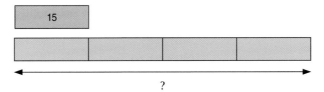

The purple quantity is four times the amount of the blue quantity when comparing them directly.

$$15 \times 4 = 60$$

Division

Using the same example of flags: There are 48 purple flags on a strip of bunting. There are four times as many purple flags than blue flags. How many blue flags are there?

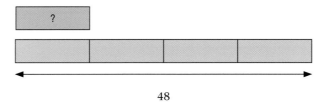

Using the inverse operation, we can compare the bars. Identifying that the number of blue flags is a quarter of the number of purple flags leads to dividing to calculate the number of blue flags.

$$48 \div 4 = 12$$

Bar method 3: Fractional

The fractional method can also be used to represent different types of calculation.

Example 1

There are 30 children in a class. Three-fifths of them walk to school. How many walk to school?

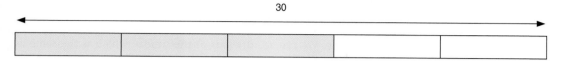

The bar is divided into five bars to represent each fifth. If we divide the number of children in the class by 5 we will know the amount of children in each fifth.

$$30 \div 5 = 6$$

We can now work out 3×6 to find out how many children walk to school.

We can then apply this method to questions with a different mathematical focus.

Example 2

A poster sold at a museum is a copy of a painting, but its dimensions are only 75% the size of the original. If the poster is 60 cm wide, how wide is the original painting?

This bar model represents the information from the problem. From this we can then consider that the orange portion is 60 cm and visually the 75% is clearly divided into three parts. Each part is worth 20 cm.

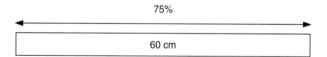

The width of the painting is therefore 80 cm.

Once children have grasped these basic methods they can then apply them to more complex problems.

Example 3

Lucy makes a fruit sundae. She places fruit into a glass and the combined weight is 105 g. Her friend Mary also wants to make a fruit sundae. Placing four times the amount of fruit in an identical glass, the total weight of her sundae is 300 g. What is the weight of the fruit that Mary uses for her sundae?

This bar model represents Lucy's sundae.

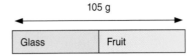

This bar model represents Mary's sundae. We can see the part of the sundae which is the same as Lucy's (105 g).

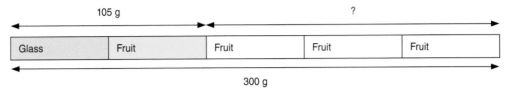

Taking that away from the total weight, the unknown quantity can be calculated as 195 g. If we calculate 195 ÷ 3 we can find the weight of one portion of fruit, which is 65 g. Therefore, four portions of fruit is the total amount of fruit that Mary has in her sundae, which is 65 × 4 giving an answer of 260 g.

Looking for patterns within bars can help us to identify relationships which help with solving the problem.

Task 1.2

Solve this problem using bar modelling.

Colette made 120 dog biscuits. She sold three quarters of them, gave one third of what was left to her neighbour and kept the rest. How many dog biscuits does she keep?

Rounding up

This chapter has introduced the concept of 'mastery'. The key message we wish to communicate here is that 'mastery' is not a new way of teaching. The best teachers of mathematics have always ensured that their children have a deep understanding of a topic before moving on. Teaching for understanding means getting away from the aquaplanic learning that is often associated with teaching each topic as a discrete element. Effective teachers of mathematics make connections between new knowledge and existing knowledge. 'Mastery' is a pedagogical approach that promotes understanding by ensuring children can apply their knowledge to a range of problems and contexts. Teaching for mastery includes rich discussion and questioning to allow children to become more confident in their application of skills.

Within this chapter we have also introduced the bar model which we feel is **one** useful tool to aid children in their thinking about number problems. Many people think that mastery equals the bar model. However, it is possible to use the bar model without developing mastery and it is also possible to develop mastery without the bar model.

WHAT MATHS CAN YOU SEE?

MASTERS
OF THE
CLASSROOM

NOT AS EASY AS 1, 2, 3

- How do children learn to count?
- Step back in time
- Starting addition
- The place of place value
- Rounding up
- What maths can you see?

Not as easy as 1, 2, 3

We can all imagine the small child wheeled out at a special occasion to demonstrate their counting skills. They stand in front of an attentive audience of grandparents, aunts, uncles and cousins. Mum or Dad says 'show everyone that you can count to 10', and off they go. Everyone smiles in anticipation, and when the child finally reaches 10 the room erupts in rapturous applause. But can that child really count?

How do children learn to count?

Gelman and Gallistell (1978)[1] explored early number acquisition and highlighted five key principles that children need to demonstrate, to show an understanding of number and how to count.

The first three principles are grouped together as the 'how to count principles'.

1.   The **Stable Order Principle** – all numbers are counted in the same repeatable order. We do not, for example, say 1, 2, 3, 4 one day then change to 1, 4, 3, 2 the next time we count.

2.   The **1 to 1 Principle** – when children count objects they need to apply the stable order principle, and then use one number name to one object. Children demonstrate this by counting on their fingers.

3.   The **Cardinal Principle** – this principle is the most important in our view. It is gaining an understanding that the last number you say, when counting a group of objects, shows the total size of the set. An ability to demonstrate an understanding of this principle is vital in proving that a child can count.

For example, suppose a child is counting some toy bricks.

| 1 | 2 | 3 | 4 | 5 |

If the child can point to each brick and say its corresponding number in order, they are evidencing the **Stable Order** and **1 to 1** principles. The teacher then asks, *How many cubes are there?* The child can respond in a variety of ways: they may start counting at the beginning again or they may keep going upwards. It is only when a child can respond to the question stating, *There are five*, that they show they have grasped the **Cardinal** principle. Without asking the follow-up question, *How many are there?*, you will not be able to assess whether the child understands or not. Just being able to point at the bricks and say 1, 2, 3, 4, 5 in order is not enough.

If we reflect back to our initial example of the child counting out loud in front of family and friends, it is now easy to see that the child knows only the stable order principle; they are reciting the repeatable order but are not counting. Counting is showing that you can find the number of elements in a set or group.

---

[1]Gelman, R. & Gallistel, C. (1978) *The Child's Understanding of Number.* Cambridge, MA: Harvard University Press.

As a teacher, you need to be aware of the mistakes children make when learning and use these mistakes to develop deeper understanding. Provide opportunities to draw these errors out so that children can learn from them.

Task 2.1

Counting to 10 on your fingers

Slowly count to 10 using your fingers to support.

1. Consider the possible errors children could make which would result in an inaccurate total.

2. The child counts all fingers but says there are only 9 instead of 10. What is the mistake they may have made?

The final two principles are the 'what to count' principles. These develop the initial 'how to count' principles, further consolidating understanding and exploring the wider contexts of counting.

4. The **Abstract Principle** – everything can be counted. The items being counted do not have to all be the same and we do not need to physically have the objects in front of us to be able to count them. For example, a child can count the number of pets they own without having to physically have the pets in class with them.

5. The **Order Irrelevance Principle** – it doesn't matter in what order you count the objects, the answer will still be the same. This will also be the same wherever you start from.

Reflection

Examine the Early Years Foundation Stage Curriculum section on number development and identify the statements which link to the five principles of counting.

In order for children to develop a deep understanding of each of these principles, it is important that the teacher provides opportunities for them to develop strategies to solve different counting situations.

Teaching idea

Developing the abstract and order irrelevance principle

Toys in a row - put a number of different objects in a row, for example, a teddy, a car and a book. Ask the child to count the objects.

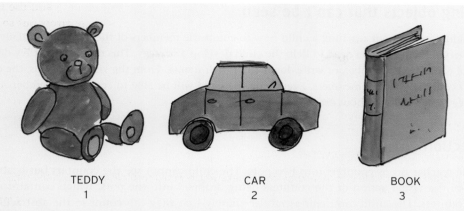

TEDDY	CAR	BOOK
1	2	3

Once they have correctly identified that there are three objects, ask the child to count them again but starting with the car. This can be a very difficult concept for children to learn. The usual pattern is to start counting in a line, left to right, but now this is not what is being asked for.

Now the car is number 1 the child has a choice for 2 and 3. The count will now be:

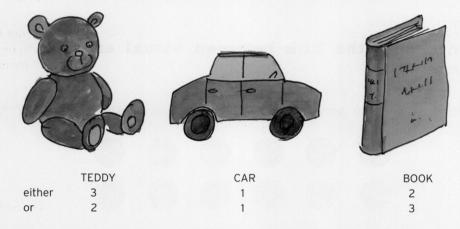

	TEDDY	CAR	BOOK
either	3	1	2
or	2	1	3

Eventually they will be able to do it, but initially the awkwardness of not counting in a row from left to right can be very confusing.

Once they have grasped this concept using three objects, extend the number of objects to four or five.

Counting objects in a circle

This teaching idea can be developed further in a number of ways. Children's initial experience of counting will often relate to objects in a straight line. As they grow in confidence it is important to use different scenarios. By placing some objects in a circle, a greater counting challenge is given. Once the child has started counting, are they able to remember where to stop? To support this, you may initially mark the start and stop points. This can be done using counters or a mark. Alternatively, you may want to approach this more creatively with start and stop signs for a race. In addition, counting both clockwise and anticlockwise introduces a further challenge.

Counting objects that can't be seen

How would you go about teaching a child how to count the members of their family? Initially this may be very difficult, so you need to help the child develop a strategy. This may be that they draw a picture of each family member, or write down all of their names. From the visual stimulus, the child can then count the family members. Eventually the child will be able to count the members using the strategy to visualise without drawing the picture.

Abstraction

Here, the teacher drops counters into two pots. The child cannot see the counters but is able to state from the visual action of the counters being dropped into the pots, which contains more or less counters. The child can demonstrate accurately that they can count in the abstract; stating how many counters are in the pot without being able to see them. You will however find that when children can see the counters they are not always as accurate. The next teaching idea explores this further.

Teaching idea

Reinforcing the link between visual and concrete

Place some counters in two identical lines and ask the child which row has the most.

The child states that they are both the same. But what happens when one row is spread out more?

The response of the child may be different here. Quite often they will say that the purple line is longer. As the teacher, you need to draw this misconception out. You cannot presume that the child will be able to grasp this. The visual image is stronger and therefore the child is wrong. What should your next response be?

Response: Ask the child to count the counters lining them up again to start to make the link between the two lines. Talk with the child once they have realised they were incorrect to get them to explain why they think they got the wrong answer.

As children develop an understanding of numbers it is important for them to count a variety of different objects to develop deeper understanding and to challenge them.

Counting actions

Ask a child to jump five times and count along with their jumps. Initially this may seem quite straightforward. If the teacher sets the beat, then, yes, the children will count along. However, if no beat is given the child has no guidance how to jump and therefore the counting will be considerably harder as they won't know the pulse and it may not be regular.

The same situation can arise when counting sounds. Say for example you are beating a drum and you want your children to count the beats. Be mindful of two things: first, the timings of your beats, and second, that they are counting the noise and not the action. We would suggest that the children close their eyes or the drum is hidden behind something. It's important to focus on the sound rather than your hand movement.

Counting pictures

There will be situations when you want children to count pictures in a book. When counting from a worksheet, or something similar, it is easy to use a pen to mark each item as you count it. However, with a book this isn't so easy. Use counters, or laminated copies of the pictures to cover the objects. Once all the pictures are covered with counters or pictures collect them together and line them up to enable the child to count them more easily.

The process is similar when trying to count objects that are out of reach: the number of lights in a room; how many windows are on a building; or tables laid out in a room.

Strategies such as standing children under the object, taking photographs or making markers as you count are all ways to support children with beginning to understand the variety of different ways that any counting situation can be solved.

Seeing patterns

Part of learning to count is developing the ability to see patterns. Children will explore this concept in various ways. First, by looking for patterns in pictures or creating their own sequence of patterns with beads.

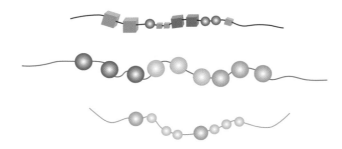

They can also create patterns by copying a given instruction. This develops other skills such as hand–eye coordination and concentration.

Recognising numbers

Whilst we develop an understanding of counting and the Cardinal Principle, we also need to develop children's ability to recognise the numerical representation.

For example:

A child can count these faces and state that there are three of them. In addition, they need to be able to match the quantity with the symbol for number 3.

This can be explored through play:

• Painting numbers with dots or patterns to represent the number.

• Making numbers using stencils.

• Decorating modelling clay numbers with the correct amount of counters.

• Jigsaws or games which encourage matching the quantity to the number.

Words don't come easy

Children start school with a wide range of levels of language development and vocabulary. Some have only a few words and some can hold small conversations. This can be affected by their home experience, number of siblings, whether they attend a nursery or if they are an only child.

Whilst we are teaching children early mathematics skills we also develop their vocabulary. It is important to remember that when we teach a child new mathematical terms, they may be thinking something completely different.

When we teach maths, we must remember that many mathematical terms have different meanings in everyday life. This can cause a barrier with children when they are using the word in a mathematical context.

Reflection

Consider the mathematical versus everyday usage of these words:

digit, take-away, volume, operation, kite, table, mean, axes, balance, difference, index, key, net, order, point, unit, face.

It is important that you are confident in your own understanding of mathematical vocabulary. This website will help you to do this and help you explain the terms at the appropriate level for children to understand.

www.amathsdictionaryforkids.com

Step back in time

Throughout time, each major civilisation had their own system for recording numbers. If this book was about the history of mathematics, then it would be really useful to explore some of these ancient systems and consider similarities. Indeed, the more studious reader may find such an investigation to be a valuable way to spend some time. Such endeavour could provide useful cross curricular ideas to directly link mathematics and history. It is also worth pointing out that some languages did not have 'numbers' as we understand them today: they may have had a word for 'one' and a different word for 'two', but anything after that would be a word equivalent to 'lots'.

A good place to start thinking about number systems is some 2,000–3,000 years ago when the Roman Empire was the centre of the civilised world. The Roman method of recording numbers is still used today for some analogue clocks/watches, or as dates at the end of films. Perhaps today, the Roman number system is only utilised for artistic effect rather than mathematical usefulness; however, this hasn't stopped politicians wanting all children to know how to write every number up to 1,000 in Roman numerals.

It is easy to see how the Roman system came about and there is logic to how the numbers are constructed. Perhaps the first step was to use a simple line (or maybe it was a notch on a stick) to represent the number one. Thus, the numbers two and three could be represented by two or three lines. It quickly becomes apparent, though, how impractical it would be to have 10, 20 or, say, 37 notches to represent those numbers. This led to important numbers such as 5, 10, 50 and 100 being given their own unique symbol. Later, 500 and 1,000 were also given their own symbol.

Number	1	5	10	50	100	500	1,000
Roman symbol	I	V	X	L	C	D	M

Every number can now be considered as either above or below the key symbol or broken down into parts that sum to the number. For example:

Number	Roman symbol	Notes
4	IV	1 before 5
7	VII	2 after 5
13	XIII	3 after 10
15	XV	5 after 10
30	XXX	Three lots of 10
48	XLVIII	10 before 50 plus 5 add 3
74	LXXIV	50 plus 20 plus 4

The National Curriculum states that, by the end of Year 4, children need to know the Roman numeral symbol for all numbers 1 to 100. By Year 5 they should know how to read all Roman numerals up to 1,000 and recognise years written in Roman numerals. In Appendix 4, we provide a full list of Roman numerals from 1 to 1,000.

Even at the time of the Romans, their number system was only of limited use. Roman numerals were a method for allocating a symbol to a numerical value. However, there was no such concept as place value and they didn't have a zero. You cannot use column addition to add XXIV to XLV. This meant it was very difficult to do any sort of calculations, no matter how simple, using Roman numerals. For calculating multiplication or division, men had to be employed to do the working out. They were known as the 'calculators'.

It is difficult for us to justify the inclusion of Roman numerals to 1,000 in a twenty-first century curriculum as Roman numerals have such a limited application. Indeed, it could be argued that what children really need to learn about is how binary numbers work, as these are fundamental to every computer, mobile telephone and electronic gadget we use. Alas, binary is not in the mathematics curriculum at all – not even in Key Stages 3 and 4.

Wanting for nothing

Once children have grasped the initial counting tools, an understanding of place value is needed and for this we need to introduce the symbol for zero. It is hard today to imagine a world without a zero, however zero was not part of Western number systems until the early 1200s, when an Italian mathematician called Fibonacci first wrote about it. Neither the Romans nor the Greeks had a symbol for zero. Fibonacci actually stole the idea from the Hindu Arabic number system which had been using a base 10 system for some 200 years.

Our counting system only works if we start counting from zero. Children also need to appreciate what the zero means in numbers such as 1,200, 120, 102, 12, 1.02, 0.12, 0.120.

In all of these numbers, zero is used as a *place holder*. Without zero, how could we write the number one hundred and two? We take zero for granted but it is of enormous importance.

Letter from Zero

A wonderful teacher, Beth Comer, who teaches in one of the schools we work with, is always thinking of new and innovative approaches to her mathematics teaching. She really wanted the children in her class to appreciate the importance of zero and so she decided to send a letter to her class from zero. Beth has kindly given us permission to replicate her letter.

Dear Year 3

My name is Zero and I have a problem. All of the other numbers are being mean to me and I feel really upset.

The other numbers have been picking on me for a while now. They keep saying I am worthless and nobody cares about me because I am nothing. I try to make friends with other numbers but I don't feel that I belong anywhere.

At the weekend I was trying to hang around with some of the other numbers but the positives say I am not one of them so I can't play with them. So I went to see the negative numbers, but they aren't much nicer. They say I don't belong to their gang because I don't have a minus sign in front of me!

The numbers say I look like a letter but I can't even hang out with the Roman numerals, who look like letters, because they don't have a zero in their number system. I mean, what kind of system do they call that?

I don't feel wanted by anyone. People keep forgetting to include me when they write numbers that have a zero in them so I'm thinking I should just give up being a number and find another job.

Am I worth nothing? Or am I important? Should I give up on being a number and find a new job?

Please help me.

Your friend

Zero (0)

Each child had to write a reply to Zero. Below is just one of the responses from Beth's Year 3 class.

I feel bad for you been left out by those misrible positive / negative numbers. When you are a place holder. I'ld be delited to help you find freinds. Just beleve in your self. becaus you are the best number ever. and you are the importint number in our sytem. also you are uniqle I don't care if you are not in the Roman numerals. I do care that your okay. Why don you come to make freinds witl the humans. because we lik you!.

best of luck

Here the child not only proves themselves to be a very caring individual, they have recognised that zero is very important as it is a place holder.

Starting addition

As children develop an increased understanding of the five principles of counting, they start to explore simple addition and subtraction. Children need to use resources to support the stages in order to develop an understanding through visual representation. For example, suppose a child is using counters to find 4 + 7.

The child will initially be taught to put together both groups and then to count all of the counters.

Eventually they will come to realise that it is much quicker to start with the four and then add on the seven.

As the children develop their understanding further, they then move to the even more efficient method of starting at the largest number first and adding the smallest number.

Addition is **commutative**, which means the numbers can be added in any order and the outcome will be the same. So, 4 + 7 = 7 + 4.

Reflection

Mal completes the following addition and shows how she has worked it out using a number line.

What does this response tell you about Mal's understanding?

4 + 3 + 5 =

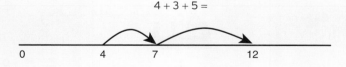

0   4   7   12

The place of place value

Our number system works using base 10. Children can find the concept of place value hard to understand. We use the numerals 0, 1, 2, 3, 4, 5, 6, 7, 8, 9 and where we place them, and in what order, determines their value.

Hundreds	Tens	Ones
		□ 1
	▭▭▭▭▭▭▭▭▭ 1	0
[10×10 grid] 1	0	0

When we start to teach children place value it is often hard to understand why in some cases they 'don't get it'.

To explore this further we are going to teach you numbers. To give you a feel for the complexities of learning place value for the first time, let us assume that base 10 doesn't exist. We are going to teach you in base 6. This is a fun activity based upon eggs.

Trays	Boxes	Eggs
		  1
	  1	0
  1	0	0

In base 6 we have ones, boxes and trays. There are six eggs in one box and six boxes in one tray.

Looking at the above diagram the number representing one box is 10. Here the numeral 1 represents the one box and zero is a place holder. This is not 10 as 'ten' as this does not exist in base 6, but 'one zero'. Six boxes then become one tray represented by 100; one zero zero.

Exploring this further, the number 23 in this number system is represented in the following way:

Boxes	Eggs
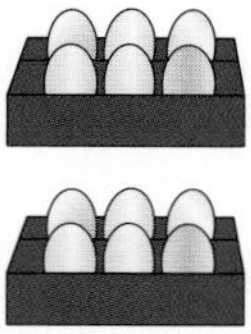 2	 3

Once an understanding of this is established we can move on to simple addition and subtraction. We begin with adding the base 6 numbers, 23 and 5. In pictorial form this would look like:

	Boxes	Eggs
	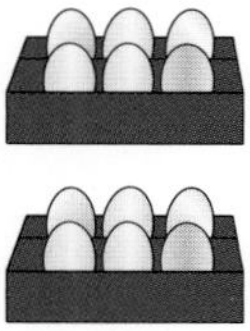 2	 3
+		
		 5
=		
	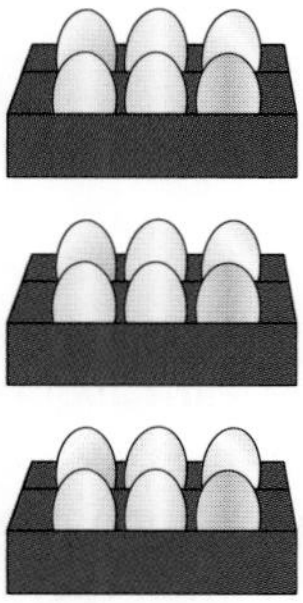 3	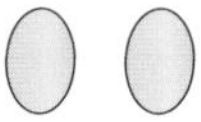 2

Thus, in base 6: 23 + 5 = 32

Let us now look at subtracting the base 6 numbers 5 from 23 again in pictorial form:

	Boxes	Eggs
	  2	 **3**
−		 **5**
	Starting on the right, 5 cannot be taken from 3 so we exchange one box for six eggs.	
	  1	 **6 + 3**
−		 **5**
=	 **1**	 **4**

Thus, in base 6: 23 − 5 = 14

The purpose of using base 6 rather than the more familiar base 10 was to enable you to feel something of what the children you are teaching may feel as they learn about place value. Working these through with pictorial representation, or using blocks or counters, is exactly what children need to do to understand base 10 and how to undertake calculations. All too often we assume that children should be able to jump into working without these supports when they are not ready to do so, and this has an impact on how children understand.

Task 2.2

Now try some of your own calculations using the base 6 egg counting system. Try mentally first, and then work them through using pictures or another means of representation.

- 31 + 5
- 45 + 23 =
- 122 + 42 =
- 43 − 4 =
- 53 − 22 =
- 215 − 142 =

Reflection

Reflecting upon the previous task:

- Did you find the work difficult and, if so, what was it that was difficult?
- Did you answer all questions correctly and, if not, do you understand where you went wrong?
- How did using resources or pictures support your understanding?

Understanding how you approached the questions and the errors you made will support you in understanding why children make mistakes and don't all understand how to work out the solutions at the same pace.

Back to base 10

In your own schooling, you may recall the terms **hundreds**, **tens** and **units**. Many teachers still use the term **units** for single-digit whole numbers. However, today many schools are using the term **ones** instead of units. There are obvious reasons for this as the name 'ones' provides a perfect description of what they are.

Children need to understand what each digit in a number represents. For example, in the number 327, the 3 represents 300 and the 2 represents 20. Splitting numbers up into their component parts is known as **partitioning** the number. Partitioning is a very useful tool for mental calculation and we will explore this in Chapter 3.

Multiplication and division by 10 and 100

We now wish to address some important issues linked to place value.

One of the most common misconceptions children have is describing the effect on a number of multiplying or dividing by 10 or 100. For example, consider $632 \times 10 = 6,320$. When you look at the answer it is easy to fall into the trap of using the rule that to multiply by 10 you 'add a zero'. Indeed, the answer does look like that happens, but as a teacher it is important you look beyond what the answer looks like and you reinforce deep understanding of the maths involved.

If we look more closely at the question represented in the diagram below, think about what physically happens to the digits when we multiply by 10.

	ten thousands	thousands	hundreds	tens	ones
632			6	3	2
632×10		6	3	2	0

What happens, therefore, when we divide by 10? For example, $78,650 \div 10 = 7,865$.

	ten thousands	thousands	hundreds	tens	ones
78,650	7	8	6	5	0
$78,650 \div 10$		7	8	6	5

These examples demonstrate clearly that when we multiply by 10, the digits all move one place to the left and zero is used as a place holder. In the division example, all the digits move one place to the right and zero is no longer required to hold the place. Visually, it does look like a zero is added and taken away but if children are taught to use this language, this can lead to problems when working with decimals. There will inevitably be situations in a classroom when a child might say, *We add a zero*, or *We move the decimal point*. This can lead to a child writing $2.5 \times 10 = 2.50$. As a teacher, you need to ensure that children appreciate what is really happening when multiplying/dividing by 10 and 100.

A deep understanding of place value is vital to ensure children can manipulate numbers confidently and build a solid foundation on which to develop understanding in mental strategies, decimals and other aspects of mathematics.

Before the introduction of the National Numeracy Strategy (1999), mathematics teaching was more rule focused. Children often did not explore the 'why' and the 'how' relating to maths. It is important to ensure any mathematics that we may have been taught in this way does not transfer into today's primary classroom.

Mastery Task

Enter a six-digit number into a calculator. Using subtraction, make the digits disappear one at a time.

For example:

Starting with the number 826,439 what number would you need to enter to remove the digit 6?

Rounding up

Counting isn't as easy as saying 1, 2, 3, hence the title of this chapter. There are several principles a child must understand to demonstrate they know how to count and are not just counting by rote, which we have identified in this chapter. We need to be mindful that each stage must be explored in a variety of ways to give a deep understanding and prepare children to move to the more complex number concepts of place value.

Too often, teachers are anxious to move children on to the abstraction principle before a child has fully grasped the concepts of numbers and counting. We cannot overestimate how important it is for children to have physical resources to support their learning.

WHAT MATHS CAN YOU SEE?

NOT AS
EASY AS
1, 2, 3

A RAY OF SUNSHINE

- Classifying numbers
- Accentuate the positive, eliminate the negative
- A ray of hope
- All square
- Prime time
- Feel good factor
- A sequence in time
- Higher powers
- Rounding up
- What maths can you see?

A ray of sunshine

In this chapter, we will explore the different types of numbers we need to be aware of in Key Stage 1 and Key Stage 2 and some of the patterns within the number system. We will also consider how these can be used to support deeper mathematical understanding and efficiency.

Classifying numbers

Let us first consider the different types of number, before applying them in different contexts. **Natural numbers** are often referred to as the positive counting numbers, such as 1, 2, 3, 4. **Whole numbers** are all the natural numbers plus zero. **Integers** are all the whole numbers plus all negative numbers.

This diagram shows how the definitions of natural numbers, whole numbers and integers fit together.

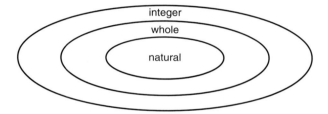

Accentuate the positive, eliminate the negative

Developing a broader understanding of the number system means exploring negative numbers.

Children can often find it quite hard to visualise this aspect of counting, so we suggest thinking of the image of a lift in a car park. The diagram below is a visual representation of this.

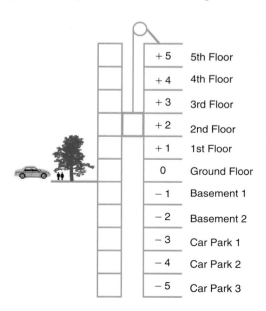

Working with this visual representation can help children understand the concept of crossing the zero. For example, a woman leaves her car in Car Park 3, then takes the lift up seven floors; which floor does she end up on? Starting at –5 (Car Park 3), if we move up seven floors we stop at +2, the second floor.

Once the concept is modelled in this way, children can move on to using a more traditional number line.

The same question would be represented on this line like this:

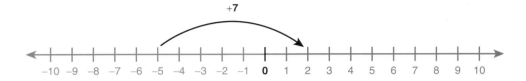

If we can confidently work with a number line in this way, then we can try more challenging questions, such as Task 3.1.

Task 3.1

Use a number line to work out the mid-point between –10 and 6.

A ray of hope

An *array* is a set of numbers or objects placed in rows and columns to represent multiplication facts.

Arrays may be made by arranging the objects to be counted in a way that enables children to count them more efficiently.

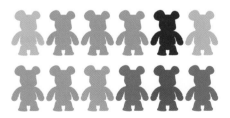

It is important that, from an early age, children learn to recognise quantities of numbers by their shapes. Arrays underpin this concept.

If we recognise ⬚ as 4 then it is easy to double this to recognise ⬚⬚ = 8.

Similarly, when we consider the number 6, we start to develop an understanding that it will be the same quantity whichever way we turn it:

2 + 2 + 2 = 6 or 3 + 3 = 6

The process of recognising these simple patterns without having to count the objects is known as being able to **subitise**. This is a vital skill when developing the ability to count efficiently. However, children with dyscalculia find subitising difficult as they do not process patterns in the same way.

An array is a useful tool to reinforce understanding of odd and even numbers. For example, if young children are given a list of numbers to identify which are odd and which are even, immediately arranging counters in an array of the number quantity creates a visual representation to support the concept.

3: Odd

8: Even

11: Odd

14: Even

The children line the counters in two rows and if they create two equal rows with the same number of counters then the number is even. If there is one row with more counters than the other, then the number is odd. The visual supports the eventual memorisation of the number facts linked to odd and even.

Teaching idea

Developing understanding of arrays (1)

Children can begin to make arrays using everyday objects as frameworks using ping-pong balls. We can place the balls in a tray to explore various arrays.

For example, 12 balls could be arranged as

Two rows of six (or six rows of two)

Three rows of four (or four rows of three)

By exploring how the number fits into equal length rows children start to see the link with times tables.

Arrays are not only a useful tool to help children understand times tables in pictorial form, they also support the commutative nature of multiplication, which is then developed further in their mental and written strategies work. By using an array, we can see how the number facts can be derived, as well as the links with the inverse operation of division.

Three rows of six = 3 × 6

Six rows of three = 6 × 3

From these arrays we can see that 3 × 6 = 18 and 6 × 3 = 18. We can then derive the division facts of 18 ÷ 3 = 6 and 18 ÷ 6 = 3. Teaching children to manipulate numbers in this way reinforces the relationships between operations, which underpins the development of mental agility in mathematics. We will explore this further in Chapter 4.

We will explore this further in Chapter 4.

Teaching idea

Developing understanding of arrays (2)

The children will work in pairs with two dice.

Ask the children to throw the two dice. Multiply the two numbers on the dice together and record this number in various arrays.

For example:

A double four would give a product of 16.

The children can record various arrays from this throw:

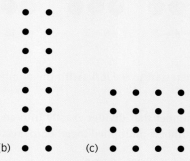

(a)   (b)   (c)

Once the children have drawn the arrays they should then write the number facts they can derive from the array.

For example, for (a) they could derive the following:

$$8 + 8 = 16$$

$$2 + 2 + 2 + 2 + 2 + 2 + 2 + 2 = 16$$

$$16 - 8 = 8$$

$$16 - 2 = 14$$

$$2 \times 8 = 16$$

$$16 \div 8 = 2$$

Mastery Task

How many numbers below 50 can only be represented using 4 arrays?

What do you notice about these numbers?

All square

Once we have a grasp of arrays and how they link to multiplication, we can start to explore those arrays that are 'special'.

By arranging counters in squares, we generate the pattern of numbers which are the **square numbers**. The result of multiplying an integer by itself.

$1 = 1^2$ $4 = 2^2$ $9 = 3^2$ $16 = 4^2$ $25 = 5^2$

Using arrays, we can then start to see links with the number of arrays a number has, and the number of factors.

A **factor** is a whole number that divides exactly into another number. We can then create **factor pairs** which are two numbers multiplied together to create their product.

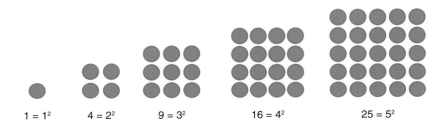

The number 12 has arrays of:

1×12 and 12×1 = factors 1 and 12

2×6 and 6×2 = factors 2 and 6

3×4 and 4×3 = factors 3 and 4

Therefore 12 has 6 factors.

Prime time

A **prime number** is a number that can only be multiplied by itself and therefore has two factors. Let's think of this in terms of arrays. A prime number can only have one array pattern. The number 1 is not prime as it IS one, so only has one factor. Therefore, the prime numbers below 10 are:

Feel good factor

We can now start to bring together all the concepts we have looked at so far to represent the factors of numbers in factor trees. Every number is the product of prime factors.

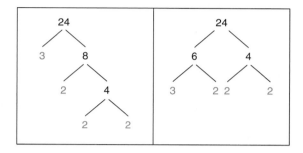

These are both factor trees for the number 24. The red numbers are the ends of the branches where it finishes with a prime number. Even starting with different factors results in the same prime numbers.

The prime factors which make 24 are therefore $3 \times 2 \times 2 \times 2$.

Task 3.2

Complete the factor trees with different factor starting points, to find the prime factors of each number.

81   15   45   49   82   77   42   56

A sequence in time

Mathematicians will often explain mathematics as the study of patterns. An understanding of the patterns generated within our number system is vital if children are to develop the ability to manipulate numbers to help them solve problems.

For example, if we know 6×8 then using our knowledge of factors, we know it is also the same as 3×16, by halving 6 and doubling 8. It's also equal to 12×4 by doubling the 6 and halving the 8.

$$3 + 7 = 10 \text{ so } 30 + 70 = 100 \text{ and } 300 + 700 = 1,000$$

Similarly, $12 + 8 = 20$ so $120 + 80 = 200$ and $1,200 + 800 = 2,000$

Task 3.3

A number sequence is generated by multiplying each integer by 5 and then adding 1.

Which of the numbers below won't be in the sequence and why?

5,671; 8,346; 57,902; 9,746; 1,111; 6,347; 4,453

We should explore patterns wherever possible to enable a deep understanding of the number system.

Reflection

Consider these statements. How can you prove whether they are correct?

1. All answers in the 4 times table are even numbers, therefore all answers in the 8 times table are even.

2. If we add the digit of a number together and the answer is divisible by 3 then the number is divisible by 3.

3. All digits in the 9 times table add up to 9.

4. The answers of the 3 times table end alternately odd then even, therefore the answers in the 6 times table will also alternate odd, even.

Statement 1 is correct. The 4 times table always ends in an even number because every number is multiplied by an even number. We explored this earlier in the chapter with the even number arrays. The 8 times table will also end in even numbers, as the answers will be the 4 times tables, doubled.

Statement 2 is correct. It is one of those special cases and children will enjoy exploring larger numbers to prove it works.

Statement 3 is known to be true up to 9×11, but again, exploring it beyond this will enrich not only children's mathematical understanding, but give them the opportunity to discuss mathematics and develop a more enquiring mind.

Statement 4, when explored, is partly true. The 3 times table does alternate odd and even, but once we double the responses to create the 6 times table, all answers are then even.

Teaching idea

Exploring times tables

Give children some of the statements in the reflection activity. Ask them to work in pairs or groups to prove that they are true or false.

Taking statement 3 further, children can explore numbers beyond the 12 × 12 times table expected in Year 4. For example, is this number divisible by 9? 123,003.

If we add the digits together, the answer is 9. If we then divide 123,003 by 9 the answer is a whole number, so it is therefore divisible by 9.

Number sequences are a useful way to begin developing children's abilities to recognise mathematical patterns. Children need to be confident at predicting what may come next and why. A good way to start this is to look at sequences where the difference between consecutive numbers is the same. These are called **_linear sequences_**. Also, note it is important to include number sequences that go down as well as up.

Teaching idea

Sequences

Key Stage 1

Ask the children to extend number sequences within the numbers they are working with.

1	3	5	7				
20	18	16	14				
2	5	8	11				
42	52	62	72				
13	18	23	28				
70	60	50	40				

Key Stage 2

We can now begin to extend the same idea of linear sequences to include non-integer numbers, negative numbers and even square numbers. Adjust the numbers you use to the children's ability.

2.5	3	3.5	4				
3.8	4.2	4.6	5				
5	3	1	−1				
17	$14\frac{1}{2}$	12	$9\frac{1}{2}$				
2.6	2	1.4	0.8				
1	4	9	16				

Teachers often resort to worksheets at this point. It is very easy to find and use worksheet after worksheet on this topic and the internet is full of such work, should you think this is best for your class. There are times when a worksheet can be helpful, however, you should be aware that as far as we know, no child has ever run to their parents at the end of the day and said, *We did a brilliant worksheet today.*

There are many other ways to develop the same skills, such as oral work, and using mini whiteboards or number cards. Number sequences can also be developed by looking at patterns made from 'straws'. For example:

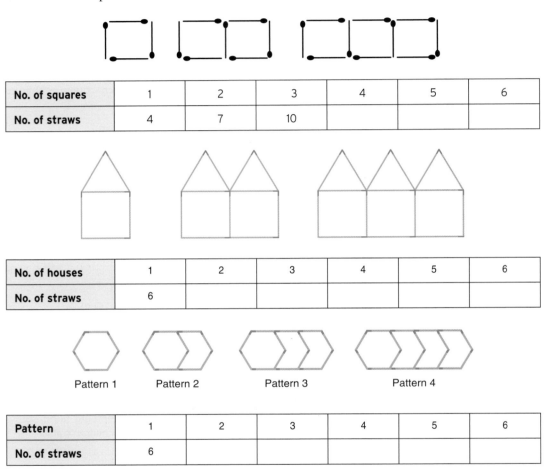

No. of squares	1	2	3	4	5	6
No. of straws	4	7	10			

No. of houses	1	2	3	4	5	6
No. of straws	6					

Pattern 1   Pattern 2   Pattern 3   Pattern 4

Pattern	1	2	3	4	5	6
No. of straws	6					

To find out how many straws are in each diagram, children will begin by counting and by extending the pattern, to find how many straws are needed for the next pattern. However, by appreciating the number sequences they will not need to draw or make the next shape or pattern to make a correct prediction.

Higher powers

By the end of Year 5, children are expected to know, recognise and use both square numbers and cubic numbers, including the notation for each. We looked at square numbers earlier in this chapter – as we demonstrated, these are square numbers because they can be represented as a square array (it is surprising how many people do not know this is why we call them square numbers).

The square of each integer is found by multiplying it by itself. To denote squaring we use the **superscript 2**, meaning to **the power of 2**.

Thus, the fifth square number is $5^2 = 5 \times 5 = 25$

and the tenth square number is $10^2 = 10 \times 10 = 100$.

This enables us to generate, say, the first ten square numbers:

1, 4, 9, 16, 25, 36, 49, 64, 81, 100

Now consider this list of numbers as a sequence and the difference between each term:

Can you see that the differences in successive terms increase by two each time? In fact, the differences are the odd numbers. We could use this to evaluate the next number in the sequence. The next odd number after 19 is 21, so the next number in the sequence is $100 + 21 = 121$ (which is 11^2).

The cubic numbers are derived from raising each number to the power of three. That is, multiplying each number by itself three times.

Hence, one cubed is $1^3 = 1 \times 1 \times 1 = 1$ (note many children think one cubed is three), two cubed is $2^3 = 2 \times 2 \times 2 = 8$, etc.

This gives us the first eleven cubic numbers as:

0   1   8   27   64   125   216   343   512   729   1,000

Reflection

Can you see the sequence in the cubic numbers and use it to predict the next two cubic numbers?

Although higher powers of numbers are not included in the Key Stage 2 curriculum, it is worth knowing that the power of the number indicates how many times together that number should be multiplied.

$$2^5 = 2 \times 2 \times 2 \times 2 \times 2 = 32$$

$$5^4 = 5 \times 5 \times 5 \times 5 = 625$$

$$10^6 = 10 \times 10 \times 10 \times 10 \times 10 \times 10 = 1,000,000$$

We will consider powers in more detail in our final chapter.

Mastery Task

Consider the following:

$$1 \times 10 + 1 = 11$$
$$11 \times 10 + 11 = 121$$
$$121 \times 10 + 121 = 1331$$
$$1311 \times 10 + 1331 = 14641$$

Can you extend the pattern?

Now calculate 11^1, 11^2, 11^3 and 11^4. What do you notice?

Triangular numbers

Triangular numbers are a special sequence of numbers that can also be generated in many ways. Like square numbers the sequence is generated by creating a shape with counters – in this case a triangle – and then looking at how adding an extra row has an impact on the sequence.

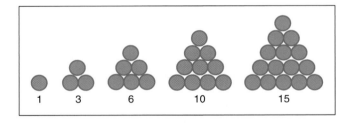

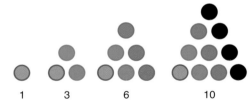

This diagram shows more clearly how the numbers increase by the number added in the next row of each colour.

Fibonacci sequence

This, too, is an exciting way of developing understanding of patterns and number sequences. Fibonacci lived in Italy at the end of the twelfth century. He came across this sequence when considering how fast rabbit populations could grow. Why this sequence is so exciting for children is that these numbers occur throughout nature – for example, in the numbers of leaves on a plant and seeds in a pod.

To generate the sequence we start with 0 and 1. The next number is found by adding the last two numbers; thus the second number is 0 + 1 = 1, the third number is 1 + 1 = 2, = 3 and so on … this gives us:

0, 1, 1, 2, 3, 5, 8 …

Children love extending the series as it is such an easy concept to grasp.

The number of petals on a flower is often one of the Fibonacci numbers, or a multiple of it.

Mastery Task

What is the highest two-digit Fibonacci number?

What is the lowest three-digit Fibonacci number?

Incidentally, Fibonacci is acknowledged as the person who popularised the use of the Hindu-Arabic numeral system that we use today throughout the world. Prior to Fibonacci, Europe was still using Roman numerals.

Rounding up

It's great fun exploring all the different patterns within our number system. Using investigations to explore patterns shows children the variety of ways in which numbers can be generated.

Once these patterns are mastered, they will help to support children in their development of number operations, both mentally and in their written methods.

We will explore how patterns can be applied in these contexts in the next two chapters.

WHAT MATHS CAN YOU SEE?

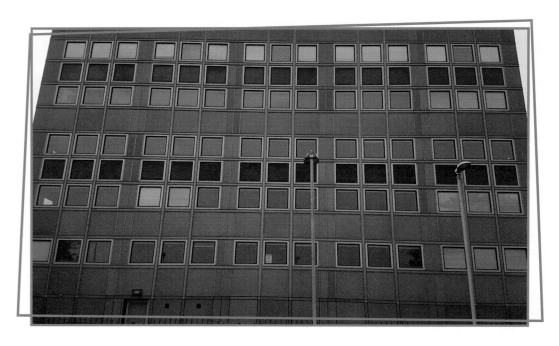

MATHS IS MENTAL

- How big is a big number?
- Developing mental calculation strategies
- Understanding the four operations
- Adding on
- Take it away
- Times are changing
- Law and order
- Rounding up
- What maths can you see?

Maths is mental

This chapter will look at mental calculation and some of the key principles of number that will aid children in their ability to calculate mentally. We also want to explore how mental methods develop differently with different children and how approaches to calculations may change, depending upon the numbers being used.

As discussed in Chapter 2, our number system is very clever. Unfortunately, many children can 'learn' about numbers and can perhaps even perform calculations with numbers, without a deep appreciation of how the number system works. If this is the case, next steps can become similar to stumbling around in the dark, unsure of where to go or what to do. In this situation, children fall back on their rules and their recipes.

First, let us think a little more about numbers. This will help you to develop a deeper understanding of numbers and allow you to become aware of some of the difficulties children can have in studying number. This aspect is sometimes overlooked in mathematics education. In order to fully empathise with children learning numbers, you need to go back to the time when you were first learning numbers. Can you remember a time before you knew how big 100 was?

<u>Mentally</u> add the following numbers:

Begin with 1,000

add 40

add another 1,000

add 30

add 1,000

add 20

add 1,000

finally, add 10 ... and write down your answer.

If you are reading this, it is likely you are hoping to become a primary teacher and you have, hopefully, already gained a GCSE in mathematics. If you are already on an ITT programme, you will have passed the Numeracy Skills Test, which all teachers need to pass before beginning their course. So, adding up these numbers should cause you no problem whatsoever ... should it?

Every time we do this activity, we find that about two-thirds of the trainee teachers in our undergraduate classes get the answer wrong. We have also given this task to postgraduate classes where none of them have got it correct. Some get it wrong because they make an error in the calculation. However, many wrong answers are because of a conceptual error.

The most common answer is 5,000. The answer is not 5,000. If you got 5,000 go back and check.

Prior to adding the final 10, the running total is 4,090. The number of people who add 10 to 4,090 to make 5,000 is amazing.

Of course, now you can appreciate your error:

90 + 10 = 100

so 4,090 + 10 should be 4,100.

Incidentally if you did get the answer 4,100 … well done! Now try it on your friends.

We trust that this activity has established whether or not YOU can add 10, which we suggest is a key skill for a primary teacher. This exercise demonstrates how easy it is for anyone to become mixed up with numbers, especially when crossing key number boundaries such as 100 or 1,000. If children are moved too quickly on to formal calculation techniques, without having a deep understanding of the number system, problems will occur later. We urge you not to move any child forward too quickly.

The best way of developing children's understanding of number is through oral and mental work. This can be achieved by getting children to think about numbers, to talk about numbers and to mentally manipulate numbers. In this chapter, we want to explore your own relationship with numbers and reflect upon your own mental mathematics skills.

How big is a big number?

Once our base 10 number system has been assimilated and understood, there is no limit to our ability to count. We can move seamlessly from tens, to hundreds, to thousands, to millions.

One million … that's a big number, isn't it? Who wouldn't want to have one million pounds? However, are you aware of exactly how big one million is? From our experiences, many adults do not have a clear concept of 'one million'. How much space would one million pounds (in ten pound notes) take up? How much space would we need to hold a crowd of one million people? Many tend to think of one million as quite a few thousand. One million is actually 1,000 thousand. We normally write this number as 1,000,000. (Note: the commas are not essential, rather they are merely a tool to help us read the number.) We can write the number one million as 1000,000. We can also write one million as 10^6, that is, 10 multiplied by itself six times. Does that help you understand how big one million is? Many students we meet, who know that one million is equal to 1,000 thousand, are still unsure what a million may 'look' like.

Now we would like you to think of one million seconds. How long would one million seconds take to pass? It is relatively easy for you to work this out with a calculator, but we do not want you to do this. Instead, gain a feel for your own concept of 1,000,000. Do you think the answer is a few hours? Or would one million seconds be a number of weeks, or months or years? This is a lovely idea to generate discussion with a group of children (or students).

When we do this activity in our sessions, suggestions for how long it would take for one million seconds to pass can range from two hours to two years. Most people do not have any real concept of 'one million' in the same way that they may have a concept of, say, the numbers 18 or 37. The answer is that, *one million seconds is approximately* $11\frac{1}{2}$ *days*. Does that help you decide whether one million is a big number?

Let us move on. We want you to think now of one billion. A number of people (including many politicians) are not sure what one billion is. Such uncertainty is compounded by the fact that a British billion used to be different to an American billion. However, we are sure that you will be happy to learn that since 1974 there has been general agreement across all countries that one billion is equal to 1,000 million. Thus, we write this number as 1,000,000,000 (or 10^9).

We have told you already that one million seconds is approximately equal to $11\frac{1}{2}$ days. So how long do you think one billion seconds will take to pass? Again, when doing this task with our students, we are never surprised at the range of responses. A very common wrong answer is 100 days and another common wrong answer is about a year. What do you think the answer is?

The surprising correct answer is that one billion seconds is almost 32 years. Yes, it is! Most people simply do not believe that answer, so it bears repetition. One million seconds is $11\frac{1}{2}$ days, but one billion seconds is 32 years. That's the difference between one million and one billion. So, does that make one billion a big number? You need to think about that. Politicians will often change their use of millions and billions depending on what they are trying to persuade us to believe. If they want us to believe that something is expensive, they may say, *We are spending twenty thousand million pounds*, but if they want us to think something is cheap they may say, *It is only costing two billion pounds*. Beware of politicians using big numbers!

We thought at this point it would be useful to try to give you some insight into some real big numbers (big numbers used in the real world) to see if we can now get a feel for what they actually mean. These numbers are changing all the time but we have tried to use the most recently published figures – although for some of these, different sources provide slightly different figures.

Look at the following data. Using what you now know about one million seconds and one billion seconds, think of each number in terms of seconds and try to estimate what time period it would be approximately equivalent to.

Approximate population of the world (UN 2015)	*7.3 billion*
The amount spent in one year on paying interest on the UK debt (2016 Budget)	*£39 billion*
The amount spent on UK education (2016 Budget)	*£102 billion*
Total bailout for Greece (source BBC)	*£200 billion*
Total US debt (2016 US Treasury)	*£19.4 trillion**
* one trillion is 1,000 billion	

At this point, it would be very easy for us to leave this with you and move on as we have complete confidence that you would be able to complete this task successfully. However, for us it is the discussion of mathematics that is important. So, we have converted these numbers into seconds and instead of thinking how far into the future they take us, we have considered how far into the past they take us. We also provide an insight into what was happening in the world at that time. This gives us some fascinating results.

	Number	Number (in seconds) converted to years	What year this takes us back to	What was happening in history at this time
Approximate population of the world (UN 2015)	7.3 billion	231 years	1787	Mozart's opera *Don Giovanni* is premiered.
The amount spent in one year on paying interest on the UK debt (2016 Budget)	£39 billion	1,286 years	781 AD	*In Anglo-Saxon England, Offa was King of Mercia.*
The amount spent on UK education (2016 Budget)	£102 billion	3,234 years	1200 BC	*End of the Bronze Age.*
Total bailout for Greece (source BBC)	£200 billion	6,341 years	4300 BC	*Beginning of the Bronze Age.*
Total US debt (2016 US Treasury)	£19.4 trillion	615,170 years	613,000 BC	*Homo-erectus man dates back to this time.*

It is interesting that even when changing these big numbers into something more manageable such as seconds, we can still end up with numbers that are really too big to fully comprehend. Does this help you decide what a big number is?

Teaching idea

How big is that?

Provide children with a selection of newspapers. Ask them to find any numbers that have been used. Get them to think about these numbers in terms of other things. For example:

(a) Seconds (as we did above)

(b) Counters ... how high would the pile of counters be?

(c) People ... how many times bigger than their class, their school, etc.

There are so many different ways to get children to think about numbers; the way you encourage their engagement will depend upon the level of your class. For children still developing their understanding, ask them to find articles that mention numbers say between 20 and 100, or between 100 and 1,000. These can also lead to interesting and useful interactive wall displays.

Developing mental calculation strategies

One of the three aims of the current National Curriculum is that pupils (of all ages, not just primary children) should become fluent in the **fundamentals** of mathematics. There is an expectation that children will be provided with regular and varied practice in mathematical problems, in order to help them develop their conceptual understanding. Children need to be able to recall knowledge and apply that knowledge, rapidly and accurately.

For you to develop children's mental mathematics skills, you must first think about your own skills. You should note that just as the best football managers were not always the best footballers themselves, the best mathematics teachers are not necessarily the best mathematicians – quite the contrary in fact. There are some people who are outstanding at mathematics but lack the ability to teach it, as they cannot understand why children may not understand the subject. Don't worry about your own mental mathematical skills. Regardless of your own mental agility you will be able to teach mathematics effectively as you WILL get better at mental calculation techniques through teaching and experience.

Skills in mental calculation are not the same as memory and recall skills. For example, children reciting their times tables are not undertaking mental calculations, they are purely using recall. Of course, if you do happen to know more number facts, then your mental skills will be enhanced. We define a 'mental calculation' as using the things you know to work out things you don't know. Further, improving your mental skills will lead to you knowing more mathematical facts:

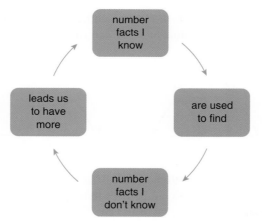

The remainder of this chapter identifies some key concepts of number and looks at how they can be developed with children in the classroom.

Understanding the four operations

The four basic 'operations' in number are: addition; subtraction; multiplication; and division. As soon as children begin to understand number you should ask them to perform these operations.

Chapter 2 looked at how this work can be introduced initially using concrete resources such as counters or other objects. As children progress and they begin to utilise bigger numbers, it becomes impractical to continue using objects. A good way to help children move away from concrete objects is to use a number line. There are essentially two types of number line we can use: a scaled number line and an empty number line.

A *scaled number line* has all the numbers, say from 0 to 10, or from 0 to 20. This is the type of number line children will use in Foundation Stage and Key Stage 1 when first learning to count. Perhaps they will be moving objects along this number line. As children become more competent and begin to use larger numbers, this becomes impractical. They come to appreciate that they do not need every number so we just use <u>some</u> of the numbers. This is known as an **empty number line.** We may have a starting number and we use labels and jumps to help us determine the answer to a given calculation.

Any method of mental calculation can be modelled using either a number line or an empty number line. Similarly, we can use a number line to develop mental calculation strategies in children. Work in the rest of this chapter will focus mainly on the empty number line.

As a primary mathematics teacher, you need to have a deep understanding of the relationship between the four number operations, which we can summarise as follows.

Repeated addition is the same as multiplication

Thus, 4×7 can be thought of as 'four lots of 7'. The number line is useful to illustrate this. Initially, children learn how to multiply by adding. So, they can calculate 4×7 by using the arithmetical sequence 7, 14, 21, 28.

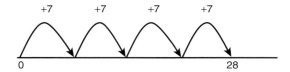

Many children also use this technique to aid recall of any times tables they have forgotten. For example, a child may not recall $8 \times 7 = 56$ but perhaps they do remember $7 \times 7 = 49$ and thus know that to find out 'eight lots of 7' they just need to add another seven onto the 49.

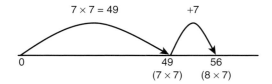

Children need also to appreciate that 'eight lots of 7' is the same as 'seven lots of 8'. This is known as the **commutative** property of multiplication. This means it does not matter which number we put first. As we stated in Chapter 2, addition is also commutative, e.g. $3 + 8 = 8 + 3$.

Addition and multiplication are the only ***commutative operations***. Subtraction is not commutative because 12 – 3 is not the same as 3 – 12 (although some children think it is).

Similarly, division is not commutative as 20 ÷ 2 is not the same as 2 ÷ 20.

Repeated subtraction is the same as division

For example, 20 ÷ 5 can be thought of as, *How many times can we subtract five from 20?*

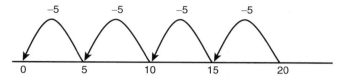

In this case, when we get to 0 we can go no further. We have taken away <u>four</u> lots of five. Therefore 20 ÷ 5 = 4.

We do not always get back to 0. For example, consider 29 ÷ 8. We begin at 28 and keep subtracting 8:

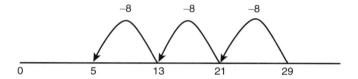

Here, we have taken away the number 8 <u>three</u> times, which takes us to the number 5. We cannot take away another 8. Our answer is 3 with a remainder of 5, which we write:

$$29 ÷ 8 = 3 \text{ r}5$$

Subtraction is the inverse of addition

In mathematics, the 'inverse' of an operation 'undoes' that operation. This may seem obvious to you but it is not obvious to children until it is pointed out. We can think of this in terms of our number line. If we, say, start at 6 and add 4 we are moving four numbers to the right, which takes us to 10.

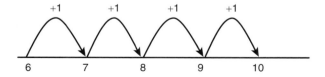

The 'inverse' of this is deciding what we would need to do to go back from 10 (where we finished) to 6 (where we started).

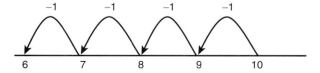

Starting at 10 and 'taking away' (or subtracting) 4 takes us back to where we started. Thus, subtracting 4 is the inverse of adding 4 (and vice versa).

Children need to be taught this relationship as they progress. Thus, for any addition fact, you should encourage them to write down the other three corresponding facts. For example:

$$8 + 5 = 13$$
$$5 + 8 = 13$$
$$13 - 8 = 5$$
$$13 - 5 = 8$$

When teaching addition, we are also teaching subtraction.

Division is the inverse of multiplication

Similarly, in multiplication the inverse is what we must do to take us back to where we started. Consider $12 \times 5 = 60$. We can think of this as five jumps of twelve (beginning at 0 using the repeated addition model). To get back from 60 to 0 in jumps of twelve will take five jumps.

We could also say, to get back from 60 to 0 in jumps of five will take twelve jumps.

From this we would advocate that all children learning about multiplication should be taught division at the same time. For example, a multiplication fact such as $7 \times 4 = 28$ leads to three other facts:

$$7 \times 4 = 28$$
$$4 \times 7 = 28$$
$$28 \div 7 = 4$$
$$28 \div 4 = 7$$

When teaching multiplication, we are also teaching division.

Adding on

Reflection

In your head, work out the answer to 27 + 28. Now think about how you actually did this and write down your method. Ask some friends to do the same and compare your methods.

This is not about establishing the correct answer, as we assume that you can do this. Rather, we are interested in the way you may have worked this out. It is always fascinating to compare different students' methods.

Some of the possible methods you may have used include:

Partitioning both numbers	$(20 + 20) + (7 + 8) = 40 + 15$
Partitioning just the second number	$(27 + 20) + 8 = 47 + 8$
Appreciating that they are only 1 apart ... so a 'near' double	$27 \times 2 + 1 = 54 + 1$
Rounding the first to the nearest 10 and then making a correction	$(27 + 3) + (28 - 3) = 30 + 25$
Rounding both up to the nearest 10 and then making a correction	$(30 + 30) - (3 + 2) = 60 - 5$
Imagining the question as a formal written method and working from right to left	$7 + 8 = 5$ carry 1, $2 + 2 + 1$ carried $= 5$

Each of you will have your own way of doing this question. No teacher has ever taught you that whenever you see the question 27 + 28, this is what you must do. Each reader will have developed a strategy they feel comfortable with. Your chosen strategy will depend upon a number of different factors including your own competence and ability with our number system. Some of these methods involve approximating and then making adjustments, which can turn an addition into a subtraction.

The final method we have listed above is used by many children who have either not sufficiently developed their mental skills, or perhaps lack the understanding of the number system we have been talking about so far. In such cases, children have probably been moved too quickly onto the formal written methods. This is the only one of the above methods that necessitates working from right to left. Children (or students) who utilise an imagined written method to undertake a mental calculation are usually prone to making errors, as they have too much information to hold in their head.

Reflection

Mentally calculate the answer to 38 + 59. Think about how you actually did this and write down your method. They key question here is, *Did your method (strategy) differ from the one you used for the question above? If so, why?*

Again, let us look at some possible strategies:

Using the commutative property to make the calculation easier	$38 + 59 = 59 + 38$
Partitioning both numbers	$(50 + 30) + (9 + 8) = 80 + 17$
Partitioning just the second number	$(38 + 50) + 9 = 88 + 9$ or $(59 + 30) + 8 = 89 + 8$

Rounding one to the nearest 10 and then making a correction	$38 + (60 - 1) = 38 + 60 - 1$ or $(40 + 59) - 2 = 99 - 2$
Rounding both numbers up to the nearest 10 and then making a correction	$(40 + 60) - (2 + 1) = 100 - 3$
Imagining the question as a formal written method and working from right to left	$8 + 9 = 17$ (7 down carry 1) $3 + 5 = 8$ plus 1 carried $= 9$

The interesting thing here is to think about whether you used the same method as you did previously. Most people change their method depending upon the actual numbers they are using.

Take it away

First, let us consider subtraction. There are two distinct models of subtraction and it is important for you to appreciate each of them, as it is something you may never have previously considered. To demonstrate these two perspectives, let us consider the calculation 62 – 25.

Subtraction as a 'take away'

This is seeing subtraction as the inverse of addition. Thus, we begin at 62 and 'go backwards' 25. We can do this in a variety of ways. We could partition the 25 and take away each part separately. Thus, we first subtract back 20 (which takes us to 42) and then go back a further 5 (finishing at 37).

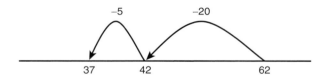

Perhaps a child would find the 42 – 5 challenging, so they can break this down further by first taking away 2 and then taking away 3. This helps with the 'bridge' of 40.

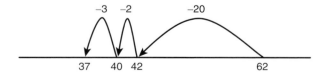

Either way we end up at 37.

$$62 - 25 = 37$$

Subtraction as a 'difference'

Considering a subtraction as a difference means that a 'take away' calculation now becomes an addition. For 62 – 25 we need to imagine the distance between these two numbers on the number line.

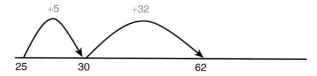

It can be seen that beginning at 25, we can add 5 to take us to 30, and then we need to add 32 to get to 62. In total, we have added 37, so the difference between 25 and 62 is equal to 37.

$$62 - 25 = 37$$

This is particularly helpful when the numbers are close together. For example, to complete the calculation 93 – 88 it is much easier to consider the difference between the numbers, rather than take the 88 away from 93.

Times are changing

Reflection

Consider the following multiplication questions:

$$37 \times 4$$

$$24 \times 30$$

Write down as many different ways you can of undertaking these calculations.

Clearly, before looking at questions such as this, children will need to be familiar with their times tables to at least 10×10.

The most common method for mentally calculating a two-digit number by a single-digit number would be to use partitioning. Thus, our first calculation becomes:

$$37 \times 4 = (30 \times 4) + (7 \times 4) = 120 + 28$$

Understanding factors can be enormously helpful when undertaking multiplication. In this case, knowing that $30 = 3 \times 10$ means that 30×4 can be thought of as $3 \times 10 \times 4$ or $3 \times 4 \times 10$.

Not only does this mean we are working from left to right, the method is also useful as it leads us directly to the formal written method that we use for long and short multiplication (see Chapter 5).

Using the same idea of factors, we can spilt the second calculation in two ways:

$$\text{either:} \quad 24 \times 10 \times 3$$

$$\text{or:} \quad 24 \times 3 \times 10$$

When we do this task with our own students, the majority of them tend to use the first method. Of course, as we discussed in Chapter 2, multiplication of a two- or three-digit number by 10 is relatively straightforward so it doesn't matter where we do the multiplication by 10.

In considering the most effective calculation strategy, we need to think whether a student is more likely to make an error in calculating 240×3, or in calculating 72×10. See what your class think of this. This links with the section entitled 'Feel good factor' in Chapter 3.

Task 4.1

Using what you now know, for each of the following questions identify as many strategies as possible to calculate the answer mentally, and for each of these strategies demonstrate the method using an empty number line.

$29 + 56$ $58 + 59$ $127 + 69$

$62 - 29$ $604 - 526$ 129×9

Teaching idea

How many ways?

Using the same ideas that we have discussed in this chapter, ask children to talk about how they would undertake a given calculation. This can be done with children of any age or ability by adjusting the numbers. It is a great activity for encouraging children to work in pairs or groups.

The power in the discussion is that children come to appreciate that mathematics can be really creative. There may be just one right answer, but there are many paths to get to that answer. Which is quickest? Which is easiest? Which is likely to lead to an error?

One of the key ideas of this chapter is that all of us use a wide variety of mental strategies, and most of these strategies have not been directly taught to us; we have developed them ourselves. Your job as a teacher is to encourage children to develop a variety of strategies and skills. This does not mean that we think children who are weaker at mental calculation will fail in mathematics. However, our experience is that having skills in mental calculation is helpful in learning other areas of mathematics and developing such skills helps to further develop children's understanding of the number system.

Mastery Task

Use the empty number line to undertake the following calculations:

$3.7 + 5.8$

$8.8 - 3.25$

1.6×5

Law and order

Task 4.2

Complete the following calculations:

1. $6 + 5 \times 2 =$

2. $9 - 15 \div 3 =$

3. $16 - 4 \times 5 =$

4. $10 + 2 \times 6 \div 3 =$

Check your answers in Appendix 2 before reading on.

If you got the answers wrong you won't be alone. This comes from a basic misunderstanding of the order in which operations should be carried out.

There is a set order for working through operations, which is often forgotten. Previously in primary schools the order was supported by using brackets but the Primary National Curriculum (2014) now expects children to be able to use the correct order without the support of brackets.

To help us remember the order there is a simple mnemonic (**BODMAS**), which stands for:

B – Brackets

O – Orders (powers, roots)

D – Division

M – Multiplication

A – Addition

S – Subtraction

If we then return to the first question in Task 4.2 of $6 + 5 \times 2$, the multiplication should be carried out before the addition. Therefore 5×2 is calculated and then we add the 6. If your answer was 22 then you completed $6 + 5$ then multiplied by 2, by just working from left to right. If we wanted to complete the calculation in that order, then we would need to use brackets: $(6 + 5) \times 2$. Using the BODMAS rule, the brackets are calculated first before the multiplication part of the calculation.

Question 4 in Task 4.2 is a little trickier.

Let's work it through in stages:

$$10 + 2 \times 6 \div 3 =$$

First, we work out the division part of the calculation: $10 + 2 \times (6 \div 3) =$

Next, we calculate the multiplication part: $10 + (2 \times 2) =$

Finally, we calculate the addition $10 + 4$ to give an answer of 14.

Rounding up

This chapter was actually one of the inspirations for this book. We felt that too many people are not appreciative of just how much bigger one billion is, compared to one million. We trust that you will now remember this. By translating big numbers into seconds and then considering what time span these equate to, we can get a much better idea of how big numbers compare with each other.

We then looked at some key elements of number that help to define the four operations and their relationship with each other. Perhaps some of these seem obvious to you, but nothing is obvious until someone points it out. It is essential that children grasp these principles of number, as it will support them in their understanding of number and the number system. These principles are also vital in supporting effective mental calculation strategies.

We hope that you now appreciate that each of us may have our own way of performing mental calculations and that these methods may change depending upon the numbers involved. The only way for you as a teacher to explore how children are developing their mental methods is to ensure you have high-quality questioning and use answers to scaffold stimulating discussion.

WHAT MATHS CAN YOU SEE?

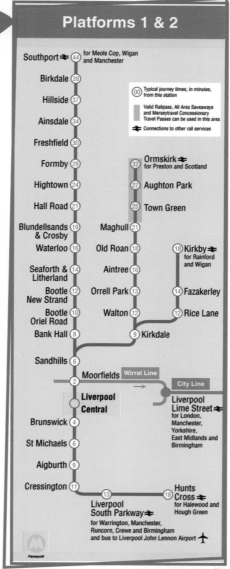

Platforms 1 & 2

Southport ⮂ (44) for Meols Cop, Wigan and Manchester

Birkdale (39)

Hillside (37)

Ainsdale (34)

Freshfield (30)

Formby (28)

Hightown (24)

Hall Road (21)

Blundellsands & Crosby (19)

Waterloo (16)

Seaforth & Litherland (14)

Bootle New Strand (12)

Bootle Oriel Road (10)

Bank Hall (8)

Sandhills (6)

Moorfields (2)

Liverpool Central

Brunswick (4)

St Michaels (6)

Aigburth (9)

Cressington (11)

(00) Typical journey times, in minutes, from this station

Valid Railpass, All Area Saveaways and Merseytravel Concessionary Travel Passes can be used in this area

⮂ Connections to other rail services

Ormskirk ⮂ (32) for Preston and Scotland

Aughton Park (27)

Town Green (25)

Maghull (21)

Old Roan (18)

Aintree (16)

Orrell Park (13)

Walton (12)

Kirkdale (9)

Wirral Line

City Line

Liverpool Lime Street ⮂ for London, Manchester, Yorkshire, East Midlands and Birmingham

Kirkby ⮂ (18) for Rainford and Wigan

Fazakerley (14)

Rice Lane (12)

Liverpool South Parkway ⮂ (13) for Warrington, Manchester, Runcorn, Crewe and Birmingham and bus to Liverpool John Lennon Airport ✈

Hunts Cross ⮂ (18) for Halewood and Hough Green

Merseyrail

MATHS IS MENTAL

MAKING SUM SENSE

- It all adds up
- Have a takeaway
- Go forth and multiply
- Divide and conquer
- Rounding up
- What maths can you see?

Making sum sense

In this chapter, we will explore the most commonly used written methods – both the informal and the formal. Whilst doing so, we will gain an understanding of the common misconceptions linked to each operation and how, as a teacher, you might deal with them in a classroom setting.

Once children have a deep understanding of place value and mental strategies they can then apply these to written methods. The National Curriculum 2014 gives examples of the formal written methods which all children need to be able to carry out by the end of Year 6.

The National Numeracy Strategy (NNS) 1999 introduced informal expanded written methods, which enabled children to explore a range of written methods and to use the method they were most comfortable with. This, however, meant that children transferring to Key Stage 3 were using a variety of methods, which were not always the most efficient.

The formal written methods in the National Curriculum 2014 focus on efficiency and speed of calculation, whereas the NNS encouraged a deeper understanding of the mathematics behind a method. As a result, many schools are using the non-formal methods as a transition to the formal methods, so that children gain an understanding of the mathematics and do not rely on learning methods by rules without any underpinning knowledge.

In Chapter 1, we asked you to reflect on the number of questions a child might answer in order to show understanding. For written methods, there is no set number of questions we should ask, but we would say that 20 similar questions, all answered correctly, first showing no carrying, then carrying units/ones and then tens etc. does not show deep understanding. Surely, if a child can answer three questions they can answer 33 questions? It is better to give a few carefully thought-out questions which, with careful planning, address possible areas where a misconception might arise, than repeat questions where a child has already demonstrated an understanding.

Children will get questions wrong: in some cases due to slips or mistakes, but in many cases where there is an underlying misconception in their understanding, or a process that must be addressed for the child to move their learning forward. As a teacher, you need to be aware of what these misconceptions may be.

There will be cases when you may not be able to identify a child's misconception. Where possible, ask the child to talk you through one of their examples to help you identify the error and draw out the misconception: with all examples, it is important that you, as teacher, design calculations which draw these out. In each of the examples we provide throughout this chapter, the child has answered questions correctly, but this is only because the numbers used do not provide the opportunity to identify the misconception.

Prior to starting any calculation, it is important to ask the children to estimate what they think the answer should be. Instilling this habit in children's working will help them identify when an answer is unreasonable. This, is turn, will encourage children to be more confident in their own ability.

It all adds up

When mentally solving an addition problem, one of the most common strategies to use is partitioning. Being able to confidently partition underpins these informal expanded methods.

Calculate: 458 + 287 =

Expanded method 1

	4	5	8
+	2	8	7
		1	5
	1	3	0
	6	0	0
	7	4	5

Answer: 745

Using partitioning, we add each column starting with the ones or units, then tens, then hundreds.

Using this expanded method, we reinforce the value of each digit.

$$8 + 7 = 15$$

$$50 + 80 = 130$$

$$400 + 200 = 600$$

Initially, children may add the three numbers using their mental strategies and then move on to adding the digits vertically – as they would with a more formal method.

Expanded method 2

4	0	0	+		5	0	+		8
2	0	0	+		8	0	+		7
6	0	0	+	1	3	0	+	1	5

This method not only links to partitioning, but also retains the horizontal layout of mental calculations. Like method 1, it reinforces the value of the numbers whilst moving children towards the more formal column method.

This method is also particularly useful when working with children who have a visual impairment or who have been diagnosed with autism.

These methods serve as transition methods prior to learning the formal column method.

Column addition

```
      3   5   6   9
  +   4   2   8   5
  ─────────────────
      7   8   5   4
          1   1
```

This is the efficient (or contracted) method which children are expected to know by the end of Key Stage 2.

Working this through, we start at the ones column adding 9 and 5. The 10 is carried into the tens column (shown in red) and the 4 placed in the units/ones column.

Next, we add the tens. Initially, it is important to focus on their full value, especially if children have not experienced a transition method.

$60 + 80 + 10 = 150$ where the 100 carries to the hundreds column (shown in purple).

Eventually this will be shortened to $6 + 8 + 1$.

The rest of the method follows the same pattern, adding each column:

Hundreds = $500 + 200 + 100$ – leading to $5 + 2 + 1$ as the child grows more confident.

Thousands = $3,000 + 4,000$ – leading to $3 + 4$.

Reflection

Examine the calculations below. Mark them and diagnose the misconceptions for each child.

Jenny

```
        6   1              4   1   6            3   8
    +   2   7          +   9   0   3        +   2   4
    ─────────          ─────────────        ─────────
        8   8          1   3   1   9        5   1   2
```

Vicky

```
        6   2              6   3   2            8   5   5
    +   3   4          +   4   8   3        +   6   2   8
    ─────────          ─────────────        ─────────────
        9   6          1   1   6            1   1   14
                             0   1                4   1
```

Michael

```
        2   3   4          3   4   5            3   8   4
    +   3   6   2      +   2   6   6        +   1   6   8
    ─────────────      ─────────────        ─────────────
        5   9   6      6   1   1            9   1   2
                           1   1                5   1
```

Jenny has two calculations correct and one wrong. Her misconception is identified in the third example. Here, she has carried the ten from adding the ones column and has not combined it with the other tens, but recorded it as if using the expanded method. She has then added the three tens and the two tens correctly, but because there is now no room in the tens column, she has placed it in the hundreds column.

Why, therefore, has she got the first two correct? The response to this is that the first two examples do not involve carrying to the next part of the calculation. Example 1 has no carrying at all and Example 2 has the hundreds adding to more than 10, although as it is the final part of the calculation it does not carry but is placed on the answer line.

Making estimations to start with, Jenny should have identified that, in example 3, the answer of 512 for 38 + 24 is unrealistic. Using rounding, a more reasonable estimate of 40 + 25 would help Jenny see that the answer should be around 65, so she could start to reason why her answer was wrong.

Vicky has the first calculation correct. Her misconception, however, is that she is working from left to right, using mental strategies she has learned. Again, by encouraging estimation before starting the calculation Vicky will realise her answer cannot be correct and will therefore try again.

Michael has two of his calculations correct. It is not until the third example that the numbers used draw out the misconception, which is that he is carrying the wrong number. This misconception can be reinforced by the language used when teaching. If we analyse example 3, the ones column is correct (4 + 8 = 12) and the 10 is carried to the tens column. When he adds the tens column, as 8 + 6 + the carried 1 = 15, it isn't surprising that here Michael wants to put the 1 in the tens column then incorrectly carries the 5. It is important that when teaching the column method, we continue to reinforce the 80 and 60 in this case to then give an answer of 140. The 1 here will then automatically be carried to the hundreds column. Example 2, although carrying in both columns, does not draw out the misconception as the numbers total 11. When planning the questions, we suggest avoiding number bonds to 11 to enable the misconceptions to be identified at the earliest opportunity.

Mastery Task

How many ways can you rearrange these digits to get the same answer?

	2	8	4
	1	7	5
+	3	9	6
	8	5	5

Have a takeaway

Mental strategies and partitioning can support children whilst learning both formal and informal written methods for subtraction.

Calculate: 776 – 253 =

Expanded method

```
    7   0   0   +   7   0   +   6
-   2   0   0   +   5   0   +   3
    5   0   0   +   2   0   +   3
```

This method uses partitioning to expand the calculation. The layout reinforces the correct value of each column and links to the mental horizontal layout.

In this example, the bottom number can be subtracted from the top number in each case, starting with the ones.

Column addition

```
    7   7   6
-   2   5   3
    5   2   3
```

This is the short column method which children in Year 6 should know by the end of Key Stage 2.

To work through it, start with the ones and calculate 6 – 3.

Next subtract the tens. To reinforce the value it's best to say, *seven tens subtract five tens, equals two tens*, or *seventy minus fifty, equals twenty*. The first way supports the understanding of the fact that only the digit 2 is entered.

Finally, the hundreds are calculated: seven hundreds, subtract two hundreds, equals five hundreds.

Subtraction starts to become more complicated when it appears it is not possible to subtract the digits. In this case we have to use decomposition to manipulate the numbers so that the calculation can be carried out. Children can find this quite difficult to understand, so visual aids such as partitioning cards will support the process. They help to reinforce both the value of each number and visually support the decomposition process.

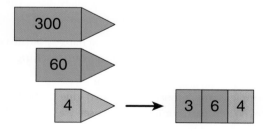

Calculate: 982 – 247

Expanded decomposition

```
                        7   0
    9   0   0   +   ̶8̶  ̶0̶  +  ¹2
-   2   0   0   +   4   0   +   7
    7   0   0   +   3   0   +   5
```

To work out this calculation we begin with the ones, saying, *two take away seven*. In this written method, it is not possible so we have to exchange from the tens. We exchange the 80 into 70 and 10 (as marked in red) thus enabling us to carry the ones (as it is now 12 – 7). Make sure that once you have exchanged, you reinforce to the children that they should add along to make sure the total is the same as the start number: $900 + 70 + 12 = 982$.

The rest of the calculation is completed in the same way as the previous example due to no more exchanging being required.

Column decomposition

$$
\begin{array}{r}
\;\;^{7} \\
9 \quad \not{8} \quad {}^{1}2 \\
- \quad 2 \quad 4 \quad 7 \\
\hline

\end{array}
$$

This is the column method of decomposition. Just as with the expanded method, the tens will need to be exchanged.

By using the language, *eight tens* and *exchanged into seven tens and one ten*, the value of each column is reinforced.

Avoid statements such as, *cross out the eight and turn it into a seven and a one* as this does not physically describe what is happening to the numbers involved and may lead to misconceptions in the future.

Exchange or borrow?

The best way to describe decomposition is to use the term **exchange**. The word accurately describes what takes place – mathematically and physically – to the numbers. For example, if we 'exchange' 700, it becomes 600 and 100.

Some still use the term 'borrow'. Using the example of 700 they would say, *borrow 100 from the 700 to make 600*. Although this does adequately describe what takes place, the term 'borrow' does infer that there should be payback at some point later in the process.

We would suggest that best practice is to use the term 'exchange', but if your school uses the term 'borrow', consider how you can use both terms within your teaching to broaden the children's understanding.

Exchanging in the next example is much more complicated, due to the fact that the top number has many zeros as place holders. When partitioning you can see we have included not just one zero at each column, but the number of zeros to retain the place value.

Calculate: 7,002 – 4,873 =

	6	0	0	0		9	0	0		9	0		
	$\not{7}$	$\not{0}$	$\not{0}$	$\not{0}$	+	$\not{}^{1}0$	$\not{0}$	$\not{0}$	+	$\not{}^{1}0$	$\not{0}$	+	${}^{1}2$
–	4	0	0	0	+	8	0	0	+	7	0	+	3
	2	0	0	0	+	1	0	0	+	2	0	+	9

Answer: 2,129

The calculation would be worked as follows (in red):

We can't do 2 – 3 = ? so we need to exchange. There is nothing in either the tens or hundreds, so we need to exchange from the thousands. 7,000 is exchanged for 6,000 and 1,000. This does not enable us to work out the calculation yet so we continue exchanging; 1,000 is exchanged for 900 and 100 and then we do the final exchange of 100 into 90 and 10.

Before completing the calculation, check the exchanges still add up to the start number: 6,000 + 900 + 90 + 12 = 7,002. Then the subtraction can be completed.

	6	9	9	
	7̶	0̶	0̶	¹2
−	4	8	7	3
	2	1	2	9

This is the column method for the end of Key Stage 2, which shows the same exchanges as above in a more efficient way.

When teaching this method, reinforce the value of each exchange – for example, not *exchange the seven into a six and a one*, but *exchange the seven thousands into six thousands and one thousand*.

Sometimes, methods involve using the inverse operation to find the answer to a calculation. To explore this, an empty number line is a good way to initially represent the process.

Calculate: 743 – 185 =

The method shown to solve this question is the ***compensation method***. It is used as a direct link with the inverse operation of counting on to calculate subtraction.

If we visualise it first on a number line we can see more clearly how the written method works.

To calculate the answer, we add the numbers in each leap.

Answer: 558

	7	4	3
−	1	8	5
			5
		1	0
	5	0	0
		4	3
	5	5	8

This is the written method which represents the number line above. It is a more formal way of showing the compensation method to solve the subtraction calculation. It is less common than the initial methods shown, but some children find the direct link to a visual context easier to follow.

Reflection

Examine the calculations below. Mark them and diagnose the misconceptions for each child.

Emma

```
     3  6          6  0          6  3  2
  -  1  5       -  4  5       -  2  8  1
     2  1          2  5          4  5  1
```

Laura

```
   2                                    6
   3̶                                    7̶
   4̶ ¹3 ¹2        5  6̶ ¹3        8̶ ¹0 ¹6
 -   1  5  6    -  2  1  9    -  4  3  7
     1  8  6       3  4  4       2  7  9
```

Emma has the first calculation correct. However, in the next two subtractions she is subtracting the smallest from the largest from each column, ignoring whether it is the number on the top or the bottom. Although estimating is always advised, she possibly wouldn't question these answers as they aren't sufficiently far away from the correct answer.

The best way to tackle this misconception is to talk the examples through with the child; reinforcing, for example, in example 2 the fact that the bottom number is taken away from the top, so 5 cannot be taken from 0 and therefore exchanging would be required.

Laura has a more sophisticated misconception. Again, one calculation is correct (the second) but understanding why and how to respond will need greater consideration. There will be times when we mark children's work when we really don't understand how they have completed a calculation; in this instance, we would advise that you either ask the child to talk you through what they have done, or ask them to complete a further example explaining the working as they do it.

Laura can obviously exchange accurately (as the second question demonstrates), so is there a misconception or just an error in the working? We can see the exchanging in red and green on the calculations so this does help in this instance. She has identified the need to exchange in the first one – however, she has exchanged from the hundreds and not the tens. Why? Well, if we look closely we can see that in the first example the tens column (3 – 5) you cannot do, so she doesn't exchange from there. In the second example the tens column (6 – 1) you can do, so she exchanges the tens.

Example 3 follows the same pattern as the first. Due to the fact the tens column (0 – 3) cannot be subtracted, Laura exchanges from the hundreds.

Mastery Task

Find the missing digits in this subtraction question:

```
      6   4   Δ
  -   2   Δ   8
  ─────────────
      3   5   9
```

Before moving on to the final two operations, complete Task 5.1 using the methods we have explored so far.

Task 5.1

Complete these calculations using a range of methods:

```
                    2   5   9
      8   5   3     1   7   6         7   5   3   9
  +   3   6   7   + 5   5   8     +   1   3   9   6
  ─────────────   ─────────────   ─────────────────


      7   2   9     8   1   4         8   0   0   5
  -   5   6   2   - 5   6   7     -   2   6   7   3
  ─────────────   ─────────────   ─────────────────

```

Go forth and multiply

When teaching multiplication, exploring informal written methods first will enable children to gain a deeper understanding of the operation and make links.

Grid method

Calculate: 178 × 6 =

×	100	70	6
6	600	420	36

```
          600
          420
      +    36
      ─────────
         1056
```

This is the **grid method** of multiplication. Many schools use this as a transition method to the more formal written method.

The number is partitioned, and then each partitioned number is multiplied by 6.

Finally, they are added together to reach the final total.

Short multiplication

```
        1   7   6
    ×     4   3   6
    _____
    1   0   5   6
```

The following method is the short method of multiplication outlined in the National Curriculum. It mirrors the parts of the grid method, but in a contracted form using the 'carrying' process used in addition.

When multiplying two-digit numbers, the process is expanded. We must be careful how we teach this to ensure that children don't develop 'short cuts', which in turn lead to misconceptions.

Calculate: 38 × 62 =

×	30	8	
60	1800	480	2280
2	60	16	¹76
			2356

The grid method reinforces the commutative nature of multiplication and addition: that the calculations can be carried out in any order and the solution would still be the same.

When calculating 60×30 it is important we don't encourage the children to think of it as 6×3 then 'add two zeros'. To teach this, we must draw on our understanding of mental methods and think of the 60 as 6×10 and the 30 as 3×10, so the calculation should be taught as $6 \times 3 \times 10 \times 10$.

Then $60 \times 8 = 6 \times 8 \times 10$, $2 \times 30 = 2 \times 3 \times 10$, 2×8.

To reinforce the fact that the four solutions can be added in any order, horizontally or vertically, children need to explore this to see that it is, in fact, always the case and then they have the choice with the final grid to choose the order that they feel is the best at the time.

Expanded long multiplication

```
            3   8
        ×   6   2
        _____
            1   6      2 x 8 = 16
            6   0      2 x 30 = 6
        4   8   0      60 x 8 = 480
    1   8   0   0      60 x 30 = 1800
    _____
    2   3   5   6
    1       1
```

This expanded method of long multiplication links directly to the grid method. It clearly shows each of the four calculations to be carried out. As this is a vertical method, we start with the ones column, multiplying first the 8 then the 30 by 2, then the 8 and 30 is multiplied by 60.

Finally, the four rows are added using the column method of addition.

Long multiplication

```
            3   8
      x     6   2
            7¹  6
  2   2⁴    8   0
  2   3     5   6
      1
```

This is the long multiplication method which children are expected to know by the end of Key Stage 2.

First, working from the right we multiply 38 by 2.

$2 \times 8 = 16$, so we place the 6 and carry the 10 (in red).

$2 \times 30 = 60$, then add to this the carried 10. As we work more efficiently we move to the shorter language of $2 \times 3 = 6$ then add 1. This should only be encouraged when the child has a deep understanding of the process and fully understands place value.

Next, we calculate 38×60.

All whole numbers that are multiplied by 10 end in zero, so we would expect 38×60 to end in zero (in red) as we can partition this into $38 \times 6 \times 10$. We can then carry out the rest of the calculation as with the first row, in the more efficient form.

Whilst teaching the various methods of multiplication we should be aware of the misconceptions which could arise so we can draw them out in the examples we use.

Reflection

Examine the calculations below. Mark them and diagnose the misconceptions for each child.

Mellissa

```
      2   5              6   8              3   9
  x   ¹   3          x   ⁵   7          x   ³   4
      2   5              3   0   6          9   6
```

(Continued)

(Continued)

Paul

```
      8   3              2   5              3   7
×  ¹      5           ×  1   1           ×  6   2
   4   1   5             2   5           2  2₄   2
                      2   5   0          7₁  4   0
                      2   7   5          9   6   2
```

Nena

```
      2   6              3   5              3   7
×  9   3             ×  6   3           ×  4   6
      1   8             1   5              4   2
   1   8   0          1   8   0          1   2   0
   1   9   8          1   9   5          1   6   3
```

If any part of a multiplication calculation is carried out incorrectly, then there is more likelihood of an incorrect response. The role of estimation is key in supporting children to assess whether the answer they have is a reasonable one.

Mellissa is completing the multiplications vertically as if they were addition questions. If we look at the first example, she has multiplied the ones correctly: $3 \times 5 = 15$. However, the carried 1 (in red) has then been vertically multiplied by the 2 (20) to result in a final answer of 25. The same method has been used to complete all three questions.

Paul has the first two questions correct. However, it is only in the third example that we see what the misconception is: he is carrying out the multiplication in the wrong order. If we look at the third question, he has multiplied 37×6 first, by saying 6×7 then 6×3. Next, the zero as a place holder for multiplying by the tens has been added to the second line as a rule, rather than understanding the process. Once the zero has been added it is then that Paul has multiplied 37 by 2. Paul has actually calculated 37×26.

Without fully understanding the reason why there is a zero at the end of the second line, this misconception cannot be dealt with. To support this, it would be useful to return to the grid method, or expanded long multiplication, to apply the correct place value to each number.

If we look at the other two examples, we can see why they are answered correctly; the first question is multiplication by a single digit and the second question is multiplied by 11, so it is not possible to identify the order in which the child has carried out the calculation unless the child talks it through.

Nena has carried out the column multiplication rules but in addition order. If we look at question one, she has first calculated $6 \times 3 = 18$ then she has added a 0 to the second row and vertically multiplied $9 \times 2 = 18$. The teaching of rules has had an impact on Nena's approach to this calculation.

The use of expanded or transition methods, before moving to the more formal written methods of short and long multiplication, enables a deeper understanding to be achieved. They also support those children in the class who need more structure and step-by-step processes to a method.

Mastery Task

Complete the missing numbers in the grid below:

×	40	?	
90	3600	720	4,320
?		56	

Divide and conquer

The methods used to teach division rely on a sound understanding and ability in addition, subtraction and multiplication. Division is the inverse operation of multiplication; however, we should also be linking division to repeated subtraction, just as multiplication links to repeated addition.

To start, we will explore short division by a single digit.

Calculate: 272 ÷ 6 =

This number line method shows how division can be carried out using repeated subtraction.

First, subtract 40 lots of 6 (240).

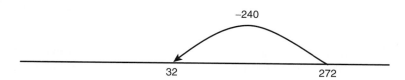

This leaves us with 32.

We can now subtract 5 lots of 6 (30).

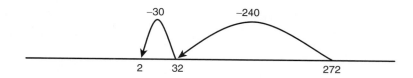

This leaves us with 2. We have now taken away a total of 45 lots of 6 and have 2 left. Therefore, the answer is 45 r2.

Expanded method

```
                4    5    r2
                _____
    6  |  2    7    2
    -     2    4    0      40 × 6
              _____
              3    2
    -         3    0      5 × 6
              _____
                   2
              _____
```

Bank
40 × 6 = 240
20 × 6 = 120
10 × 6 = 60
5 × 6 = 30

This expanded method, known as **chunking**, involves multiplication and subtraction by subtracting multiple groups of the divisor.

First, a bank is created to assist with identifying the number of groups to subtract.

Then we look at the number as a whole, which is 272, and ask how many groups of six could be subtracted from this? Forty groups of six are subtracted to leave 32. We then identify how many groups of six can be subtracted, which is five. The total number of groups subtracted is 45 with 2 left over. Therefore, the answer is 45 r2.

Bus stop/short division

```
              4     5    r2
           _____
    6  |  2   ²7    ³2
```

This is the formal method used for short division, also known as the **bus stop** method.

To start we ask how many 6s are there in 2? As the answer is zero, the 2 is carried to the next column.

Continuing the calculation, we now ask how many 6s are in 27 which gives an answer of 4 r3. The 4 is recorded (in green) and the remainder of 3 (in red) is carried to the next column.

Finally, we ask how many 6s are in 32? The answer is 5 r2. The answer 5 (in green) is placed on the top line and then, as the calculation is complete, the remainder placed at the end. It is important to remember that the remainder is $\frac{2}{6}$.

Children can struggle with this method, as the language used to work it through does not support traditional place value and is therefore hard to understand. Repeated subtraction provides a method which can be demonstrated easily with resources, thus creating a visual image to support understanding.

Long division is developed from the two previous methods. Initially children may be taught the chunking method linked to repeated subtraction, then the more formal algorithm for long division. Some schools may choose to only adopt the long division method identified in the National Curriculum.

Calculate: 786 ÷ 17 =

```
17  | 7   8   6
  -   6   8   0    40 × 17
      1   10   6
    -   6   8        4 × 17
        3   8
      -   3   4      2 × 17
            4
```

Bank
40 × 17 = 680
20 × 17 = 340
10 × 17 = 170
4 × 17 = 68
2 × 17 = 34

In total, we have subtracted 46 lots of 17 with a remainder of 4.

Answer: 46 r4

This is long division using the *chunking* method with a two-digit number as divisor.

Just like the short division version, using one digit, we identify a bank of quantities to assist. Here we subtracted 40 lots first – this could have been done as 20 lots then another 20 lots; there is no set way to subtract and the child can select different groupings. In fact, we would recommend children explore the different ways the chunks can be taken away to reinforce the range of ways available.

The final solution is found by adding the number of lots of 17 subtracted (in green).

Make sure that when children list the lots/groups removed, they check that they record them in the same order. If on one example a child had recorded 17 × 4 instead, then adding down the column to find the total would result in an incorrect answer.

Long division

```
            4   6    r4
17  | 7   8   6
  -   6   8   ↓
      1   0   6
    -   1   0   2
            4
```

Using this more traditional method of long division, although more efficient, does not reinforce the place value of the numbers; children often find this method hard to understand.

To work through it, we start by saying, *How many 17s are there in 78?* The answer is 4 (in green) which is 68. This is then subtracted from the 78 to leave 10.

Next, we bring down the 6 (in red) to make 106 and then find how many 17s are in 106. The answer is 6 equalling 102 which is then subtracted from 106 leaving a remainder of 4.

The long division method does mean that children are learning a method by rote, rather than understanding why the calculation works. It is a more efficient method, as opposed to the chunking method where producing the bank can be time consuming. We would always advise that children learn a range of methods to focus on deep understanding and then learn those which are efficient. Focusing only on an efficient method can mean that when the rote, rule-based procedure is forgotten, the children no longer remember how to do the calculation.

Reflection

Sue has completed the following division calculations. Mark them and diagnose any misconceptions.

$$
\begin{array}{r}
2\ \ 1 \\
4\ \overline{|\ 8\ \ 4} \\
\end{array}
\qquad
\begin{array}{r}
1\ \ 0\ \ 2 \\
6\ \overline{|\ 6\ \ 2} \\
\end{array}
\qquad
\begin{array}{r}
1\ \ 3\ \ 0\ \ 1 \\
3\ \overline{|\ 3\ \ 9\ \ 1} \\
\end{array}
$$

Sue is completing the bus stop method of short division. The first question is correct due to 84 being exactly divisible by 4. The next two are incorrect as the remainder is not being correctly identified. The red digits should be written r2 and r1 to show how many is left over. The routine of estimation would again draw attention to the fact that the answer is unreasonable.

To develop your own understanding further, complete Task 5.2 using as many of the methods shown in this chapter as possible.

Task 5.2

Complete these calculations using a range of methods.

$$
\begin{array}{r}
7\ \ 8 \\
\times\ \ 2\ \ 6 \\
\hline
\end{array}
\qquad
\begin{array}{r}
7\ \ 5\ \ 6 \\
\times\ \ \ \ \ 3\ \ 2 \\
\hline
\end{array}
\qquad
\begin{array}{r}
8\ \ 9 \\
\times\ \ 5\ \ 7 \\
\hline
\end{array}
$$

$$
6\ \overline{|\ 5\ \ 8\ \ 9}
\qquad
15\ \overline{|\ 6\ \ 2\ \ 7}
\qquad
23\ \overline{|\ 8\ \ 9\ \ 1\ \ 6}
$$

Mastery Task

Ask the children to prove that 15 × 15 isn't (10 × 10) + (5 × 5).

Teaching idea

When learning to teach any of the methods used in this chapter, initially it is worth writing a script to enable you to focus on the correct language to use with children, appropriate to their stage.

In addition, we would also advise practising modelling how you work through each of the methods to ensure accuracy and develop your own confidence in using the methods – especially those with which you are not familiar.

Finally, it is essential before teaching any method in school that you consult the school's calculation policy to ensure you develop the school's agreed written methods and not just the methods you want to teach.

Task 5.3

When teaching any of the four operations discussed in this chapter it is important that you broaden children's mathematical vocabulary linked to each operation.

Complete the table below with as many mathematical terms as you can for each operation.

Add	Subtract	Multiply	Divide

Rounding up

There are various written methods, both informal and formal, all of which you need to be confident in. This chapter has explored those most commonly used in a primary classroom.

It is important that you are confident not only in the method you are teaching, but how you will teach it, the language you will use and the possible misconceptions which could arise that will need addressing.

Remember to ensure the children understand why a method works – don't just teach to rules which have no context and, if forgotten, may mean they can no longer carry out the calculation.

Again, we caution you to not move too quickly to the contracted algorithm for each operation. Any teaching of calculation strategies should be in line with the school's calculation policy. It may be useful for you to discuss this policy with the lead teacher for mathematics in your school.

WHAT MATHS CAN YOU SEE?

RECURRING PROBLEMS

- Key misconceptions
- Where do I begin?
- Key concepts in fractions, decimals and percentages
- Formal calculations with fractions, decimals and percentages
- Out of proportion
- Rounding up
- What maths can you see?

Recurring problems

This chapter will look at the topics of fractions, decimals and percentages. We will look closely at the formal calculation techniques that children need to undertake, as well as explain the key conceptual understanding that these calculations require. As a teacher assigned to a specific year group, you will not be teaching every element covered in this chapter in one sequence of lessons. However, by fully appreciating the start and end points for these topics, you can ensure that your contribution is a significant part of children's learning experience.

Fractions, decimals and percentages are not some strange part of the mathematics world. They are purely numbers and are a rich and integral part of the number system. Bear in mind that children will develop their concepts and skills in fractions, decimals and percentages over six years. There is a natural order to that progression and it is up to the teacher to determine how children are navigated along that journey. We will explore different aspects of that progression, but this book is not a scheme of work. The order in which we discuss elements of this topic may not be the same as the order in which your school teaches them.

Many mathematics textbooks will have a chapter on decimals and then perhaps a chapter on fractions, followed by a separate chapter on percentages. Additionally, many schemes of work, especially in the early days of the National Curriculum, encouraged teachers to teach these as separate topics. We have seen many units of work where children are expected to do perhaps three days on fractions and then move to something else, before doing two days on percentages, etc. Thus, these very important topics can be taught and learned in isolation of each other. This should be avoided. Such separation of topics is detrimental to children's deep mathematical understanding.

Primarily, fractions, decimals and percentages are all about the numbers between the integers. It is difficult to try to explain any one of these topics without leaning on another. For example, if talking about decimals we need to relate this to fractions in terms of tenths and hundredths. When talking about percentages, we again need to talk about hundredths. Children need to be able to relate fractions to decimals. They need to be able to calculate percentages by converting to fractions. Above all, children need to continually link each of these topics to their understanding of the number system and operations with numbers.

Without doubt, the teaching of fractions, decimals and percentages is where we can see the most frequent examples of teaching rules and recipes.

I know I must turn upside down but I'm not sure why.

Rules and recipes are a shortcut. They can be a safe haven for a teacher who themselves is perhaps less confident in an area; they can also provide children with techniques to get the 'right' answer.

However, we must ask, is there a value in being able to perform such 'tricks' without the child understanding what they are doing? If the child forgets the rule or, more likely, misapplies the rule, they may become 'stuck'.

The current Primary National Curriculum for Key Stage 2 includes several 'statutory requirements' relating to teaching fractions, decimals and percentages, that were previously taught at Key Stage 3. Ensuring children gain a clear and deep understanding of the concepts involved in these topics, and can from the outset see the relationship between fractions, decimals and percentages, allows them to be moved on more successfully to learn how to calculate in each form.

Reflection

Before you read on, make a list of the rules you were taught in school, related to calculating with fractions, decimals and percentages. Do you think that the way you were taught these topics was effective?

Key misconceptions

Before we give any further consideration to the 'rules' for undertaking calculations with fractions, decimals and percentages, it is important for you to appreciate that there are a significant number of key misconceptions children can have in their understanding of these topics.

When teaching any new topic in mathematics, a teacher should first consider some of the possible difficulties a child may have with the work and what errors they may make in their understanding of the topic. The teacher then needs to address these in their teaching to ensure that children do not pick up any of these misconceptions.

One of the privileges of being a primary teacher, is that it is you who will be providing children with their first experiences of many mathematical topics. If you get your teaching right, children will become confident in their ability in that topic. However, if you get it wrong, you can confuse them and end up teaching children that they 'can't do it'. For the rest of their school lives, they may be inhibited in their progression in that topic, because their introduction to it was negative.

Once a child holds a misconception, it is surprising how they will 'stick' with it. The misconception can come back again and again – hence the title of this chapter. So, let us begin by considering just some of these common misconceptions in fractions, decimals and percentages.

The more decimal places then the bigger the number

This misconception is often associated with using the same oral notation for numbers to the right of the decimal point as those before. For example, a child can easily think 0.8 is smaller than 0.26, as 8 is smaller than 26. It is essential that numbers after the decimal point are consistently read, and spoken, as individual digits. Thus, 0.26 should not read as *zero point twenty-six* but as *zero point two six*. Similarly, a three-digit decimal such as 0.391 must be spoken as *zero point three nine one*, rather than *zero point three hundred and ninety-one*.

Larger denominators make the fraction bigger

For similar reasons, it can be entirely logical for a child to think that $\frac{1}{5}$ is bigger than $\frac{1}{3}$ as they 'know' that 5 is bigger than 3. Such a conceptual error, however, means that the child does not really comprehend what a fraction is. This type of misconception can occur when a child is moved on in a topic before they are ready.

Multiplication makes things bigger and division makes things smaller

This is true if multiplying and dividing by numbers bigger than 1. However, multiplying any number by another that is between 0 and 1 makes it smaller. Children can encounter real difficulty in understanding this. However, it is easy to demonstrate that this is so. For example, 0.5×12 is the same as half of 12: of course it is smaller! Similarly, dividing by numbers between 0 and 1 makes things bigger.

The denominator becomes the decimal

Decimals are an extension of place value. Thus, $\frac{1}{10} = 0.1 = 0.10$. Perhaps then, it is not surprising that some children may think that $\frac{1}{5} = 0.5$ and that $\frac{1}{7} = 0.7$.

The percentage becomes the denominator

This is very similar to 'the denominator become the decimal' and arises from the fact that 10% is equal to $\frac{1}{10}$. Thus, some children may believe $12\% = \frac{1}{12}$ or $8\% = \frac{1}{8}$.

Where do I begin?

There are lots of different ways to introduce children to non-integer numbers, and many teachers will disagree about which way is best. However, for us, it is sensible to begin with decimals, as they are so important to our day-to-day lives – especially in money and measure. In order for children to make any real sense of decimals, and to be able to make the links between different applications of decimal numbers, it is important to ensure they appreciate how place value works.

Base 10 again

At your level, you should appreciate that our base 10 number system is based upon 'powers' of 10:

10^4	10^3	10^2	10^1	10^0
ten thousands	**thousands**	**hundreds**	**tens**	**ones (units)**

In Chapter 2 we looked at how to develop a sense of place value, especially in Key Stage 1. We looked at multiplication of integers by 10 and why one simply doesn't just 'add a zero' as it is the place value that changes. For example, consider 36×10 and 36×100.

	thousands	hundreds	tens	ones/units	number
36			3	6	36
36 × 10		3	6	0	360
36 × 100	3	6	0	0	3,600

In the answer to 36 × 10, the three tens now become three hundreds, and the six ones/units now become six tens. In the answer, there are no units so we use 0 as a **place holder**. This is extended for multiplying by 100 or 1,000, etc.

For division, let us consider 7,800 ÷ 10 and 7,800 ÷ 100, using the inverse of the multiplication method.

	thousands	hundreds	tens	ones/units	number
7,800	7	8	0	0	7,800
7,800 ÷ 10		7	8	0	780
7,800 ÷ 100			7	8	78

Now let us consider what happens to the right of the ones/units column. Moving from right to left we divide by 10.

$$1,000 \xrightarrow{\div 10} 100 \xrightarrow{\div 10} 10 \xrightarrow{\div 10} 1 \xrightarrow{\div 10} \frac{1}{10} \xrightarrow{\div 10} \frac{1}{100}$$

To separate out the whole numbers and the non-whole numbers (or decimal fractions) we use the conventional decimal symbol, which looks like a full stop.

We can then apply this to division as follows:

	hundreds	tens	ones/units		tenths	hundredths	number
38		3	8	.			38
38 ÷ 10			3	.	8		3.8
38 ÷ 100			0	.	3	8	0.38

By Year 4, children are expected to be able to divide any one- or two-digit number by 10 or 100. They should also be able to write the decimal number for any amount of tenths or hundredths. To do this, all of the activities we have previously considered for developing children's knowledge of number and place value can be used and extended to decimal numbers.

Just add zero

You will recall that in Chapter 2 we discussed the danger of adding a zero to multiply by 10. We will now explore this rule further in relation to decimals to consider the wider implications of teaching to rules, rather than deep understanding.

If we use the 'add a zero' rule with decimals, then the following responses are possible:

Consider three different responses to 56.1×100.

response	thousands	hundreds	tens	ones		tenths	hundredths	thousandths
			5	6	.	1		
(a)			5	6	.	1	0	0
(b)	5	6	0	0	.	1		
(c)	5	6	1	0	.			

Response (a) - the child has followed the rule and just added two zeros. This response reinforces a lack of understanding of the value of each place.

For (b) - the two zeros have been added as if the question was a whole number, leaving the one tenth in its original place.

Response (c) - is correct as all digits have moved two places to the left and only one zero is needed as a place holder.

What possible answers could there be when dividing by 100?

Consider $302.5 \div 100 =$

response	thousands	hundreds	tens	ones		tenths	hundredths	thousandths
		3	0	2	.	5		
(a)			3	2	.	5		
(b)			3	3	.	0	2	5

Response (a) - the zero has been removed, misapplying the rule.

Response (b) - all digits have been moved two places to the right. The zero has been retained as a place holder between digits 3 and 2.

Note: in these examples, the decimal point has not moved, the digits have. Were you taught to move the decimal point to multiply and divide by 10 and 100? This is another quick method which is often taught, but again does not reinforce understanding of place value.

Key concepts in fractions, decimals and percentages

To help children develop their concept of a decimal number it is important to look at rounding decimals to the nearest whole number. A useful way to do this is going back to our number line and asking children to note on that line where a particular decimal number is. For introductory work your number line may just go from, say, 1 to 5 and children need to show where decimal numbers such as 3.2 or 1.9 may be. This can then help them decide, *Which is the nearest whole number?*

Teaching idea

Draw a number line spanning just two consecutive integers, for example:

```
 _____
3                                4
```

Ask children to show you where 3.2 is, and then 3.3.

Using such a diagram, it is relatively easy to decide what numbers are closer to three and what numbers are closer to four. What if we had 3.51 or 3.52? Most children are happy to round these up to 4.

However, what if we have a number exactly half way? Here we can generate much discussion about whether 3.5 is closer to 3 or to 4. The fact that we actually round such a number up is a mathematical convention.

Extension: Now ask for a number in between 3.2 and 3.3. How many answers are there?

Mastery Task

Children work in pairs or small groups. One child picks two consecutive numbers and, using a mini whiteboard, shows them on a number line. Children have to keep finding new numbers between these.

For example, suppose the first child picks 3; we would have:

```
 _____
3                                4
```

The second child may say 3.3, and can show this on same line. Now the next child needs to find another number between 3 and 4 and show it in the right position. This is repeated by each child. Very quickly, all the decimal tenths become exhausted so the children will need to consider numbers in between these. This activity very quickly helps develop understanding of second and third decimal places.

This task can be made more challenging by using more complex starting numbers - for example, 3.05 and 3.41.

Until children have an appreciation of place value in decimal numbers, there is little value in moving them on to the four operations with decimal numbers.

As we said at the start of this chapter, such an appreciation cannot be taught without talking about fractions. In fact, it may be that fractions feel like a more comfortable place to begin the study of non-integers. From an early age, children have a concept of 'half'. Interestingly, many children think there is something known as 'the biggest half'. They may be familiar with 'half an hour' (although they may not appreciate its significance). Time is actually a good way to develop understanding of fractions.

A key concept that needs to be initially acquired by children is understanding that dividing something in half is the same as dividing it into two equal parts. Similarly, they need to understand that finding $\frac{1}{3}$ of something requires division into three equal parts, and so on. There are many 'whole' objects that can be halved or divided into thirds or quarters … aren't there?

Teaching idea

Ask your class how they could divide an apple into two equal halves.

Once you have done this, ask them how we can check that the two halves are EXACTLY equal?

Can we actually have two equal halves of an apple?

You may then think about dividing a bar of chocolate, with say 12 or 24 squares, into two, three or four. This then leads us to finding a fraction of a quantity and immediately there are links to division of number. There are many ways to develop in young children the relationship between fractions of a quantity and division. Many teachers at this point reach for the 'colouring-in pencils'. Many internet resources in this area are based upon tasks requiring colouring in. We are hesitant about recommending this approach. There may be a place to encourage children to 'colour in' – especially in helping to develop their motor skills in holding a pencil – but colouring in as a mathematics activity is, in our opinion, 'time heavy'.

The sort of simple task we may ask of children at this point could be, for example, find half of 18. This may be approached in several ways. First, we could use a variety of concrete resources such as counters to show 18 of them can be split equally into two nines. We could ask children to draw a number line from 0 to 18 and ask them to find the point that divides this line into two equal parts.

If children can understand the number line image, and relate it to having two equal parts and division by two, they are likely to become more confident in a purely arithmetic approach.

In Year 2, children are introduced to **non-unit fractions**. This sounds much more complicated than it really is. **Unit fractions** are those with one as the numerator such as $\frac{1}{3}$ or $\frac{1}{4}$. A non-unit fraction has a numerator greater than one, such as $\frac{2}{3}$ or $\frac{3}{4}$.

By Year 3, we would be expecting children to know that finding $\frac{1}{5}, \frac{1}{8}, \frac{1}{10}$ of any quantity involves dividing that quantity by the value of the denominator. This then leads them to be able to undertake calculations using non-unit fractions. For example, to calculate $\frac{2}{3}$ of a quantity by first finding $\frac{1}{3}$ and then doubling the answer, or to find $\frac{3}{4}$ by first finding $\frac{1}{4}$ and then tripling the answer. The key pedagogical aspect to this is that we are not teaching children rules. The links between the denominator to division and the numerator to multiplication occur naturally.

Another objective we need to achieve is to help children appreciate that there are many fractions that are in fact the same, or **equivalent**. So, imagine we have two quarters of a whole object. We can use many methods to show that these are equivalent to one half. For example, we could divide a cake into four pieces and show children that two of those pieces is equal to one half. We can also develop this understanding numerically using a number line.

Teaching idea

This will work either as a whole-class activity, or in pairs or small groups.

Draw a straight line on a piece of A3 paper 60 cm long. Use two dice* to generate two numbers which will become our fraction, with the larger number being the denominator. For example, if 2 and 3 are thrown, our fraction is $\frac{2}{3}$ but if a double 6 is thrown our fraction is $\frac{6}{6}$, or six sixths.

For each fraction generated, children need to calculate it as a fraction of 60 and mark it on their number line. Thus, if the two numbers on the dice are 6 and 4 we find $\frac{4}{6}$ of 60 cm and mark it.

Later, children may get a 2 and a 3 and will be able to show that $\frac{2}{3} = \frac{4}{6}$ or that $\frac{3}{6} = \frac{1}{2}$ etc.

This activity is very useful in giving children practice in finding fractions of a number; the same method is helpful in showing that $\frac{1}{6} < \frac{1}{5}$ or $\frac{1}{4} < \frac{1}{3}$ etc.

The final work produced by the children can be used for your classroom display or as part of a working wall.

*Remember that the word 'dice' is a plural and that the singular is 'die'. Also, for whole-class work, it is great fun to use giant foam dice, that schools may have, to generate the numbers.

This teaching idea can lead us to exploring **equivalence**. The dice activity may demonstrate that $\frac{2}{6}$ is equal to $\frac{1}{3}$. However, we can also show this as an image using a **fraction wall**.

1 whole					
$\frac{1}{3}$		$\frac{1}{3}$		$\frac{1}{3}$	
$\frac{1}{6}$	$\frac{1}{6}$	$\frac{1}{6}$	$\frac{1}{6}$	$\frac{1}{6}$	$\frac{1}{6}$

Or for halves, quarters and eighths:

1 whole							
$\frac{1}{2}$				$\frac{1}{2}$			
$\frac{1}{4}$		$\frac{1}{4}$		$\frac{1}{4}$		$\frac{1}{4}$	
$\frac{1}{8}$	$\frac{1}{8}$	$\frac{1}{8}$	$\frac{1}{8}$	$\frac{1}{8}$	$\frac{1}{8}$	$\frac{1}{8}$	$\frac{1}{8}$

By using fraction walls, it is very easy to see that $\frac{4}{6} = \frac{2}{3}$ or $\frac{4}{8} = \frac{1}{2}$. Once this has been established, we can show that the same result can be obtained by simply dividing the top number (numerator) and the bottom number (denominator) by the same number. You will probably remember this as **cancelling down.**

We then need children to explore fractions such as $\frac{24}{36}$.

$$\frac{24}{36} = \frac{12}{18} = \frac{6}{9} = \frac{2}{3}$$

(Here we have cancelled by 2 three times, and then by 3.)

A key message here is that we can 'cancel down' by any number we like and as many times as we like: however, you may realise that we could have got from $\frac{24}{36}$ to $\frac{2}{3}$ in one jump if we cancelled by 12. (Note: $2 \times 2 \times 2 \times 3 = 12$.)

It is very easy to compare decimal numbers or percentages with each other. However, comparing fractions is much more difficult. Which is bigger: $\frac{1}{3}$ or $\frac{2}{5}$? If you are not sure then you need to complete the teaching idea above and it will become clear. However, we need a more efficient approach. This takes us further in understanding equivalence of fractions as we require the two fractions to have the same denominator. We call this **cancelling up**. It works on the same principle that the fraction remains equivalent, provided we are dividing both the numerator and denominator by the same number. Now we are multiplying both by the same number.

For example:

$$\frac{3}{5} = \frac{6}{10} = \frac{60}{100}$$

or

$$\frac{1}{4} = \frac{12}{48} = \frac{24}{96}$$

To compare $\frac{1}{3}$ with $\frac{2}{5}$ we need to 'cancel up' both fractions so that they have the same denominator (you may recall this as finding the **common denominator**). Any number that is a multiple of both 3 and 5 will do, such as 60 or 30. However, it is much easier if we can spot the smallest number that is a factor of both 3 and 5, which as you know is 15. This is our **lowest common denominator**.

Thus, for $\frac{1}{3}$ we can multiply numerator and denominator by 5:

$$\frac{1}{3} = \frac{5}{15}$$

For $\frac{2}{5}$ we can multiply numerator and denominator by 3:

$$\frac{2}{5} = \frac{6}{15}$$

Hence, we can now see that $\frac{2}{5}$ is just a little bigger than $\frac{1}{3}$.

Suppose we hadn't spotted that 15 is the best number to use as the common denominator and had used 60 instead.

For $\frac{1}{3}$ we can multiply both numerator and denominator by 20:

$$\frac{1}{3} = \frac{20}{60}$$

For $\frac{2}{5}$ we can multiply both numerator and denominator by 12:

$$\frac{2}{5} = \frac{24}{60}$$

It still shows that $\frac{2}{5}$ is bigger – so it is not an incorrect method, it may just take longer.

Mastery Task

Arrange these numbers in order, from the smallest to the largest:

$$\frac{4}{5}, \frac{5}{6}, \frac{3}{4}, \frac{5}{8}$$

We begin your understanding of percentages in a simple way. First, we need to establish that 'percentage' means 'out of 100'. The word 'percent' actually comes from the Latin *per centum* which means 'per 100'. The word 'cent' is used in the same way as in 'cents', 'century', 'centimetre', etc.; each referring to 100 parts. The use of 'parts of 100' goes back to the ancient Romans. This then, provides us with a simple link to fractions and decimals. Further, our work on decimal place value allows us then to convert percentages to decimals.

$$1\% = \frac{1}{100} = 0.01 \qquad 5\% = \frac{5}{100} = 0.05 \qquad 85\% = \frac{85}{100} = 0.85$$

This allows us to look at simple fractions and their percentage and decimal equivalent. For example, to represent $\frac{1}{5}$ as a percentage, we find $\frac{1}{5}$ of 100, which is 20. Thus $\frac{1}{5} = 20\% = 0.20$. We can proceed using any fraction, where the denominator is a factor of 100. In the same way, we can get children to compile a list of the most common fraction/percentage/decimal equivalences.

Fraction	Percentage	Decimal
1 whole	100%	1.0
$\frac{1}{2}$	50%	0.5
$\frac{1}{4}$	25%	0.25
$\frac{3}{4}$	75%	0.75
$\frac{1}{5}$	20%	0.2
$\frac{2}{5}$	40%	0.4
$\frac{3}{5}$	60%	0.6
$\frac{4}{5}$	80%	0.8

We would hope that by the time children are being taught this they will have become comfortable in recognising that $\frac{2}{10} = \frac{1}{5}$ or that $\frac{5}{10} = \frac{1}{2}$. If so, we can look at the other multiples of 10% not covered above.

Fraction	Percentage	Decimal
$\frac{1}{10}$	10%	0.1
$\frac{3}{10}$	30%	0.3
$\frac{7}{10}$	70%	0.7
$\frac{9}{10}$	90%	0.9

If you were sitting in one of our lectures, we would perhaps at this point explore which of these conversions YOU are secure in. Can you make such conversions quickly?

We believe that as a teacher, you should have instant access to all of the above conversions; with this information, one can undertake a great many calculations. Sometimes, converting from, say, a percentage to a fraction, or a decimal to a percentage, enables us to compute faster and more accurately. It is from this point we can move towards those calculation strategies.

A really important milestone in developing children's number skills in percentages is for them to appreciate that 10% is the same as $\frac{1}{10}$ and then use their knowledge of fractions to scale up for other multiples of 10, allowing them to find a percentage of a much larger quantity.

For example:

Find 60% of £480

10% of £480 = £48   (We know 10% = 1/10)

So:

60% of £480 = £288   (6 × 48)

It is important to point out here that a number of children may correctly compute the numerical answer to 60% of £480, but write it as 288%. As we are finding a 'percentage' of a quantity, the answer must be in the same units as the initial quantity.

A question such as this doesn't dictate one single solution strategy and can open up many wonderful opportunities for exploration and discussion. Another approach may be to find 20% (£96) and triple it, or perhaps find 10% (£48) and add it to 50% (£240).

The photograph below shows how a Year 5 child considered various percentage facts of £480.

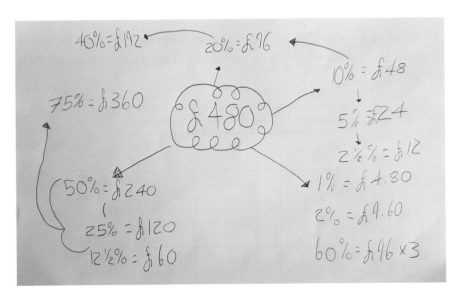

Before we move on, it is useful to talk about expressing one number as a percentage of another. This is perhaps most successfully undertaken by first expressing the numbers as a fraction, and then considering that fraction 'of 100'.

For example, to express 16 as a percentage of 64, we first write this as $\frac{16}{64}$. This is equal to $\frac{1}{4}$, which is equal to 25%.

At Key Stage 2, when children are asked to express one number as a percentage of another, the fraction will usually cancel down to one of the key fractions we gave earlier. However, even if it is not one of these fractions, it is likely to lead us to a denominator which is a factor of 100.

For example, express 54 as a percentage of 360:

$$\frac{54}{360} = \frac{9}{60} = \frac{3}{20}$$

We now find this fraction 'of 100':

$$\frac{1}{20} \text{ of } 100 = 5$$

$$\frac{3}{20} \text{ of } 100 = 15$$

$$\text{thus, } \frac{54}{360} = 15\%$$

Mastery Task

Arrange these numbers in order, from the smallest to the largest:

$$\frac{4}{5}, \quad 0.5, \quad \frac{3}{4}, \quad 70\%, \quad 0.775, \quad \frac{5}{8}$$

Formal calculations with fractions, decimals and percentages

Before we consider some of the formal calculation methods children need to know in this area, let us return to the reflection at the start of this chapter. We asked you to think about your own experiences of learning about fractions, decimals and percentages.

What rules do you remember? Was the way you were taught fractions, decimals and percentages highly effective? As stated earlier, this topic lends itself very easily to applying rules and recipes to generate correct answers. One of the issues that arises from relying on teaching rules and recipes is that children can mis-remember a rule, or they try to use a rule for one calculation for a different calculation where it doesn't apply.

The following represents a list of some of the ways children can be taught fractions, decimals and percentages through rules. We present this as indicative and not exhaustive and the reflection task at the beginning of this chapter may enable you to supplement this list from your own experiences.

Rule	Used for	Possible misuse
Turn it upside down and multiply.	Division of fractions.	Some children use this for other operations on fractions.
Put the percentage over 100 and multiply.	Find a percentage of a given number.	Children get really mixed up between these two rules and many use the wrong one.
Put the first number over the second and multiply by 100.	Express one number as a percentage of another.	
Move the decimal point to the right/left.	Multiplication/division by powers of 10.	Children forget which way to move the point and can end up doing a division for a multiplication and vice versa.
Find a common denominator.	Addition/subtraction of fractions.	Many with weak number skills find this difficult and make arithmetical errors but also some children try to use this for multiplication.
Keep the decimal points lined up underneath each other.	Standard method for addition/subtraction of decimals.	These are two completely different strategies that are often not understood, mixed up or conflated.
Ignore the decimal point and multiply then count the number of decimal places and put it back in.	Standard method for long multiplication of decimals.	
Times the numerators and then times the denominators.	Standard method for multiplication of fractions.	Often misapplied to addition and subtraction of fractions.
Put the decimal point before the numbers.	This can successfully change a two-digit percentage into a decimal e.g. 24% = 0.24	Doesn't work for single-digit percentages. For example, many children can write 1% as 0.1 rather than 0.01. Can also be very confusing if there is a fraction in the percentage e.g. $2\frac{1}{2}$ %

As a teacher, you need to understand the limitations and common errors in using rules. It is often the case that when teachers provide children with such rules, they fail to explain the HOW? and WHY? of where the rule comes from. For us, this is one of the reasons why children can have difficulty in using rules ... they don't really understand them. We want you to understand that if the teacher understands the mathematics, the quality of their teaching will be better.

Reflection

For each of the 'rules' that we state above, can you explain WHY the rule works?

The remainder of this chapter explores some of the standard formal methods for calculating with fractions and decimals. If you cannot explain the WHY? for every rule above, then read on. As with everything in this chapter, the order in which we address the various calculations is not suggesting an order for them to be taught. That is a decision for your school and will also be based upon where the children are up to in their learning.

Addition/subtraction of fractions

The addition and subtraction of fractions is one of the easiest things to teach badly. In our experience, many children have real difficulties in successfully recalling and applying the approaches and methods for addition/subtraction of fractions that they have been taught. The most common error that you will see again and again is children adding/subtracting both numerators and denominators.

$$\frac{2}{3} + \frac{1}{4} = \frac{3}{7} \quad \text{or} \quad \frac{3}{5} - \frac{1}{2} = \frac{2}{3}$$

A really easy way to evidence to children that this cannot be correct is to ask them, what if we have $\frac{1}{4}$ and add it to another $\frac{1}{4}$? Children will be able to picture this in their head and will appreciate that the answer is $\frac{1}{2}$. However, using the above logic we get:

$$\frac{1}{4} + \frac{1}{4} = \frac{2}{8} = \frac{1}{4}$$

This can lead to a rich discussion. How can we double a number, yet it stays the same?

When children first learn to add, they are adding concrete objects. For example, *one chair plus four chairs equals five chairs*, or *one car plus four cars equals five cars*, or *one sweet add four sweets equals five sweets*. We would not say, *What is one table plus four chairs?* They are different things. (The actual answer to this question is that one table plus four chairs makes a dining suite!)

To introduce children to addition and subtraction of fractions, you should begin by keeping the denominators equal. Also, it is really useful if the children can see the denominator as 'the things' we are adding and the numerator as the amounts of these 'things'. To add, say, $\frac{1}{5}$ and $\frac{3}{5}$, emphasise the numerators. If denominators are equal, the numerators are telling us how many similar things we have. Thus, our question is now spoken as, *What is **one** fifth add **three** fifths?* When heard in this way, children are much more likely to say, **four** fifths.

You may perhaps now progress to examples where the answer exceeds one whole, such as *What is **four** fifths add **three** fifths?* Again, this is another task that leads to rich discussion. The answer, of seven fifths, is relatively easy to evaluate, but what does this mean? What does it look like? Is there another way we could write it? This then leads us into exploring **improper fractions** (you may know these as **top heavy fractions**). The children may have already explored improper fractions in their foundation work on the topic, but it is important for you to always keep referring back to earlier work to help them assimilate new knowledge and make connections from this to their existing knowledge. This approach to pedagogy helps develop children's mastery of fractions.

By Year 5, children should feel comfortable in doing this, in both subtraction as well as addition, and it is time to move on to mixed denominators. The best way to begin this is to have examples where one denominator is a multiple of the other. This will enable us to refer back to our fraction wall.

For example: $\dfrac{1}{4} + \dfrac{3}{8}$

1 whole							
$\dfrac{1}{2}$				$\dfrac{1}{2}$			
$\dfrac{1}{4}$		$\dfrac{1}{4}$		$\dfrac{1}{4}$		$\dfrac{1}{4}$	
$\dfrac{1}{8}$	$\dfrac{1}{8}$	$\dfrac{1}{8}$	$\dfrac{1}{8}$	$\dfrac{1}{8}$	$\dfrac{1}{8}$	$\dfrac{1}{8}$	$\dfrac{1}{8}$

$$\dfrac{1}{4} \quad + \quad \dfrac{3}{8} \quad = \quad \dfrac{5}{8}$$

or $\quad \dfrac{1}{3} + \dfrac{1}{6}$

1 whole					
$\dfrac{1}{3}$		$\dfrac{1}{3}$		$\dfrac{1}{3}$	
$\dfrac{1}{6}$	$\dfrac{1}{6}$	$\dfrac{1}{6}$	$\dfrac{1}{6}$	$\dfrac{1}{6}$	$\dfrac{1}{6}$

$$\dfrac{1}{3} \quad + \quad \dfrac{1}{6} \quad = \quad \dfrac{5}{6}$$

As with any model or image, we want the children to use it to help them, until they are confident enough to work without it. The key concept for you to emphasise here is that we can add or subtract fractions, provided they have equal denominators. If denominators are not equal, we use our knowledge of equivalent fractions to convert them.

Thus: $\frac{1}{4} = \frac{2}{8}$ so: $\frac{1}{4} + \frac{3}{8} = \frac{2}{8} + \frac{3}{8}$

$$= \frac{5}{8}$$

and: $\frac{1}{3} = \frac{2}{6}$ so: $\frac{1}{3} + \frac{1}{6} = \frac{2}{6} + \frac{1}{6}$

$$= \frac{3}{6}$$

In Year 6 we finally extend this to cover all denominators. First, we need to decide what denominator we wish to convert to. For example, consider the question $\frac{1}{3} + \frac{1}{4}$. We need a denominator common to both 3 and 4. Remember, we can use any number that is a multiple of both, such as 24 or 60, but the easiest one (the lowest) is 12.

$$\frac{1}{3} = \frac{4}{12} \text{ and } \frac{1}{4} = \frac{3}{12}$$

So: $\frac{1}{3} + \frac{1}{4} = \frac{4}{12} + \frac{3}{12}$

$$= \frac{7}{12}$$

At this point, it may be useful to consider what would happen if we didn't use the lowest common denominator. Let us demonstrate by using a much bigger one, 60:

$$\frac{1}{3} = \frac{20}{60} \text{ and } \frac{1}{4} = \frac{15}{60}$$

So: $\frac{1}{3} + \frac{1}{4} = \frac{20}{60} + \frac{15}{60}$

$$= \frac{35}{60}$$

$$= \frac{7}{12}$$

It doesn't matter if children do not spot the lowest common denominator, as we still get the same result. It just means we have a few extra steps in the calculation.

Multiplication of fractions

The principal error that we identified above in addition and subtraction of fractions can come about because children are moved too quickly onto multiplication of fractions where such a rule does work. To multiply together two fractions, we can simply multiply together the numerators and then multiply together the denominators. For example:

$$\frac{1}{2} \times \frac{1}{4} = \frac{1}{8}$$

$$\frac{2}{3} \times \frac{4}{5} = \frac{8}{15}$$

So, how can this be? We suggest that once again, the use of imagery is a much more secure way into this topic. It is also useful to link back to our initial concept of multiplication as being repeated addition, so the multiplication sign and the word 'of' mean the same thing.

Thus, $\frac{1}{2} \times \frac{1}{4}$ can be thought of as $\frac{1}{2}$ of $\frac{1}{4}$.

Imagine a shape divided into four equal pieces. Each piece is $\frac{1}{4}$.

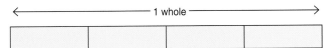

To find $\frac{1}{2}$ of $\frac{1}{4}$ we need to halve one of these pieces.

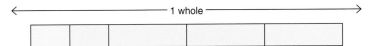

By linking this to our fraction wall, we can see that this is equivalent to $\frac{1}{8}$.

Another really useful image for the same problem of $\frac{1}{2} \times \frac{1}{4}$ is to consider a rectangle to represent the whole.

We spilt our rectangle vertically into four (our second denominator).

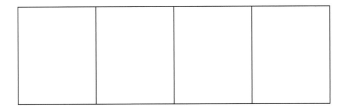

Each part is $\frac{1}{4}$. We want to take one of these quarters.

We now horizontally divide the rectangle into two (our first denominator).

Now we want to find half of one of these quarters.

The orange represents one half of our one quarter and it is immediately clear that this represents $\frac{1}{8}$.

This method works for other products of fractions, for example $\frac{2}{3} \times \frac{4}{5}$.

We begin with a block to represent one whole.

We now vertically divide our whole into five parts, but this time we need four of them.

We now need to find $\frac{2}{3}$ of this so we now divide our whole into three, horizontally.

We have now divided out $\frac{3}{5}$ into thirds. Each row is a third, but we want two thirds, so we want 'two rows' worth' of our $\frac{3}{5}$.

Thus, we have now selected 8 out of a total of 15. Thus $\frac{2}{3} \times \frac{4}{5} = \frac{8}{15}$

Mastery Task

Use this idea to consider other multiplication problems, such as:

$$\frac{1}{3} \times 1\frac{1}{2}$$

or

$$2\frac{1}{4} \times 1\frac{1}{2}$$

Division of fractions

This is perhaps the topic that causes the most conceptual difficulties for children and for students. To begin with, let us define **a reciprocal**. This is 'inverting' the fraction. The reciprocal of $\frac{2}{3}$ is $\frac{3}{2}$, the reciprocal of $\frac{3}{5}$ is $\frac{5}{3}$. Likewise, the reciprocal of $\frac{1}{2}$ is $\frac{2}{1}$ (i.e. 2) and the reciprocal of $\frac{1}{4}$ is $\frac{4}{1} = 4$. The concept of 'reciprocal' is where the rule about 'turning it upside down' comes from. We think you should know this word. Although children at Key Stage 2 are not required to know it, they need to understand how to divide fractions by whole numbers and the word comes in useful in explaining the concept. The progression to dividing a fraction by another fraction is actually covered in Key Stage 3 and we will discuss that in our final chapter.

Let us go right back to our original concept of a fraction being a division. To find half of something, we divide by 2, to find a quarter of a number we divide by 4, etc. Also remember that multiplication is the same as 'of'. Thus, multiplying by half is the same as dividing by 2 ... its reciprocal. It is the same for any fraction. However, we do not want to stop here as it would just be providing a rule. We want the children to explore problems, initially using imagery to develop their understanding of what is actually happening. It is possible to use imagery for questions about both simple and complex division of fractions.

Dividing a whole number by a fraction

First, let us state another conceptual error children can make. Consider the question $6 \div \frac{1}{2}$. Many children will give this as the answer 3. If so, they are confusing multiplication and division. If we were to ask, *What is half of six?* or *What is* $6 \times \frac{1}{2}$ *?* we know the answer is 3 and we have already discussed how we can verify that answer. However, $6 \div \frac{1}{2}$ is not multiplication, it is division.

There are two ways we can look at this:

1. Using physical objects (or imagining them). The question could be phrased, *If we have six cakes and divide them all into halves ... how many pieces of cake would we have?*

2. Using a number line. As we know that division is repeated subtraction, we could rephrase this question as, *Starting at 6, how many times can we subtract $\frac{1}{2}$ in order to get back to zero?*

In both of these approaches we can see the answer has to be 12. The same result as multiplying 6 by the reciprocal of our divisor $\frac{1}{2}$.

Dividing a fraction by a whole number

Let us begin by considering $\frac{2}{3} \div 4$.

First, we need to find a multiple of 3 and 4, e.g. 12. Now we use a bar to represent the whole and divide it into 12 equal sections:

We begin by showing what $\frac{2}{3}$ looks like:

We want to divide this into four. We currently have eight sections, so that means we need two of them (out of a total of 12).

$$\longleftarrow \quad \frac{2}{12} \quad \longrightarrow$$

Thus, we can demonstrate that $\frac{2}{3} \div 4 = \frac{2}{12}$ (or $\frac{1}{6}$).

Alternatively, dividing by 4 is the same as quartering, so we would have thought of this as $\frac{2}{3} \times \frac{1}{4} = \frac{2}{12}$.

Converting fractions to decimals by division

Having looked earlier at finding decimal equivalents to a number of key fractions, we now want to explore a method for less common fractions. We said earlier that $\frac{1}{2}$ can be thought of as one whole divided into two equal pieces. In general, any fraction can be considered as the dividing of the numerator and the denominator. You will now need to recall some of the formal division strategies we discussed in Chapter 5. This skill begins with a natural extension of the short division algorithm.

We know that 1 = 1.0 = 1.00 = 1.000. So, in order to consider $\frac{1}{2}$ as a division calculation of 1 ÷ 2, we need to think of one whole as being the same as 1.0 and we then can apply our 'bus stop' method.

$$\frac{1}{2} = 1 \div 2$$

$$2\overline{)1.0}$$

Leading to: $2\overline{)1.^10}$ with $0.\,5$ above $\frac{1}{2} = 0.5$

Sometimes, we need to include two or three zeros after the decimal point in order to complete the calculation.

For example, $\frac{3}{4} = 3 \div 4$

Leading to: $4\overline{)3.^30^20}$ with $0.\,7\,5$ above $\frac{3}{4} = 0.75$

Let us now try this method with some less familiar fractions.

$\frac{3}{8} = 3 \div 8$ $8\overline{)3.^30^60^40}$ with $0.\,3\,7\,5$ above

$\frac{1}{3} = 1 \div 3$ $3\overline{)1.^10^10^10^10}$ with $0.\,3\,3\,3\,3$ above

In the second example, we can see that no matter how many iterations we complete, we will always have a remainder of 1. This is why $\frac{1}{3}$ is classified as a recurring decimal. The recurring element can be a single digit, or two or more digits such as 0.1212 or 0.628628628.

To show clearly which part of a recurring decimal number is being repeated, it is convention to use a dot above the recurring element. Two dots indicate the start and end of the recurring part.

Thus: $0.\dot{6} = 0.6666666666$

$0.\dot{1}\dot{6} = 0.16161616$

$0.\dot{3}1\dot{6} = 0.316316316$

Task 6.1

Use the method described above to convert the fraction $\frac{7}{8}$ to a decimal.

Mastery Task

The sevenths are a very special family of fractions. By writing 1 as 1.000000, use the above method to convert $\frac{1}{7}$ to a decimal. Repeat for $\frac{2}{7}, \frac{3}{7}, \frac{4}{7}, \frac{5}{7}$ and $\frac{6}{7}$. What do you notice?

The result here is magical ...

Addition/subtraction of decimals

Understanding place value is the key to being able to add and subtract decimals. For example, if you were to ask a child to add 3.7 to 7.5, many would have no problem at all applying the formal contracted addition algorithm:

$$
\begin{array}{r}
3.7 \\
+ \ 7.5 \\
\hline
11.2 \\
\hline
{\scriptstyle 1}
\end{array}
$$

However, if they are asked to use the same method with, say, 8.65 + 0.2, a common mistake is to line the numbers up on the right-hand side:

$$
\begin{array}{r}
8.65 \\
+ \ 0.2 \\
\hline
8.6\ 7 \\
\hline
\end{array}
$$

You will appreciate that this doesn't make sense, but a child with weak understanding of place value may consider this logical. This error can be easily avoided by suggesting that we write both numbers with equal length of decimal places, so 0.2 becomes 0.20, which gives:

$$\begin{array}{r} 8.6\,5 \\ +\,0.2\,0 \\ \hline 8.8\,5 \end{array}$$

Mastery Task

Enter any number that has at least five decimal places into a calculator. Using subtraction, make the digits disappear one at a time.

For example:

Starting with the number 7.281439, what number would you need to enter to remove the digit 4?

Multiplication of a decimal by a whole number

We need to begin this topic, working within our times tables, by looking at multiplying a single place decimal number by a single integer, such as 0.3×4.

You will immediately see that this links directly back to using repeated addition on our number line, as we can think of this as four 'jumps' of 0.3.

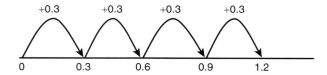

This gives us $0.3 \times 4 = 1.2$. We need the children to see how this links to their times tables. In order to help us do that, we can also think of the same question in a slightly different way. For this we need an appreciation that 0.3 is the same as $3 \div 10$:

$$0.3 \times 4 = 4 \times 0.3 = 4 \times (3 \div 10) = (4 \times 3) \div 10 = 12 \div 10 = 1.2$$

This will, at first sight, seem very long-winded to you. However, this is what mastery is all about: getting the children to think about new information by linking it in with information they already know. We wouldn't suggest that you will do this for every similar question. However, we want children to apply knowledge of their times tables with confidence and be able to use these with decimal numbers that contain the same digits.

For example:

$6 \times 3 = 18$

$6 \times 0.3 = 1.8$

$0.6 \times 3 = 1.8$

$0.6 \times 0.3 = 0.18$

Leading to:

$60 \times 3 = 180$

$60 \times 0.3 = 18$

$0.6 \times 30 = 18$

$600 \times 0.3 = 180$

Mastery Task

Given that $189 \times 27 = 5{,}103$: use this fact to work out the answers to:

18.9×27

$1.89 \times 2{,}700$

18.9×2.7

1.89×2.7

$51{,}030 \div 189$

$5{,}103 \div 18.9$

$5{,}103 \div 0.27$

When children are secure in questions of this type, we can move forward to consider questions that would be impractical to compute mentally or to use a number line for, such as 23.4×8.

There are two distinct ways we can look at these types of question, both of which are extensions of the methods we looked at in Chapter 5.

First, we could consider this as an extension of the **_grid method_**.

Example: 23.4×8

×	20	3	0.4
8	160	24	3.2

$160 + 24 + 3.2 = 187.2$

The most likely place a child will make an error with this method is in the final column 8×0.4, or in the addition, which is why it is important that they are not moved on too quickly from the column addition and simple multiplication of decimals discussed above.

A second way to consider this question is as a formal multiplication. The standard method here is to write each number without the decimals:

$$\begin{array}{r} 2\,3\,4 \\ \times\quad 8 \\ \hline 1\,8\,7\,2 \end{array}$$

However, this is the answer to 234 × 8, but we want the answer to 23.4 × 8. Securing children's understanding of the work we discussed at the start of this section will ensure that children will appreciate that the answer must be 187.2.

$$234 \times 8 = 1872$$

$$23.4 \times 8 = 187.2$$

Another element you should bring in here is verifying that this seems like a 'sensible' answer, using estimation. For this example, if we round each number to the nearest 10, we would get 20 × 10 = 200. Thus, our answer ought to be near to 200. Such estimation skills are important in helping children to develop a sense of confidence in their working.

Dividing a decimal by a whole number

This is a relatively straightforward and simple extension of the work we did converting fractions to decimals, for example 13.5 ÷ 3:

$$\begin{array}{r} 4.\,5 \\ 3\,\overline{)13.^15} \end{array}$$

Again, we may need to add an additional zero at the end of the decimal, for example 29.2 ÷ 5:

$$\begin{array}{r} 5.\,8\,5 \\ 5\,\overline{)29.^42^20} \end{array}$$

Of course, one could always use a calculator to undertake investigation work in this area. Politicians unfortunately do not see the value in using calculators below Key Stage 3, which is a pity.

Out of proportion

It is useful to conclude this section by considering the topic of ratio and proportion, as their study has close links to fractions. Children are only taught about ratio and proportion in Year 6, but these are usually taught at the same time. It is important for you to appreciate that they are very different things.

A **ratio** compares the quantities in two or more parts. A **proportion** compares a part to a whole. Children will often mix these up which leads to conceptual errors in their working.

Look at this shape:

There are twelve squares altogether: three red squares and nine blue squares. The ratio of red to blue squares is written 3:9 or 1:3. However, the proportion of each colour is calculated as a fraction of the total. Thus, the proportion of red squares is $\dfrac{3}{12}$ $\left(=\dfrac{1}{4}\right)$ and the proportion of blue squares is $\dfrac{9}{12}$ $\left(=\dfrac{3}{4}\right)$. The most common incorrect answer here would be that a ratio of 1:3 gives a proportion of $\dfrac{1}{3}$.

Recipes are sometimes given as ratios. To make pastry you may need to mix two parts flour to one part butter: this means the ratio of flour to butter is 2:1. Mixing cordial may need one part cordial to four parts water: this means the ratio of cordial to water is 1:4.

Bar modelling is often helpful in looking at ratio and proportion questions.

Example

In a box of chocolates, for every dark chocolate there are four milk chocolates. If there are 40 chocolates altogether, how many of each type are there?

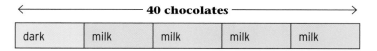

The ratio of dark chocolate:milk chocolate is 1:4.

Thus, the proportion of dark chocolates is $\dfrac{1}{5}$ and the proportion of milk chocolates is $\dfrac{4}{5}$.

$\dfrac{1}{5}$ of 40 = 8 (there are **8 dark chocolates**)

$\dfrac{4}{7}$ of 40 = 32 (there are **32 milk chocolates**)

Task 6.2

1. There are 35 children in a class and 15 are boys. What is the ratio of girls to boys?

2. A bag of 30 sweets contains only strawberry and orange flavours. There are 2 strawberry sweets to every 3 orange sweets. How many strawberry sweets are there?

3. Miyuki had a bag of sweets that contained just blue and red sweets. For every blue sweet, there are 3 red sweets.

   (a) What is the ratio of red to blue sweets?

   (b) If there are 60 sweets in a large bag how many are blue?

   (c) If there are 48 sweets in a medium bag how many are red?

Rounding up

In terms of our own students, it is the topics of fractions, decimals and percentages that often frighten them the most. Certainly, in terms of auditing their own subject knowledge, it is clearly an area where many have gaps. It is our belief that these gaps often stem from poor teaching that failed to explain the relationships between fractions, decimals and percentages. Additionally, it is within these topics that teachers will often resort to rules and recipes for the associated calculations. These rules are great if you can remember them, but many don't. Why these rules work is understood by even fewer students.

Being able to solve a problem or undertake a calculation by using a rule is not, in our opinion, mastery. We hope that reading this chapter has made you think about how fractions, decimals and percentages relate to each other and how it is possible to teach children how to undertake calculations without resorting to giving a rule.

WHAT MATHS CAN *YOU* SEE?

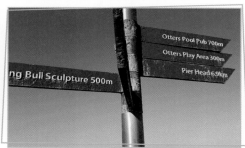

6

THE JOY OF X

- **Abbreviations and shorthand**
- **What is algebra?**
- **Solving equations**
- **Using algebra to create sequences**
- **Problems with two unknowns**
- **Rounding up**
- **What maths can you see?**

The joy of x

In case you had not realised it, this chapter is about algebra. Like other topics we have previously considered, algebra is something that many children and, indeed, many students, have a real phobia about. Many people's memories of their secondary school mathematics lessons are often clouded by remembering that they 'hated' algebra. They were 'taught' that they 'couldn't do it'. We need to ensure that teachers' worries, shortcomings or even perhaps their own phobias of algebra are not passed on to the children in their class.

If you do have such concerns, do not worry. In the same way that you perhaps get a sense of panic with percentages or decimals, if you think you 'cannot do' algebra it is not your fault, rather it is the fault of a teacher failing at some point. Algebra is another area of mathematics that can be taught by using many rules and recipes. Learn the rule, remember the recipe, learn the rule, remember the recipe ... etc. As we have pointed out several times in this book, this is not mastery and this is not the way we want children to learn mathematics. Nor is it the way we want you to teach mathematics.

To be a successful teacher of algebra requires an understanding of what algebra is, what it is not and why we should be concerned with it: in short, understanding its purpose. It is our belief that every primary teacher can achieve this. For the purpose of this chapter, we will assume that your own algebraic skills and confidence are perhaps not as developed as they could be. By reading on you will gain real insight into algebra and will be able to deliver high quality lessons in this topic. (Although we do hope that is the case for every other chapter as well!)

At Key Stage 2, algebra is really an extension of the number system. Many children have difficulties with algebra, but these often stem from a weakness in their knowledge of the topic of number. The bridge from number to algebra must be crossed carefully, and before beginning that crossing, children must be confident in their understanding of numbers, number bonds, operations on numbers and their inverses. As primary school is where these are all first encountered, this is your responsibility.

Abbreviations and shorthand

We begin by considering the laziness of all mathematicians. Every mathematician likes to use a form of shorthand ... it's quicker. For example, have you ever seen this symbol?

$$\therefore$$

Mathematicians looking at proofs or developing mathematical arguments often use this symbol instead of the word 'therefore'. Did you know this was the symbol for the word 'therefore'? Well you do now. If you are the sort of inquiring student that we are hoping will read this book, you will now be saying, *Why are three dots used to represent the word* therefore? We are glad you asked that and the answer is nobody really seems to know. However, we do know that this symbol has been used in texts as far back as the seventeenth century.

A better example of mathematical shorthand is the sign for 'equality'. Perhaps you may write $3 + 4$ is equal to 7. But most likely you would write $3 + 4 = 7$.

We use the = sign without thinking about it. Everyone knows what it means. It may be hugely interesting for you to learn that the symbol was not invented until 1557, when a Welshman named Robert Recorde first used it. He suggested that there is nothing in the world more equal than two parallel lines of the same length. Now you may be wondering what we did use for 'equals' before this symbol was invented and that takes us into the wonderful world of the history of mathematics, which is not part of the primary mathematics curriculum (apart from Roman numerals) so we will leave this with you.

Everyone, whether they realise it or not, uses mathematical abbreviations, as can be seen in our notations for measures such as mm, ml, cm, g, L, km, kg, etc. We did once observe a lesson where a student teacher used these as an introduction to algebra, suggesting that algebra is about abbreviations. THIS IS NOT TRUE. Do not confuse the use of symbols and abbreviations as being algebra.

You may say, *The area of a triangle is equal to half the base times the height*. But you may prefer to write $A = \frac{1}{2} b \times h$. This is fine if you understand that each letter represents a numerical attribute of the triangle. It further assumes that you appreciate 'h' represents the perpendicular height, that both 'b' and 'h' must be measured in the same units and that the area represented by 'A' will be in square units. Although the letters within such formulae correspond to certain attributes of the shape, you need to appreciate that these attributes can change in different triangles. Thus, the letters are used to represent a **parameter** or a **variable** within the triangle. We discuss this much further in Chapter 10.

When one writes down all of the assumptions that are contained in such a simple formula as $A = \frac{1}{2} b \times h$, it becomes easier to appreciate that we can often take much for granted. It is easy to see how teaching without being aware of these assumptions, and clearly clarifying them for children, may lead to confusion.

There are actually very few formulae that children in primary school are expected to know and these are confined to Year 6. However, if a child gains a deep understanding of what they should know by Year 6, this will put them at a significant advantage when they move into Key Stage 3.

This discussion leads us quite naturally to considering substitution into formulae. Many of the formulae used by primary children relate to measures and thus will be discussed in much more detail in Chapter 10.

What is algebra?

This leads nicely to identifying what algebra actually is. The word 'algebra' derives from the Arabic term 'al-*jabr*' meaning *reunion of broken parts* and can be found in work dating back to the ninth century. For us though, algebra is about using letters or other symbols to represent unknown numbers or numbers that can vary.

Here is the answer … what is the question?

Another way of thinking about algebra at this level is to consider the difference between the following questions:

* What is the sum of 6 and 4?

* What numbers do I add to 4 to make 10?

In the first case, we are seeking the 'answer' to the sum of the two numbers. In the second case we are seeking the value that 'gives us' the answer of 10. The study of what number do I need to 'input' in order to get a specific answer leads to the study of equations, which is a fundamental aspect of primary algebra.

Algebra starts at an earlier age than you think. Consider the expression:

$$4 + \boxed{} = 10$$

This typifies something you may see in a Year 1 or even a Reception class. Questions such as this are designed to help children learn and understand number bonds. We know that you could complete this task if required. You will find this easy as you (hopefully) know your number bonds to 10. This task is not designed for you, but what if we change this question to:

$$24 + \boxed{} = 73$$

Or even:
$$18.87 + \boxed{} = 37.93$$

How would you cope? What strategies would you use? You could apply some of the techniques we covered in earlier chapters by considering inverse operations.

Now consider these expressions:

$$4 + x = 10$$
$$24 + x = 73$$
$$18.87 + x = 37.93$$

All of these are known as **equations** because they contain an 'equals' sign. However, conceptually these are exactly the same as the expressions above. In one case, we are using a square to represent a missing number and in the second we are using the letter x to represent an 'unknown' number. This type of expression is known as a **linear equation**, because there is only a single number that can make the statement true. You may recall other types of equations from your GCSE work. Quadratic equations usually have two answers (although many have no answers), and cubic equations can have up to three answers. However, for our primary curriculum, we need only focus on linear equations.

This brings us to the next dilemma. What should we use to represent an unknown number? Well there is no set answer. Use whatever you like. Some examples may be:

$$13 + \Delta = 42$$
$$13 + ? = 42$$
$$13 + \bigstar = 42$$

In primary school, you should only use letters or symbols that children are already familiar with and can reproduce easily. If a symbol is unknown to a child, it can make the question seem harder.

This can even be the case with our humble x. It is sometimes the case a child would find $13 + x = 42$ much more difficult to solve than $13 + a = 42$.

A good method is to allow a child to select their own symbol or use the first letter of their own name.

Teaching idea

Ask Jenny to pick a number and add, say, 27 to it. Jenny tells you that the answer is 46. So, we can write down the equation:

$$j + 27 = 46$$

The class now has to solve the equation and only Jenny knows the right answer ... so she can tell you if the rest of the class is correct.

However, some letters will always lead to confusion.

Do not use these letters to represent missing numbers	Because ...
B	Young children often write the letter b as a 6
l (lower case L)	Looks too much like the number 1
O (the 15th letter)	Looks like a zero

It is equally valid to use other symbols to represent unknown numbers. We have already shown how a little square is often used, especially in Key Stage 1. However, we can easily extend this idea to extend understanding in Key Stage 2. For example:

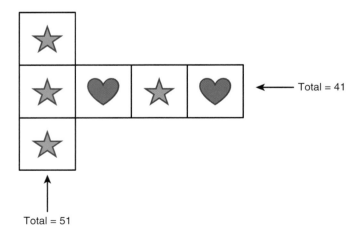

Here, the vertical column shows three stars that sum up to 51. Each star, therefore, must represent the number 17. Now looking horizontally, we have two stars and two hearts which sum to 41. We already know that the star represents the number 17, so two stars represents 34. If the rest of the row sums to 41, then the two hearts must represent the difference between 41 and 34, which is 7. If two hearts represent seven, one heart represents 3.5.

Task 7.1

Find the value for each symbol:

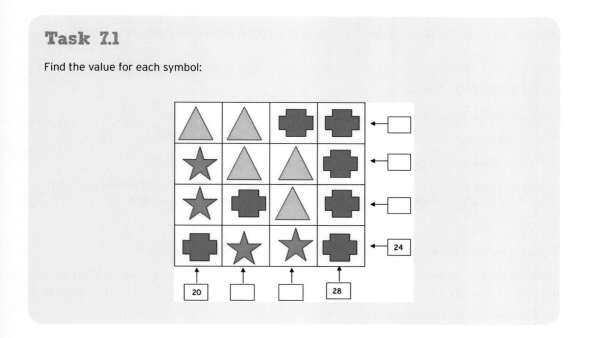

Solving equations

Now having introduced equations, we want to discuss how children may consider solving them. As we have already said, some answers can easily be identified because children know their number bonds or times tables – but what about when the answer is not so apparent? Here is where you may need to 'unlearn' whatever method you were taught at school.

Using the empty number line

In Chapter 4 we looked at how the empty number line can be used to model multiplication. Thus, 7×4 can be thought of as four jumps of seven.

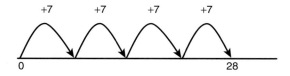

Similarly, we can use the empty number line to show the meaning of $3x$ as three jumps of x. This is the same as saying, *I think of a number and triple it.*

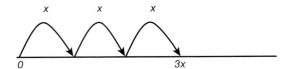

Note: We are using x to represent an unknown number. Other letters are available.

Teaching idea

By considering different values for x we can link this to various times tables.

For example, if $a = 4$ then $3a = 12$; if $b = 7$ then $3b = 21$; if $c = 9$ then $3c = 27$ etc.

If children are learning their five times table, can they solve $5x = 25$ or $12x = 60$?

This can lead into discussions on the inverse relationship between multiplication and division to solve the equation. There is a direct link here to the work we covered in Chapter 3.

Now suppose we want to consider the equation $3x + 8 = 23$.

Children need to understand that the left-hand side of this equation means we are thinking of a number, we multiply it by 3 (or make three jumps of this unknown number) and we then add 8 to it.

On a number line this would look like:

However, the right-hand side of the equation tells us that doing this takes us to 23.

Thus:

Now we can consider the number corresponding to the three jumps of the unknown number, which must be 8 less than our finishing point, i.e. 8 less than 23.

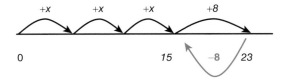

Now we have three equal jumps of an unknown number to make 15.

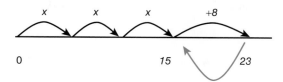

Using our knowledge of the links between multiplication and division, it is easy to see that each equal jump must be 5.

We have found that this approach really cements the relationship between the different inverse operations. Additionally, we are not teaching a series of rules and recipes to solve the equation. It is easy to appreciate the links between this approach and more traditional algebraic methods and thus works well as an introduction to linear equations at Key Stage 3.

The table below models how the above approach to solving $3x + 8 = 23$ links at each stage to the traditional method taught at secondary school.

	Solve $3x + 8 = 23$	
	Number line	**Algebraic equivalent**
1.		$3x + 8$
2.	+5 +5 +5 +8 23	$3x + 8 = 23$
3.	+5 +5 +5 +8 15 23	$3x = 23 - 8$ $3x = 15$
4.	3 equal jumps make 15 x x x +8 15 23 each equal jump must be 5. **Check your answer.**	$x = \dfrac{15}{3}$ $x = 5$

Note: there is no 'take it to the other side and change the sign'.

So far, we have considered just a single missing number. However, there are many variations.

Task 7.2

How can you find the missing number?

$$4 + \boxed{} = 10 - \triangle$$

What assumptions are you making? How many solutions are there to this problem?

Mastery Task

How can you model the following on the empty number line?

Vicky thinks of a number. She multiplies it by 5 and then subtracts 6. Her final answer is 29.

Using algebra to create sequences

In Chapter 3 we introduced you to a variety of linear sequences. This type of work enables children to gain confidence in sequences, before we begin using any form of algebraic generalisation. The links from sequences to algebra are only considered in upper Key Stage 2.

By developing their ability to substitute numbers into simple formulae, we can help children gain confidence in their algebraic ability and to use formulae to generate a sequence.

Example: Consider the formula **3n + 5**.

The first number in this sequence is obtained by substituting in the number 1 for n. The second number in this sequence is obtained by substituting in the number 2 for n. For the fifth number substitute 5, etc.

We get:

n	calculation	answer
1	$3 \times 1 + 5$	8
2	$3 \times 2 + 5$	11
3	$3 \times 3 + 5$	14
4	$3 \times 4 + 5$	17
5	$3 \times 5 + 5$	20
6	$3 \times 6 + 5$	23

Thus, our number sequence is 8, 11, 14, 17, 20, 23 ...

Our initial formula is often known as the ***nth term***. When we have the nth term, it is easy to find the tenth or the twentieth or the one hundredth number in any sequence, by substituting in that value.

Teaching idea

Find the first eight numbers in the sequences defined by the following nth terms:

(a) $4n + 1$

(b) $3n + 4$

(c) $6n - 3$

(d) $5n - 8$

(e) $4 - 2n$

(f) $6 - 3n$

(g) $\frac{1}{2}n + 10$

(h) $12 - \frac{1}{4}n$

What do you notice?

What would be the twentieth number in each sequence?

If you are unsure what children should notice, then you should complete this task before you read on.

Problems with two unknowns

Reflection

Think of two numbers that add up to 10. Write down some possible answers.

Find the pair of numbers that add up to 10 and have a difference of 3.

This reflection activity stumps many of our students. They often find a solution to one condition that does not satisfy the second condition. For example, they may say 8 and 2. These add up to 10 but the difference is not three. Or, they may say 5 and 2. These have a difference of three but their sum is not 10. They make the assumption that the numbers must be whole numbers or integers. We did not say that the two numbers had to be integers, so it is not a trick question.

As soon as we state that the two numbers are not necessarily integers, it is easy to appreciate the fact that it is not possible to think of all pairs of numbers that sum to 10. For example, some pairs of answers include:

$$3 + 7$$

$$10 + 0$$

$$8\tfrac{1}{2} + 1\tfrac{1}{2}$$

$$7.2 + 2.8$$

$$12 + (-2)$$

There is an **infinite** number of solutions to this condition. However, as soon as we provide a second condition – that the difference of the numbers must be 3 – there is now a unique solution: $6\tfrac{1}{2} + 3\tfrac{1}{2}$.

We could express this problem with two equations:

$$a + b = 10$$

$$a - b = 3$$

The variables a and b represent the two unknown numbers. In looking for the solution we find the value for **a** and the value for **b** *at the same time* (or simultaneously). Hence the phrase **simultaneous equations**. Hopefully, you can immediately see the link to another mathematics topic you will have studied at GCSE. The formal name is somewhat foreboding and is not used at Key Stage 2. At Key Stage 2 we would expect the children to find the two numbers, not using the algebraic approach that will be taught in secondary school, but by trial and error. However, we would want to encourage the children to become systematic in their thinking. For example, they may present their working like this:

$a + b = 10$		
values for *a*	values for *b*	*a* − *b*
10	0	10
9	1	8
8	2	6
7	3	4
6	4	2
5	5	0
4	6	−2
3	7	−4

Such working allows the children to immediately see that for integer values, the difference is always even. Inspection leads to noticing that the pair 7 and 3 have a difference of 4 (too big) whereas the next pair, 6 and 4, have a difference of 2 (too small). Our solution must then lie between.

Further work may consider non-integer pairs between these values, perhaps by looking at decimals with steps of 0.5:

values for *a*	values for *b*	a – b
7.5	2.5	5
7	3	4
6.5	3.5	3
6	4	2
5.5	4.5	1

Approaches such as this all lead to deeper mathematical understanding. This is a really good example of how developing a 'mastery' approach to mathematical learning does not necessarily mean making the children undertake really difficult mathematics. Rather, it is tweaking activities that you may already do, to encourage the children to think more about them.

Mastery Task

Pick any two numbers. We will call your larger number the **target sum** and the smaller number the **target difference**.

Now, find two other numbers that when added give your target sum, and when subtracted give your target difference.

If you can find a correct answer to your own question, then give yourself a different one and keep going until you can see how to quickly find the correct answer.

Can you always find a solution?

Rounding up

The key to understanding algebra is appreciating its links to number. In this chapter, we have shown how these links are developed from the earliest work on number, such as number bonds. We have distinguished between algebraic expressions and shorthand and looked at how algebra may be used in generating sequences. We have discussed here that many children are put off algebra by fear of symbols and letters; if you use symbols that the children recognise and understand, such fear is minimised.

By considering equations as an extension of number problems, and using an empty number line to approach their solutions using inverse operations, we have demonstrated that algebra is nothing to be worried about. Further algebra does not need to be taught by providing a series of rules for children to follow.

Hopefully, you will have also gained from reading this chapter a deeper insight into your own subject knowledge and perhaps some of the algebra you were taught in secondary school now makes just a little more sense.

Finally, you will have seen from this chapter that there is very little formal algebra in the primary curriculum. However, the algebra work that there is in primary school is key for progression in Key Stage 3.

THE SHAPE OF THINGS TO COME

- **2D or not 2D**
- **2D shape in a 3D world**
- **What's my line?**
- **The right angle**
- **What's your angle?**
- **Going in circles**
- **Rounding up**
- **What maths can you see?**

The shape of things to come

In this chapter, we will consider the properties of two-dimensional and three-dimensional shapes and how they can be classified using a range of properties. The National Curriculum groups this part of the mathematics curriculum under a broad heading of 'geometry'.

When teaching children to identify properties of shapes it is important to provide opportunities for children to hold them, explore them, fold them, open them, rotate them and link them to real-life objects and images. Many students feel they are secure in their subject knowledge of shape. However, it is our experience that many have forgotten some of the basic shape names and their properties. In this chapter we will ensure that your subject knowledge is complete in all aspects of shape, to enable you to teach the topic successfully in both Key Stage 1 and Key Stage 2.

Pick up a piece of A4 paper. What shape is it? Most people will say it is a rectangle. However, they are wrong. If you can pick an object up, it has three dimensions (3D). A **two-*dimensional*** (2D) object has no depth (thickness). It has only two dimensions: width and height. A ***three-dimensional object*** does have a depth and can be picked up. This may sound a little pedantic and it is easy to feel confused. A piece of paper is actually a 3D object with a very small depth.

| 0 dimensions: No length, no width. | 1 dimension: Has a length but no width. | 2 dimensions: Has a length (or height) and width. | 3 dimensions: Has length, width and height. |

Reflection

Draw the following shapes with the first thing that comes into your mind:

1.   A triangle

2.   A rectangle

3.   A trapezium

We will return to your response later in the chapter.

2D or not 2D

The mathematics National Curriculum uses the term **polygon** in reference to Year 2. This leads us naturally to the oldest maths joke in the word:

Question: What is a polygon?

Answer: A dead parrot.

Once the children have finished laughing at this, which won't take long, you can make sure they fully understand what the term means. A 'polygon' is a 2D shape that is constructed with only straight sides. Thus, a circle is not a polygon.

Task 8.1

Name all these polygons and ensure that you know how to spell each one correctly.

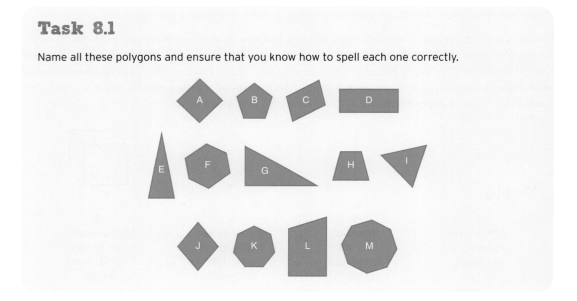

If we look in more detail at these 2D shapes, we need to understand any issues relating to why children cannot correctly identify them. Each shape is a polygon as it is an enclosed shape with straight sides. Having worked through the task yourself, do you know where you made the mistake and why?

Let's first look at the triangles, E, G and I. It is important to know their names and key properties to be able to identify them correctly.

  E – **isosceles triangle**. A triangle with two equal length sides and two equal size angles.

  G – **right-angled scalene triangle**. A scalene triangle has three different sides and three different sized angles. In this case, one of the angles is a right angle but this does not always have to be the case.

We can also have a **right-angled isosceles triangle.**

I – *equilateral triangle*. A triangle with three equal length sides and three equal sized angles.

Next, we will explore the quadrilaterals – the four-sided shapes. The most common error in identifying the shapes in Task 8.1 is naming shape A. Children do not always recognise this as a square, as it is not in its usual prototypical orientation. The moment the orientation changes, children may incorrectly name it as a diamond.

When learning about polygons we need to keep encouraging children to reason and think about the properties of these shapes by asking questions such as, *Can you have a right-angled equilateral triangle?*

The other quadrilaterals are named as follows:

C – *parallelogram*. A parallelogram has two pairs of parallel sides with opposite sides of equal length. Using this description, we note that rectangles and squares can also be parallelograms.

J – *rhombus*. A rhombus has four equal sides, with opposite sides and opposite angles equal length. The sides are parallel to each other and the diagonals bisect at right angles. A rhombus is also a type of parallelogram.

Shapes H and L – *trapezium*. A trapezium has one pair of parallel sides. Children are often shown shape H as a trapezium, with shape L being used less frequently as an example. (Note: the plural of trapezium is *trapezia*.)

Reflection

Having explored the definitions of these shapes, we will now return to the initial reflection and consider your answers.

These are the most common responses:

1.   2.   3.

If you responded in the same way it is important to understand why.

1.   It is easier to draw a triangle with a horizontal base so when we draw them or represent them in the classroom that is how they are displayed.

2.   Similarly, to response number 1, the longer side is easier to draw so often we print or draw this orientation.

By always showing shapes in a prototypical orientation, children come only to identify them in this way. Shape A in Task 8.1 is often not identified as a square for the same reason. When you display shapes in your classroom or on a screen, vary the orientation to help support children's understanding.

(Continued)

(Continued)

If children can manipulate the shape themselves into various positions it helps them to gain a better understanding of how the shape looks from a variety of viewpoints.

3.   The trapezium must have one pair of parallel sides. Although it is useful to link shapes to real life, it is vital that you don't exclude other versions of the shape.

The trapezium is sometimes, for ease, described as looking like a roof. This is partly helpful, as the most common example does in fact look like that. There have also been examples of a trapezium being described as looking like the bottom of a boat. If we turn the example above round the other way, it does appear that way.

However, the other example of the trapezium in Task 8.1, shape L, and its variations must not be forgotten.

When sharing examples with children it is important that they don't start to believe that a trapezium also should have a line of symmetry, which shape H would encourage.

Part of exploring the properties of shape is helping children to visualise shapes. Children need to be able to create mental images of the shapes and manipulate them without the support of the actual image as they develop a deeper understanding.

Teaching idea

Ask your class to close their eyes and visualise a rectangle. Once you have given time for this, ask them to imagine that one of the corners is being cut off with a pair of scissors. Finally, ask them to draw the image that remains.

Depending upon how the children visualise the corner being cut off, there will be one of three responses. These are worth discussing as a class and making sure that children understand that various solutions are possible.

1.   The child cuts a small corner as marked to leave a pentagon.

2.   The child cuts the corner to leave a trapezium.

3.   The child cuts the corner to leave a triangle.

The final classification for the polygons that we need to explore is to identify which are regular and which are irregular. **Regular polygons** are those where all the sides are the same length and all the angles are the same size. Therefore, from Task 8.1, shapes A, B, F, I, K and M would be described as regular polygons.

Task 8.2

What are the names of these 3D shapes? Check the accuracy of your spelling.

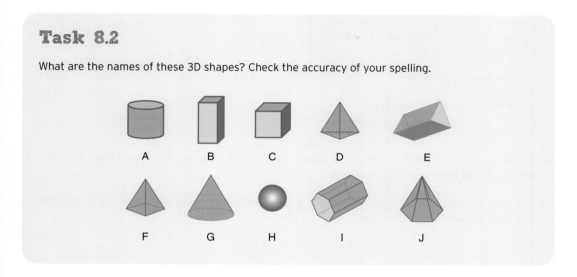

We will now explore the definition of a prism and a pyramid.

A **prism** is a solid 3D shape with identical polygon ends which are parallel to each other, separated by rectangles. The number of rectangles in the shape is equal to the number of sides on the polygon.

A **pyramid** is a solid shape with the base of a polygon and triangular faces that meet at a common point. The number of triangles is equal to the number of sides on the polygon base.

When we teach children, it is important to reinforce the correct vocabulary; when referring to 2D shapes we talk of 'corners' and 'sides', but when describing 3D shapes, we refer to 'vertices', 'faces' and 'edges'. A **face** is the flat surface of a 3D shape. An **edge** is where two faces meet. A **vertex** is where three or more edges meet.

Mastery Task

Complete the following table about 3D shapes.

Name of 3D shape	Number of vertices (V)	Number of edges (E)	Number of faces (F)	V − E + F

(Continued)

(Continued)

Name of 3D shape	Number of vertices (V)	Number of edges (E)	Number of faces (F)	V − E + F

What do you notice?

Are there any patterns?

What conclusions can you make?

Whilst children work with 3D shapes they should link them to real life, which will help them visualise the number of faces, edges and vertices.

For example, a cube is a dice, a cylinder a tube, a cuboid a box of cereal and a triangular based prism is a box for a popular bar of chocolate.

Reflection

What happens to 3D shapes when you cut through them?

Imagine a cuboid which you then cut in half, horizontally or vertically.

What does each half look like?

Do the properties of the cuboid change?

Are the remaining halves still cuboids?

Consider the same for a triangular prism.

Now imagine cutting a square based pyramid in half, horizontally or vertically.

What does each half look like?

Do the properties of the pyramid change?

Are the remaining halves still pyramids?

If children reflect upon these, or we model the process to children, then visual images are developed which reinforce understanding.

When children have a deep understanding of 3D shapes then they can recreate them by building models. This is very useful when developing the ability to recognise 3D shapes from a 2D representation.

Teaching idea

Show a 3D model from a 2D representation

Give the children some modelling clay or sticky tack and a pile of plastic straws or sticks. Ask them to produce a 3D model from a 2D representation.

For example:

Ask the children, in pairs, to describe the properties of their 3D shapes and name them.

2D shape in a 3D world

Although our world is a three-dimensional one, we need children to see the shapes that are all around us. We give just two examples here.

This building is a Victorian brewery. Victorian bricklayers were very proud of their skills. Many Victorian brick buildings evidence a wide range of elaborate design and skilful use of bricks to create very intricate designs. Here, we can see many of the 2D shapes we have talked about in this chapter.

This photograph comes from Cuzco in Peru, where much of the architecture dates back to the Incas in the sixteenth century. All stones were hand cut, which is an amazing feat in itself, and were so perfectly made they did not require any mortar. The central stone in this photograph is known as the twelve angle stone as, if you look carefully, there are twelve sides. The stone is believed to have once been part of an Inca palace and is a national heritage object. Perhaps the most interesting fact about Inca design was that the most commonly used shape in their buildings was not based upon rectangles, but upon a trapezium.

Network

We can develop this further when we look at the nets of 3D shapes. A **net** is the pattern created when a 3D shape is opened and laid flat. For example, a cuboid can be opened to create this net:

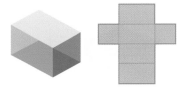

Children can explore nets in various ways: encourage them to use resources which snap together to show that there isn't just one way to produce a net for each 3D shape.

Once the various nets are put together to produce the 3D shapes, we can link the 3D forms to every-day objects: a cube to a dice; a cuboid to a box of cereal; and a sphere to a ball.

Reflection

Below are various nets. Do any of them fold to make a cube? How do you know?

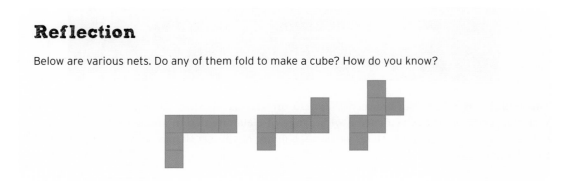

When considering 2D shapes, we discussed the issues that occur when children only have access to a shape in a prototypical orientation. It is the same with nets of 3D shapes; if they are only shown nets in a certain orientation, children will not be able to explore the wide range of possibilities.

Task 8.3

Which of the following nets will fold to make the cube shown?

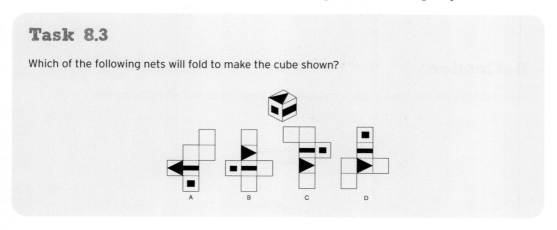

The use of nets will be looked at further in Chapter 10, when we explore using nets to calculate surface area.

What's my line?

One of the key ways to identify properties in polygons is to explore the angles and lines.

We have already identified features of polygons in Task 8.1 linked to parallel lines. **Parallel lines** are two lines which are the same distance apart and don't meet. Parallelograms and a trapezium have two pairs of parallel lines. When working with children we often look for ways to help them relate to the mathematics. We sometimes say to think about comparing them to a railway line, but look at this picture:

Looking down a track, the lines appear to meet, so this isn't useful. The best object to use to make the link is a ruler.

Children have this readily available in the classroom and can use it as a comparison tool to check as they work.

Orientation and how you represent parallel lines to children can have an impact on whether they can identify them correctly. We suggest that if you always show the children examples with horizontal orientation of the same length you are not giving children the knowledge to identify parallel lines in different settings.

Reflection

Are these lines parallel? How might a child respond when asked to identify the parallel lines?

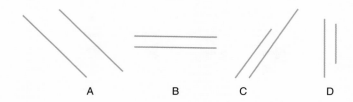

All the examples in the reflection box are parallel, however, not all children will identify them. A and C are not in a prototypical orientation which hinders their identification. In addition, C and D are often not identified as the lines are not the same length. Offering children a range of examples not only draws out these misconceptions, but allows for rich discussion to deepen their understanding.

The right angle

A *right angle* is a quarter turn. Children should be able to identify a right angle from Year 3. From this, children start to make the link between quarter and half turns; that two quarter turns are the same as a half turn – in addition, that you would end up in the same place by turning three right-angle turns clockwise, as you would by turning anticlockwise one right angle. If children physically make the turns themselves, it creates a visual and physical image to draw upon when working to solve written questions.

Teaching idea

Identifying right angles

Children do not measure angles accurately in degrees until Year 5, so in Year 3 they need a means to identify and measure right angles.

A simple right-angle measurer can be made by folding a circle into four and fitting it into corners. Alternatively, you can get your children to make a right-angle muncher. Children design a monster on card using a template like this

They then use the shapes to see if they fit into the monster's mouth to identify the right angles.

Alternatively, rather than using the 2D shapes, you could use card slices of pizza to feed the monster, who will only eat slices which are a right angle!

Perpendicular lines are two lines which meet at a right angle. As with parallel lines, how they are represented to children can have an impact on their understanding.

Reflection

How would children respond when asked to identify the perpendicular lines from the examples below?

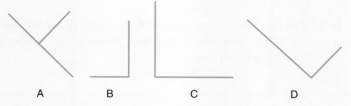

A   B   C   D

Think about the misconceptions which could lead to children not identifying them.

What's your angle?

In Year 4, children start to identify acute and obtuse angles leading to identifying reflex angles in Year 5.

An **acute angle** is an angle which is less than 90°. An **obtuse angle** is more than 90° and less than 180°. Developing an understanding of these first helps children link the concept of two right angles being a half turn, and therefore equal to 180°, or a **straight angle**. Children could initially use the right-angle measurer to identify whether the angle is smaller or greater than 90°. A **reflex angle** is greater than 180°.

Teaching idea

Proving the angles of a triangle add up to 180°

Get the children to work in pairs, drawing various triangles. Then label each angle a, b and c.

Rip off each corner and arrange them so they meet along a straight line. It is important to reinforce the need to rip the corners to identify clearly the angles to be used.

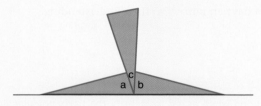

The same task can be used in the classroom to prove that the angles of a quadrilateral total 360°. We would suggest using a range of quadrilaterals: a trapezium, rhombus and various parallelograms, as well as quadrilaterals without any parallel sides.

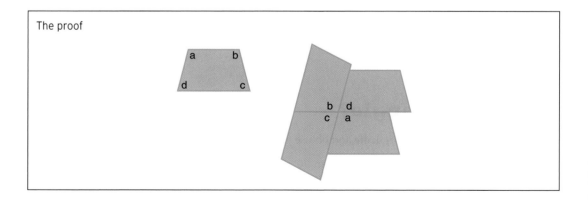

The proof

Once children understand these mathematical concepts, they can apply them to identify missing angles.

Task 8.4

Find the missing angles in the following shapes:

1.

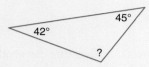

2.

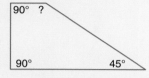

3.   A right-angled triangle has an angle of 37°. What is the size of the missing angle?

4.   A rhombus has an angle of 65°. What size are the three missing angles?

Mastery Task

This is a regular pentagon. If we draw lines from each corner to its centre we can calculate the size of each angle.

Repeat the task for other regular polygons.

The Key Stage 2 curriculum expects children to be able to draw and measure angles. When teaching children to measure angles accurately you should make sure you are familiar with the **protractors** in the school and can model how to use them.

The three types below are like those you could find in any primary classroom.

Type A is probably the most common; type B is useful as the numbers of degrees are different colours, reinforcing which side you start to measure the angle from; type C is more sophisticated and has a small arm which can be moved to assist with both drawing and measuring the angles.

A

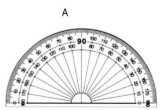

B

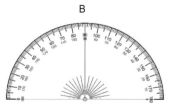

C

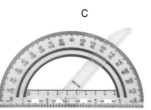

Children should initially use the visual provided in the reflection box to order angles in size to reinforce estimation skills. Then you should test their estimation by using the protractor to measure the angles accurately.

Reflection

Order the angles below, from smallest to largest. Look at the responses given and consider whether they are correct and, if not, what any possible misconceptions are.

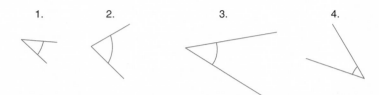

1.   2.   3.   4.

Avril's response was: 1, 2, 4, 3

Kathy's response was: 1 and 3, 2, 4

Avril has ordered the angles by the length of their sides, rather than the size of the angle.

Kathy has identified 1 and 3 as being the same size and that angle 2 is larger than them both. She has not identified angle 4 as the smallest due to its orientation. She needs to focus on the marked angle, not the orientation.

Going in circles

The National Curriculum has introduced to Year 6 the requirement to know how to label and illustrate the parts of a circle.

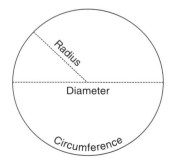

When teaching children to 'know that the diameter is twice the radius' you cannot just tell them. It is vital that they investigate this and prove it through visual exploration.

Ensure that any circle given to children has the centre marked so that accurate measurements can be taken.

Rounding up

2D shapes can be classified in a variety of ways: regular or irregular, by angle, lines and number of sides. We need to provide children with opportunities to explore these shapes in many contexts and various orientations, so children do not only recognise them in a prototypical form.

We can have a deeper understanding of 3D shapes when we think of them in terms of everyday objects, then we can visualise them more easily in their net form and recognise their 2D faces.

WHAT MATHS CAN YOU SEE?

THE SHAPE
OF THINGS
TO COME

LOSING THE PLOT

- **Coordinates**
- **The real transformers**
- **Rounding up**
- **What maths can you see?**

Losing the plot

In this chapter, we explore geometry further by examining the positions of shapes. This develops from a sound understanding of the properties of shapes, particularly 2D shapes.

Coordinates

Coordinates were originally developed as a mathematical idea by René Descartes in the seventeenth century. Descartes was not only a great French mathematician; he was also a famous philosopher, who thought a great deal about what he could believe with complete certainty. He decided that as he could think, he 'existed' and thus created probably the most philosophical phrase, 'I think therefore I am'. Descartes' analytical geometry linked it to algebra. His system stated that any point in a 2D plane could be represented as two points. It is because of Descartes that we refer to these as ***Cartesian coordinates***.

The numerical coordinates represent first the number on the horizontal (***x axis***) and then the vertical (***y axis***). Two axes – horizontal and vertical – divide the plane into four ***quadrants***. The point where the two axes intersect (0,0) is known as the ***origin***.

Single quadrant

When working with children initially, we plot points using the first quadrant. It is important that children can both read points from the grid and plot the points. Sometimes, difficulties arise in remembering the order in which to plot the coordinate and for this reason teachers will teach various sayings or visual cues to support this.

For example, 'along the corridor and up the stairs', or x is 'across' and y 'to the sky'.

Teaching idea

Supporting children plotting coordinates

Children who find it difficult to remember the order in which to plot points can be supported by colour coding both the axes and the coordinate.

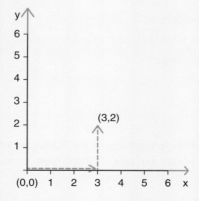

So when plotting the point (3,2) the colours provide a visual cue to the order.

Once children are confident with the concept of plotting coordinates we can move to applying this to wider mathematical context, such as constructing shapes. For example, we can now plot the coordinates (2,2) (7,3) (5,7) (3,5) and join them to make an irregular polygon.

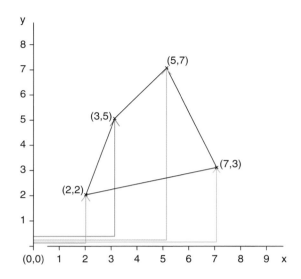

Task 9.1

Plot the coordinates (2,0) (4,0) and (5,5).

Find a fourth coordinate to make a parallelogram shape.

Mastery Task

Plot these two coordinates: (2,2) and (5,2).

Find two coordinates that can be joined to (2,2) and (5,2) in order to create a trapezium.

Can you find other solutions to this problem?

Four quadrants

The next stage in developing an understanding of the Cartesian system is to explore coordinates plotted in the four quadrants. It is essential that children have a good understanding of the number line, including negative numbers.

We explored negative numbers in Chapter 3, when we considered a lift moving up and down a building above ground, into a car park below. By using this vertical image and the horizontal empty number line, children will be supported in labelling the axes accurately.

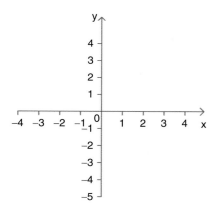

The four quadrants labelled here can extend to an infinite number on each axes.

Task 9.2

Plot the following points: (4,3) (−3,3) (4,−3) (−3,−3)

Consider the difficulties children may have when completing this task.

Now join the four coordinates and name the image.

Look at Appendix 2 to check your solution before reading any further.

Reflection

If you thought the answer to Task 9.2 was a rectangle, do you know where you went wrong? If you got the correct answer then well done!

When plotting the coordinates, you cannot just plot the points, then visually join them around the outside to make the image. In the task, we purposely asked you to plot them then think about the difficulties before joining them – so you would possibly make the mistake of just joining them around the outside to make the image.

The reason for this was to reinforce the teaching point that the coordinates should be joined in order. By guiding you into potentially making the mistake you are more likely to remember this when teaching children.

Children have three main difficulties when drawing and plotting coordinates using the four quadrants.

1. Drawing and labelling the axes.

2. The order in which to plot the coordinates.

3. Joining the points.

Always think about the objective of the lesson when considering how to manage potential difficulties.

*   If the objective is to label the axes, then the support could be that you have the axes already drawn so the focus is on the labelling. Some children find it hard to manipulate a ruler and thinking ahead to eliminate this aspect of the task will help.

*   If the objective is to accurately plot the coordinates, then for those children who find drawing and labelling time consuming, give them a grid already completed. The important thing here is that the children demonstrate an understanding of how to plot the coordinates and have time to show they can do this correctly. It is also useful, as with the single quadrant, to colour code the axes as an additional level of support.

*   If the objective is to join coordinates to create a polygon, then reinforce the need to join the points in order. Model to the children joining the points immediately after they have plotted each one to improve accuracy in this area.

The real transformers

There are four transformations we need to understand in the National Curriculum: reflection, rotation, translation and enlargement.

Each transformation has specific features and obtaining the skills required to both complete and identify these transformations begins in Key Stage 1.

As we work through each of the transformations we will be considering the final image in relation to the starting image. Is it **congruent** to the original? A shape will be 'congruent' if we turn it, flip it or move it and it would still fit exactly onto the original.

Reflection

Reflection is first taught in its simplest form with the concept of symmetry. **Symmetry** is having one side which is an exact mirror image of the other side. It is included in the **properties of shape** objectives for the National Curriculum but we see a natural progression to reflection so have included it here.

Using symmetry to classify a group of shapes is still a concept which is essential, so direct links between properties and positioning of shapes is crucial.

Often, symmetry in Foundation Stage takes the form of creating butterflies by painting one side and folding to create a symmetrical image.

Starting in this way reinforces the physical aspect of folding and the visual image created, with both sides of the fold being identical. The term 'symmetry' may or may not be used at this point.

In Key Stage 1 we suggest that children should physically work with the shapes, as discussed in Chapter 8. Cutting or tracing a shape, then folding to see if the sides will match helps children to identify the many patterns – especially when examining regular and irregular shapes.

Below are four regular polygons. We can see from the lines of symmetry marked that the number of equal sides and angles in this case is also the same as the number of lines of symmetry.

It is different for irregular shapes. We often find that when working with triangles children will say there is only one line of symmetry for both equilateral and isosceles triangles, as marked below.

 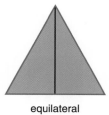

isosceles   equilateral

This misconception is based on orientation. When we turn the page and the equilateral triangle has a different side as the base we can see another line of symmetry. Therefore, it is so important to encourage children to manipulate the shapes.

Looking at further 2D shapes we can see instances where, depending on how the shape is drawn will impact on the number of lines of symmetry. It is important that we don't generalise and therefore create misconceptions in how shapes can be classified.

This parallelogram has two lines of symmetry as its sides are of equal length and it's therefore a rhombus, whereas the parallelogram next to it has no lines of symmetry due to its irregular shape.

This also needs to be considered when calculating lines of symmetry on a trapezium, as shown below.

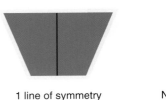

1 line of symmetry   No lines of symmetry

Part of the fun of exploring symmetry in Key Stage 1 is also exploring letters and other shapes.

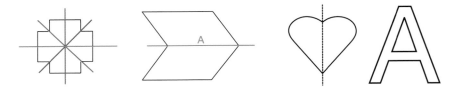

Teaching idea

Exploring symmetry and reflection

Give the children part or all of a shape or pattern and ask them to use a mirror to explore symmetry. This links to the topic of reflection.

Which letters of the alphabet still read the same when reflected? For this task, one could consider if the answers are different when using capital and lowercase letters.

Identify the letters this could be when reflected. This may or may not be a mirror line of symmetry.

We will now look at the transformation reflection using a Cartesian grid. To carry this out we need to know one piece of information: the mirror line.

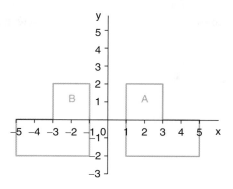

First, we have plotted the following points in order: (1,–2) (5,–2) (5,0) (3,0) (3,2) (1,2) to create Shape A.

Next, we have reflected Shape A with the y axis as the mirror line and labelled it Shape B.

Shape B is congruent to Shape A, but reversed.

We have chosen this shape to reflect because it is important to be able to immediately identify if an accurate reflection has been made.

If we look at the example below, the choice of Shape A does not clearly help you to assess if the reflection to Shape B is correct. The shape could have been slid across and the outcome would have been the same.

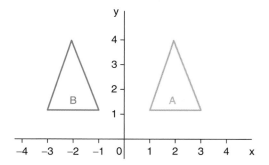

As discussed in Chapter 5, when planning your activities you should be looking to draw out any misconception at the earliest opportunity. Geometry activities are no different from number activities in this way.

Mastery Task

Plot the following coordinates onto a Cartesian grid to make Shape A:

(1,3) (3,–3) (3,–1) (4,–1) (4,1) (5,1) (5,3) (3,3) (3,1) (2,1) (2,–1) (1,–1)

Reflect Shape A in the line x = y and label the reflected image Shape B.

Rotation

In Chapter 8 we discussed angles of rotation and how a quarter turn is 90°, or a right angle, and a half turn is 180°, or a straight angle. This early work in Key Stage 1 prepares us to carry out the transformation of rotation in Key Stage 2.

If we explore angles of turns, both clockwise and anticlockwise, in Key Stage 1 then we will start to make direct links. For example, recognising that a three-quarter turn clockwise will end in the same place as a quarter turn anticlockwise.

To successfully carry out a rotation we need three pieces of information.

1. The centre of rotation.

2. The direction of rotation.

3. The angle of rotation.

Question: Plot the coordinates (1,1) (3,2) (3,4) and (1,4) on a Cartesian grid and label this Shape A. Rotate Shape A 90° anticlockwise about the point (1,1) and label this new shape, Shape B.

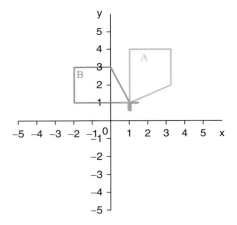

First, plot the coordinates on the grid. We have chosen a starting shape which will immediately identify if the final rotation is correct.

The next step is to identify the centre of rotation – in this case the point (1,1). To help visualise the rotation we have marked a right angle in blue. It is often difficult to visualise where the whole shape will finish. By marking a right angle, we can focus on the relationship with one of the sides of the shape and then where the right angle would move to, marked in red on the diagram above. The final Shape B can then be drawn.

Another way to support understanding of this type of rotation is to trace Shape A, mark the right angle, then rotate the tracing paper and map where the image has moved to. The new image is congruent to the original.

Task 9.3

Plot the coordinates (2,–1) (3,4) (0,1).

Rotate the shape 270° clockwise about the point (2,–1).

Mastery Task

Describe the single transformation that maps Shape A onto Shape B.

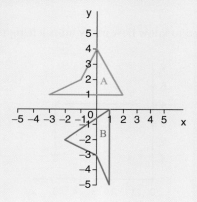

Rotational symmetry

If a shape is rotated around its centre and it matches the original image at least once, then the shape has an order of **rotational symmetry**.

This star has rotational symmetry of the order five. It can be rotated about its centre five times and fit exactly. As it is a regular star it will also have five lines of reflective symmetry.

This links with regular polygons, as they have the same number of lines of symmetry as their order of rotational symmetry. For example, a square has four lines of symmetry and rotational symmetry order four.

Translation

To **translate** a shape or object it is moved in a given direction, a given distance, without turning it or flipping it.

We start to develop skills linked to this concept in Foundation Stage and Key Stage 1 with simple map work, navigating a robot or a friend around a maze by giving directions. We learn that with instructions we can move in a straight line forward or backward: a translation.

If we turn whilst navigating around a maze then we are also carrying out a rotation and we can easily start to link the two concepts.

We then explore translations using a Cartesian grid. To begin with, we work with a single quadrant translating individual points.

To carry out a translation we need to know how many units left/right and up/down to move.

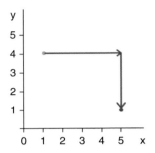

Translate the red point four units to the right and three units down. Like plotting coordinates, the horizontal movement is carried out before the vertical movement.

Once we have mastered translating single points we can apply this skill to translating shapes.

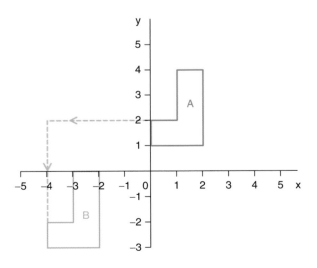

Plot the following coordinates to make Shape A: (0,1) (2,1) (2,4) (1,4) (1,2) (0,2).

Translate Shape A four units to the left and four units down.

By translating each single point on Shape A we can build the new Shape B.

Here, point (0,2) is translated four units to the left and four units down.

We can carry on with each individual point, or use the new point to plot the rest of the new translated shape. The image of Shape B is congruent to the original shape.

Mastery Task

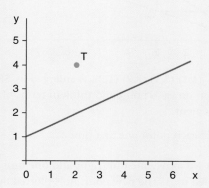

Draw a line parallel to the one shown, which will pass through point T. What is the coordinate where the new line meets the y axis?

Point T is translated two units to the right and three units down, making point S.

Draw another line parallel to the others. What is the coordinate where the new line crosses the x axis?

Enlargement

Enlargement is not part of the National Curriculum at Key Stage 1 and Key Stage 2. However, to develop your own subject knowledge it is important that we explore all four transformations.

If we consider the word 'enlargement' we visualise shapes getting larger. As we explore this further we will see that to **enlarge** a shape it can become either larger or smaller. Also, it does not change position or direction.

To carry out an enlargement we need to know the following two pieces of information.

1. The scale factor (SF).

2. The centre of enlargement.

Example

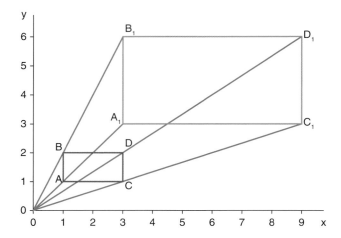

The original shape, coordinates (1,1) (3,1) (3,2) (1,2), is enlarged by SF3 from the origin. It is important to carry out the enlargement on each point and think in terms of enlarging the distance to each point from the centre of enlargement.

For the example above, let's take each point one at a time.

- From the origin to point A we move one unit right and one unit up, so for an enlargement SF3 these distances are multiplied by 3. The new point Ai is plotted by moving three units right and three units up.

- From the origin to point B we move one unit right and two units up, so the new point Bi will be three units right and six units up.

- From the origin to point C we move three units right and one unit up, so the new point Ci will be nine units right and three units up.

- From the origin to point D we move three units right and two units up, so the new point Di will be nine units right and six units up.

A line can be drawn from the centre of enlargement through each point (in green) to show that our enlargement is accurate. We can see that the new image is not congruent to the original.

Reflection

What happens to the area and perimeter of a rectangle enlarged by SF2 and SF $\frac{1}{2}$?

The first response is to say that they double for SF2, and halve for SF $\frac{1}{2}$ but let's work through a specific example to fully understand what happens.

Using the point (1,1) as the centre of enlargement, the blue rectangle is enlarged SF2 (green rectangle) and then SF $\frac{1}{2}$ (red rectangle).

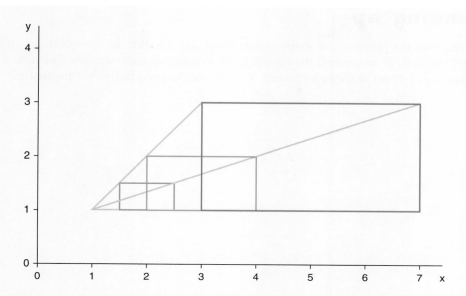

This clearly shows that enlargement does not always make shapes bigger. The enlargement SF $\frac{1}{2}$ has made the shape smaller.

If we calculate the perimeter and area of each rectangle we can see the impact of each enlargement.

Rectangle	Dimensions	Perimeter	Area
Blue	2×1	6 units	2 units^2
Green SF2	4×2	12 units	8 units^2
Red SF $\frac{1}{2}$	$1 \times \frac{1}{2}$	3 units	$\frac{1}{2}$ unit^2

From these results, we can see that when we enlarge SF2 the perimeter doubles but the area is four times bigger. This is because both the length and the breadth are doubled.

The enlargement of SF $\frac{1}{2}$ halves the perimeter but the area is $\frac{1}{4}$ of the original rectangle.

Mastery Task

Plot the following points and label it Shape A: (3,1) (6,1) (6,2) (4,2).

Reflect Shape A in the line y = x and label the image Shape B.

Reflect Shape B in the line y = −x and label the image Shape C.

Translate Shape C seven units to the right and one unit down and label the image Shape D.

Enlarge Shape D by SF2 centred on (−1,−1) and label the image Shape E.

Rounding up

By linking both the properties of shape with position and direction we have explored all of the geometry concepts. To understand the skills required to complete transformations we need a broad understanding of shapes in multiple contexts. We will consider these further in Chapter 10.

WHAT MATHS CAN YOU SEE?

MADE TO MEASURE

- **Non-standard units**
- **Metric units**
- **Learning to measure length**
- **Around the outside**
- **What's inside?**
- **Scratching the surface**
- **Turn up the volume**
- **It's similar**
- **Putting it on the map**
- **Mass and capacity**
- **Measuring equipment**
- **Imperial units – it's complicated**
- **It is all about the money**
- **Time after time**
- **Rounding up**
- **What maths can you see?**

Made to measure

This chapter will explore the world of measure. We measure all sorts of wonderful things such as length, mass, time, temperature, etc. In one sense, measure is a practical application of number, so a teacher introducing topics in measure needs to have a real insight into their children's ability in number. Without this, children may be presented with work beyond their capability.

A key element of being proficient at measure is to have a deep understanding of the different units of measure we use for length, height, mass and capacity. This includes metric – and some imperial – units of measure. In addition, children need to know about time and money.

Non-standard units

Young children begin their understanding of measure by comparing objects and deciding which is longer or shorter, which is quicker or slower, which is heavier or lighter. Initially, they may be comparing just two objects before moving on to sorting three or more.

We then move children on to measuring lengths of different objects. Before we move to 'standard units of measure' which allows us to use rulers or tape measures, children will be encouraged to use non-standard units, such as measuring the width of their desk using their hand span, or the length of the room using their number of footsteps. It is then easy to show that different children do not always get the same answers, as their hands and feet are all different sizes. We therefore need to use a measure that will ensure every child gets the same answer. This can be done with cubes or other types of building bricks. Such work will then lead naturally to the introduction of the 'centimetre'.

Metric units

Before we consider the teaching of metric units, it is worth considering the nature of metric measures in order to appreciate how different types of metric measures are related.

When do you think the idea of the 'metre' was developed? Surprisingly, the concept of a metre was introduced in 1668 by the great architect Sir Christopher Wren, who defined a metre as *the length of a pendulum that takes one second to swing*. We now know that the length of such a pendulum is actually 997 mm, so Wren was quite accurate. Later, a metre was defined as one ten millionth of the distance between the equator and the poles. (Note: make sure you get the spelling correct. A **metre** is a unit of length, whereas a **meter** is for monitoring electricity, gas or car parking.)

A useful way to help children in their understanding of metric measure is to ensure they are aware of these prefixes:

'Milli' meaning $\frac{1}{1000}$

'Cent' meaning $\frac{1}{100}$

'Kilo' meaning 1,000

The three most common standard metric units are **metre** for length, **gram** for mass and **litre** for capacity (the way we measure liquid). We can summarise these as follows.

	length	mass	capacity
Standard unit	**metre (m)**	**gram (g)**	**litre (l)**
$\frac{1}{1000}$ of the standard unit	millimetre (mm)	milligram (mg)	millilitre (ml)
$\frac{1}{100}$ of the standard unit	centimetre (cm)	centigram (cg)	centilitre (cl)
1,000 of the standard units	kilometre (km)	kilogram (kg)	kilolitre (kl)

Some of these units are used only rarely (those in red). For capacity, in everyday use we tend to use only litres and millilitres and it would be very rare to hear of a mass measured in centigrams.

The metric units for length, mass and capacity are connected to each other. Many of our students are surprised to learn this, yet these relationships are fascinating and rather clever. To explain this, consider a cube of side 10 cm.

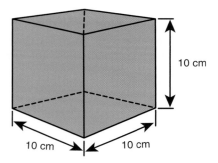

The volume of this cube is 1,000 cubic cm ($10 \times 10 \times 10 = 1,000 \text{ cm}^3$). We will look at this in more detail later in this chapter.

- The amount of water that such a cube could hold is defined as one litre.

- The weight of one litre of (cold) water is defined as one kg.

- Equally, therefore, one cubic centimetre of cold water weighs one gram.

Learning to measure length

Once children are introduced to units and are aware of the differences between measuring length, mass and capacity, they need to understand which units are most appropriate for measuring different objects. For example, to measure the width of a book the best unit is centimetres, whereas for measuring the width of a playground, metres would be more useful. To measure the distance from, say, Liverpool to Manchester, kilometres is the most sensible unit. Many children can find the selection of appropriate units very challenging.

The best way to get children thinking about measure is to get them measuring. This leads us to something you have perhaps never previously considered, *How do we teach children to measure length?* It is important that they are provided with some meaning to each of the units when they are first introduced; practical work is essential for this. Children need to use a ruler to accurately measure lengths. Probably one would begin with objects that are common in the classroom, such as a pencil, a paper clip, the width of the desk, etc. However, it is at this point that many students start to realise that teaching children to measure lengths is much harder than they thought.

A child may never have been taught how to draw a straight line between two points. Before you begin teaching measuring distances with a ruler, you need to ensure that children have the motor skills necessary to hold a ruler: to first draw a straight line, then draw a straight line between two given points, then draw a straight line of a given length. Try getting the children to draw lines of different lengths. Giving them squared centimetre paper can be helpful here.

Types of rulers

You will find different types of rulers in the primary classroom.

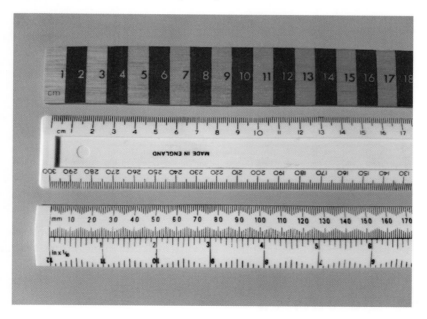

The top type of ruler in this image is labelled in cm 'blocks'. You will often see these in Early Years classrooms. There are two potential problems here. First, as there is no zero, children need to measure from the end of the ruler. This can create problems when moving to other rulers where there is a blank space before the numbers start. Second, the numbers are aligned to the left of each unit.

This can cause significant conceptual difficulty in accurate measuring. For example, any line between 3 and 4 cm long can be recorded as 4 cm.

The second ruler is perhaps the most common ruler in primary schools. This has centimetres on one side and millimetres on the other. This immediately creates problems for some children who are not sure which side of the ruler to use. In the picture, the side scaled in centimetres is uppermost but the subdivision of each unit into 10 mm also causes significant problems for many children. The children also have to appreciate where the (invisible) zero is and begin their measuring from there rather than the end of the ruler.

The third ruler is a mixture of imperial and metric, which itself can cause problems. A common mistake is to measure in inches instead of centimetres. Again, there is a gap to the 'invisible' zero but you will notice this is a bigger gap than in the second ruler. The problems with not measuring from zero are summarised in the next picture where each ruler has been used to measure a line 10 cm in length.

Incorrect use of the ruler gives different results. Understanding that we can only measure from zero – and knowing where zero is on the ruler – is an essential skill in measuring. Teaching use of a ruler is not easy!

Around the outside

In Year 3, children are introduced to the concept of 'perimeter' and need to be able to measure perimeters of simple two-dimensional shapes. (Note: Again, be careful with spellings. Having got used to the fact that metre is spelt 're' there will be many students who spell the word 'perimetre'. The correct spelling is **perimeter**.)

One way to introduce perimeter is using a trundle wheel to measure the distance around the school field or school playground. This secures the concept that 'perimeter' is the 'distance all the way around the edge of the shape'. Physically walking around the edge of the field/playground/hall will help children when they are presented with simple 2D shapes on paper to measure. Encourage the children to think about taking their pencil on a journey around the outside of the shape, as they did on the playground with the trundle wheel. We would anticipate that this paper-based approach would begin with rectangles, before moving to other shapes. To begin with, children will measure all four sides and then add these numbers together. However, you could develop this activity later to try to encourage children to use their understanding of the properties of rectangles, i.e. that opposite sides are equal. Thus, we only need to measure two sides and add them together, then double the answer.

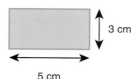

3 cm

5 cm

(i)   (children measure four sides)
      Perimeter = 3 + 5 + 3 + 5 = 16 cm
(ii)   (children measure just two sides and double)
      Perimeter = (5 + 3) × 2 = 16 cm

Another important concept to cement here is that **perimeter is a length** and therefore the units we use must be cm or mm, etc.

It is tempting to get children to begin such introductory work by asking them to draw rectangles on squared paper. However, you need to be careful here; a very common mistake that children make when looking at perimeter of shapes on squared paper is to count the number of squares around the edge rather than the actual length. For example, imagine a child has a 5 × 3 rectangle, drawn on squared paper. They may do this:

	1	2	3	4	5		
	12				6		
	11	10	9	8	7		

Children may think the perimeter is 12 cm rather than 16 cm. Asking the question, *Why do we get a different answer?* is a useful discussion task.

You need to ensure that children are confident with the concept of perimeter and can accurately measure the perimeters of simple 2D shapes, especially those discussed in Chapter 8, before getting them to work with shapes drawn on squared paper. Once children appreciate that a perimeter may be measured by adding up the length of each side then the complexity of the shape is not important, provided we are using polygons.

In Year 5, children need to consider the perimeter of **rectilinear shapes**. These are shapes that can be constructed using two or more rectangles of different sizes, such as:

One of the things you need to consider here is how much information you give the child in the diagram and how much you expect them to deduce. For example:

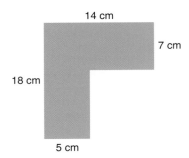

You will often see this type of diagram given to children who are working on perimeter.

Inexperienced teachers may assume that a child will know how to find the lengths of the two sides which aren't given by using subtraction. This is incorrect. Many children will be puzzled by this diagram and will just add up the lengths that are given (18 + 14 + 7 + 5).

You must teach children how to find the missing lengths.

Mastery Task

Draw a square of sides 20 cm.

At one corner you cut out another square of sides 10 cm.

How does this affect the perimeter of the new shape?

What happens to the perimeter if you cut away a number of pieces?

What's inside?

The study of area goes back to the ancient Greeks and many aspects of the topic that we teach in school today can be traced back to this time. *Area* may be thought of as the amount of space that is contained within a shape. As a concept, the topic of area is introduced in Year 4 by counting squares. Here, the use of squared paper really is useful.

Draw some rectangles on cm squared paper.

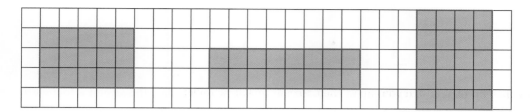

Children will begin by counting the number of squares inside the shape. As we are counting **squares** and as the width of each square is (in this case) 1 cm, ***our unit of area is 'square cm' or cm²***. We feel it is important to mention this and for you to explain why this is the case to children. You will find children continually confuse the units of perimeter (mm, cm, m, km) with the units for area perimeter (mm², cm², m², km²).

There is a clear link here to the work we did in Chapter 3 on ***arrays***. It does not take children long to see that instead of counting each square, they can think of three rows of five, or two rows of eight, etc. This also makes good links to Year 5 work when the formal method for calculating area of rectangles is introduced (area = base × height).

It's all about the base

When you think about rectangles, do you think of the sides being 'length' and 'width', or 'base' and 'height'? Certainly, for triangles, most people think of the dimensions in terms of base and height, and these are the terms used in the standard formula for the area of a triangle. So why do many teachers confuse children by not using base and height as the key dimensions for rectangles? Even more confusingly, some refer to the dimensions of a rectangle as breadth and width. We believe that this variation in terminology comes from the orientation of the shape being considered.

Think of the playing area of a football or hockey pitch. This is a rectangular shape and it is clear it has a width and a length. Nobody talks about the breadth of a football pitch or the base of a hockey pitch. Now think of a rectangular wall. Here we would probably all agree that the wall has a height, not a length. However, what would you call the second dimension of the wall? The 'width' of the wall or the 'base' of the wall? It is perhaps when we consider two-dimensional shapes from above we use the terms length and width – whereas when looking at objects that are upright, such as a wall or door, we think of base and height. There is no agreed correct answer here, but hopefully, just by thinking about this, you can see how some children can be confused and develop misconceptions. Whichever terminology you use, be consistent and ensure that all children appreciate what each word means.

Irregular shapes

Children will then be moved on to consider the area of irregular shapes by counting squares. As you can see in the diagram below, here it is not possible to be exact and thus we can only have approximate answers.

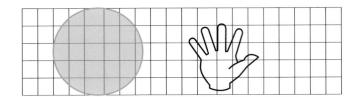

By the end of Year 6, children are expected to know how to calculate the area of a triangle and a parallelogram. Of course, you could just give the children the formulae and show them how to apply it, but a much stronger pedagogical approach is to show them where each of the formulae come from. In each case we can do this relatively easily.

Area of a triangle

Let us begin with a right-angled triangle, formed from a rectangle of the same dimensions. By simply cutting the rectangle along one of the diagonals, we can show that we have two triangles of identical size.

Hence the area of each triangle is half of the area of the original rectangle. This leads to our formula $A = \dfrac{1}{2}$ base × height.

A similar process can be used to consider non-right-angled triangles.

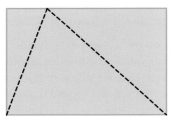

We begin with a rectangle and, from any point along the top edge, draw lines to the two vertices at the base. This gives us a non-right-angled triangle along the base and two right-angled triangles on the top edge.

Now cut out the right-angled triangles. We have shaded them yellow so it is easier for you to see.

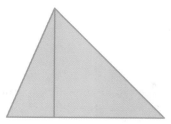

The two right-angled triangles can now be inverted to fit perfectly inside the non-right-angled triangle. Thus, again, the area of the non-right-angled triangle must be half that of the rectangle.

'Real mathematicians' would not call this a 'proof' but it is a child-friendly way of verifying to children where that well-known formula comes from.

It is worth making a few points about how some children interpret the formula:

$$A = \frac{1}{2} b \times h$$

Let us suppose we are calculating the area of a triangle of base 12 cm and height 8 cm. There are several ways to consider performing the calculation.

$A = \frac{1}{2}$ of (base × height)	$A = \frac{1}{2}$ of (12 × 8) $= \frac{1}{2}$ of 96 $= 48$ cm²	This is the most common method children use, especially when the formula is first introduced.
$A = \frac{1}{2}$ of the base multiplied by the height	$A = \frac{1}{2}$ of 12 × 8 $= 6 \times 8$ $= 48$ cm²	This is equally successful, provided the base is an even number. Where the base is an odd number, the calculation is much more complicated than the top version.
$A =$ base multiplied by half the height	$A = 12 \times (\frac{1}{2}$ of 8) $= 12 \times 4$ $= 48$ cm²	Used less frequently but this is helpful if the base is odd and the height is even. Children need to appreciate that the values for b and h are commutative.
$A = \frac{1}{2}$ of the base multiplied by half the height	$A = \frac{1}{2} 12 \times \frac{1}{2} 8$ $= 6 \times 4$ $= 24$ cm²	You will see this many times. Children often halve both numbers before multiplying. This gives an **incorrect** answer because by halving twice, they have actually quartered the product instead of halving. This error is the algebraic equivalent of stating: $\frac{1}{2} (b \times h) = \frac{1}{2} b \times \frac{1}{2} h$

Area of a parallelogram

In order to find the area of a parallelogram, we can use very simple technique to demonstrate where the formal formula comes from.

We begin with a parallelogram and we drop a perpendicular line from one edge to the vertex below, in order to form a right-angled triangle.

Now cut out the right-angled triangle and move it to the opposite end. We now have a rectangle which has the same length base as the parallelogram. The height of the rectangle is the perpendicular height of the parallelogram.

Thus, area = base × perpendicular height.

The most common error children make here is to use the length of the sloping edge as the height, instead of the perpendicular height.

Scratching the surface

Having discussed area and perimeter in relation to two-dimensional shapes, we now turn our attention to three-dimensional shapes. However, before we completely finish our work on area, it is useful to think about how the topic relates to three-dimensional shapes. As discussed in Chapter 8, every three-dimensional object has a number of faces. For the purpose of this discussion, we will only consider shapes that have faces that are squares, rectangles or triangles. Each of these faces has an area, and the sum of the area of all faces in the shape is called the ***surface area***. Although the topic of surface area is principally a Key Stage 3 topic, it is useful to discuss the concept with children in Key Stage 2 to help cement deep understanding of the topic of area.

The easiest way to do this is to consider a cube of, say, 5 cm.

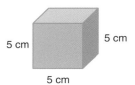

The cube has six faces. Each face is a square and each square has an area of 25 cm². Thus, the total surface area of the cube is 6 × 25 = 150 cm².

Developing this idea for cuboids requires a little lateral thinking. It is best to begin with a square-ended cuboid before thinking about prisms with three different lengths. Then perhaps consider a triangular prism.

Cuboid 3 cm × 3 cm × 12 cm

There are two square ends, each 3 cm × 3 cm

There are four rectangular sides, each 12 cm × 3 cm

Surface area = 2 × (3 × 3) + 4 × (12 × 3)

           = 18 + 144

           = 162 cm²

Cuboid 10 cm × 2 cm × 3 cm

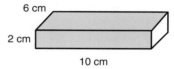

Children need to consider this very carefully.

Front / back two rectangles 10 cm × 2 cm

Each side two rectangles 6 cm × 2 cm

Top / bottom two rectangles 10 cm × 6 cm

Surface area = 2 × (10 × 2) + 2 × (6 × 2) + 2 × (10 × 6)

           = 40 + 24 + 120

           = 184 cm²

Using a real cuboid will help if children have difficulty visualising each rectangle.

Triangular prism 3 cm × 4 cm × 8 cm

Sloping length = 5 cm

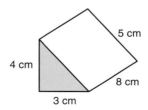

This shape consists of three rectangles (all different dimensions) and two equal triangles.

Two triangles 3 cm × 4 cm

Base of shape is a rectangle 3 cm × 8 cm

Side of shape is a rectangle 4 cm × 8 cm

Sloping face is a rectangle 5 cm × 8 cm

$$\text{Surface area} = 2 \times [\frac{1}{2}(3 \times 4)] + (3 \times 8) + (4 \times 8) + (5 \times 8)$$
$$= 12 + 24 + 32 + 40$$
$$= 108 \text{ cm}^2$$

Another way to consider surface area of prisms is to look at the nets of each shape. For some children, this is an easier way to appreciate the shape and area of each face.

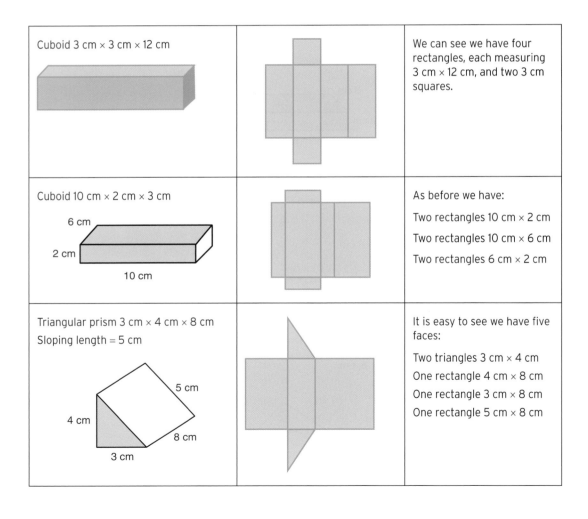

Cuboid 3 cm × 3 cm × 12 cm		We can see we have four rectangles, each measuring 3 cm × 12 cm, and two 3 cm squares.
Cuboid 10 cm × 2 cm × 3 cm 6 cm 2 cm 10 cm		As before we have: Two rectangles 10 cm × 2 cm Two rectangles 10 cm × 6 cm Two rectangles 6 cm × 2 cm
Triangular prism 3 cm × 4 cm × 8 cm Sloping length = 5 cm 5 cm 4 cm 8 cm 3 cm		It is easy to see we have five faces: Two triangles 3 cm × 4 cm One rectangle 4 cm × 8 cm One rectangle 3 cm × 8 cm One rectangle 5 cm × 8 cm

Turn up the volume

Volume is informally defined as the amount of space contained within a given three-dimensional shape. A useful way to begin this topic is to look at boxes of stock cubes. This also provides a helpful way to introduce children to the units we use for volume. We are trying to find out how many single cubes fit into the box. If each box measures say 2 cm × 2 cm × 3 cm and each stock cube is 1 cm × 1 cm × 1 cm then we can demonstrate that we have three 'layers' of four cubes which means we have a total of 12 cubes (12 cubic cm, or 12 cm³). Such an introduction will also quickly lead to establishing how the volume of a cube can be calculated.

Teaching idea

How many cuboids?

Take 36 cubes and ask the children to use them to build a cuboid. How many different cuboids can be made?

Repeat with different numbers of cubes. For example, 12, 48, 96 ... (Note: it is important to use numbers that have plenty of factors.)

We want the children to appreciate that the volume of any cuboid can be calculated by multiplying the length of each side, often recorded as length, breadth and height. Of course, just as in area and perimeter, all sides need to be measured in the same units.

Task 10.1

A cube is made using 27 blue centimetre cubes. The large cube is then painted yellow.

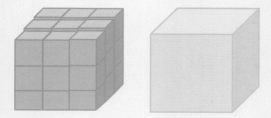

If the large cube is then split back into centimetre cubes, how many of the cubes will have three faces painted yellow? How many will have two yellow faces? How many will have just one yellow face?

Mastery Task

How can you calculate the volume of a single piece of A4 paper?

It's similar

Children in Year 6 are expected to understand the properties of similar shapes and solve problems where the scale factor is known, or can be found. Similar shapes have the same shapes but are different sizes. If two shapes are ***similar***, they have all their sides in the ***same ratio***. The ***scale factor*** is defined by how much each side has been enlarged.

In these rectangles:

Ratio of height = 3:15

= 1:5

Ratio of base = 4:20

= 1:5

Corresponding sides are both in the same ratio, therefore **the rectangles are similar**. In this example, the scale factor is 5.

In these rectangles:

Ratio of height = 4:12

= 1:3

Ratio of base = 5:20

= 1:4

Corresponding sides are **not** in the same ratio therefore, **the rectangles are not similar**.

We now wish to consider some associated properties of similar shapes with respect to other measures we have discussed.

Reflection

Carolyn is asked to calculate the area of a rectangle with sides of 30 cm and 40 cm.

She writes:

Area = base × height

$\quad$ = 30 × 40

$\quad$ = 1,200 cm²

$\quad$ = 12 m²

Is Carolyn correct?

Before we consider this question, let us look at the two similar rectangles we discussed above. For each rectangle, we will calculate the area and perimeter.

3 cm

4 cm

Perimeter = 3 + 4 + 3 + 4 = 14 cm

Area = 4 × 3 = 12 cm²

15 cm

20 cm

Perimeter = 15 + 20 + 15 + 20 = 70 cm

Area = 20 × 15 = 300 cm²

We now consider the ratio of each of these measures:

Ratio of sides $\qquad$ = 3:15

$\qquad\qquad\qquad$ = 1:5

Ratio of perimeters $\quad$ = 14:70

$\qquad\qquad\qquad$ = 2:10

$\qquad\qquad\qquad$ = 1:5

Ratio of areas $\qquad$ = 12:300

$\qquad\qquad\qquad$ = 4:100

$\qquad\qquad\qquad$ = 1:25

The ratio of the perimeters stay the same as the ratio of the sides. ***This is because perimeter is a length***. However, the ratio of the areas has changed to 1:25. ***This is because area is measured in square units*** – the ratio has been squared.

Now consider two identical squares. We measure the sides of each, one in metres and the other in centimetres.

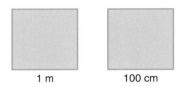

1 m   100 cm

Both squares are identical, so their areas are equal.

If measuring in metres: area = 1 × 1 = 1 m²

If measuring in centimetres: area = 100 × 100 = 10,000 cm²

This shows: **1 m² = 10,000 cm²**

At Key Stage 2, children are not required to convert square units. The units we measure in determines the units for the answer. Referring back to the reflection, if we wanted Carolyn to give an answer in square metres we should ask her to convert each side into metres before she multiplies them together. Carolyn's calculation would then have become:

Area = base × height

= 0.3 × 0.4

= 0.12 m²

Now consider two equal cubes:

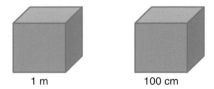

1 m   100 cm

Both cubes are identical, so their volumes are equal.

If measuring in metres: volume = 1 × 1 = 1 m³

If measuring in centimetres: volume = 100 × 100 × 100 = 1,000,000 cm³

This shows: **1 m³ = 1,000,000 cm³**

In general, if two similar shapes have sides in the ratio a:b, their areas are in the ratio a²:b² and their volumes are in the ratio a³:b³.

Task 10.2

1. Two similar rectangles have sides in the ratio 1:3. If the first measures 10 cm x 6 cm, what are the dimensions of the second rectangle? What is the ratio of their areas?

2. Two similar triangles have areas in the ratio 1:16. If the largest triangle has a base of 24 cm and a height of 36 cm, what are the dimensions of the smaller triangle?

Putting it on the map

Before we move on from measuring length, it is important to make links with the topic of ratio and how it is applied to maps.

A number of years ago, map scales were given using specific units such as 'one inch to the mile' or 'one centimetre to the kilometre'. Today however, all map scales are usually given as a ratio. This means map scales are independent of units.

A typical example may be a map using a scale of 1:10,000. This means that one of any unit on the map is the equivalent to 10,000 of the same units in real life. Thus, one inch on the map would be equivalent to 10,000 inches; one centimetre on the map would be equivalent to 10,000 cm. Equally, if the real distance between two points is 500 metres, on the map they would be a distance of 1/10,000 of 500 metres apart (which is 5 cm).

Example

A map has a scale of 1:500,000.

(a) If the distance between two points on the map is 4 cm, what is the real distance between them?

(b) Two cities are actually 95 km apart. How far apart do they appear on the map?

Scale 1:100,000

(a) 1 cm = 500,000 cm

    4 cm = 2,000,000 cm

        = 20,000 m

        = 20 km

(b) 95 km = 95,000 m

          = 9,500,000 cm

Dividing by 500,000, 95 km corresponds to 19 cm on the map.

Task 10.3

1. A map scale is 1:100,000. A road appears to be 12 cm long on the map. What is its real length?

2. The distance between two towns is 8.3 km but appears as 5 cm on a map. What is the scale of the map?

Mass and capacity

It's mass-ive

Before we proceed any further, it is worth spending a few minutes talking about the concept of mass. You may notice that the National Curriculum talks about 'mass' rather than 'weight'. There is a technical difference here that you need to be aware of. You will appreciate that heaviness is not dependent upon size. We can have small heavy objects and large light objects. The 'mass' of an object is a measure of how much matter that object contains. For most people 'mass' is commonly measured by how much something weighs. However, weight can change in different locations. For example, an object will have a different weight on the moon (because of differences in gravity), while its mass stays the same. In everyday use, mass and weight are seen as the same but we do need to distinguish between them, as it is important in precise scientific measurement.

As mentioned at the beginning of this chapter, developing a sense of measure for mass and capacity begins with ordering objects. For example, can children identify the lighter/heavier of two (or more) objects simply by picking each of them up? If you are doing such an activity, try to ensure that you use objects that have a different order for size and mass. We do not want children to develop the misconception that the larger object is always the heaviest. This activity soon moves on to using balances to decide which is heaviest. At this stage, you can begin to use objects that have masses which are closer to each other and where the question, *Which is the heaviest?* is difficult to securely answer by just picking each object up.

At Key Stage 1, children are expected to be able to undertake tasks such as this.

Here are three glasses. Sort the glasses from least full to most full.

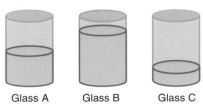

Glass A   Glass B   Glass C

A key element to teaching this topic is to ensure that children are fully appreciative of the associated vocabulary. Children may know which glass has the most liquid in, but some may not appreciate that the question is asking them to write the names of the glasses in a specific order, smallest to biggest. As a teacher of mathematics, it is important that you not only teach children new words, but that each child must also know how to say the word, to read the word and to comprehend the use of the word when it is given in an instruction or sentence.

Measuring equipment

Developing understanding in measure is moved forward by introducing children to a variety of instruments that they can use, such as measuring scales, measuring cylinders (or beakers) and thermometers. Many students do not initially appreciate just how difficult it is for a child to read from a simple scale. Consider the following question, which comes from the 2016 Key Stage 1 Mathematics Paper 2, Reasoning.

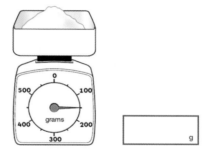

Until you have tried to teach this, you will not appreciate the difficulty it can cause many children. Just as in teaching children how to use a ruler, teaching them to read scales correctly can be fraught with difficulties – principally because it requires children to understand a wide range of different number scales. As we have said several times, all mathematics is based upon developing in children a sense of number. Children who are weak in their number skills are quickly exposed in other areas of the curriculum, thus limiting their progression. Measuring is such an area.

Before we discuss measuring equipment any further, let us briefly go back to some of the number work we discussed in Chapter 2. We need children to be able to count forwards and backwards, first in ones, then twos, threes, fives, tens, etc. A similar and useful oral exercise that can be used to support children in being able to successfully read any measuring equipment is to get them to count up and down in fives, tens, twenties, twenty-fives, fifties, etc. This will help when introducing, say, a scale labelled in 100 g intervals, a measuring cylinder labelled in 50 ml intervals or a thermometer labelled in 5°C.

We then want children to be able to identify missing numbers on a variety of scales. The following examples may be helpful.

Teaching idea

Scaling up

For each of the following scales label each of the missing numbers.

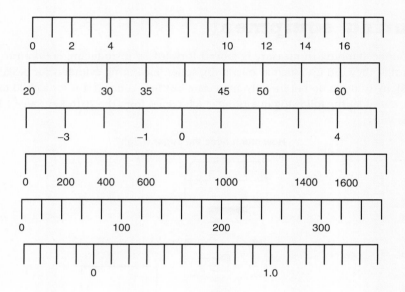

A variety of such activities will enable children to apply their number skills when reading scaled values on an assortment of measuring instruments.

This will lead us to tasks that encourage children to read out specific values from a scale without having to fill in each missing number.

Task 10.4

For each diagram, read the values that correspond to each letter.

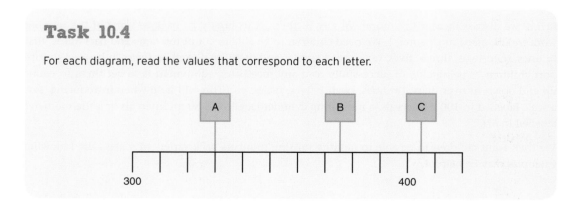

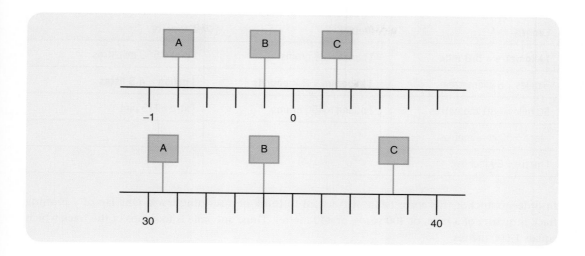

Imperial units – it's complicated

What is your height? What is your weight? If anyone asks you these questions, do you answer in imperial measure (feet/inches, stones/pounds) or in metric measure (metres/cm, kg/g)? The vast majority of our students who were brought up with metric units still answer these questions in imperial units.

The imperial system of units developed over many hundreds of years and numerous imperial units of measure were developed in isolation to each other. This probably explains their complexity, especially when converting from one unit to another.

To anyone brought up with a metric system, the imperial system can be confusing, not least in the range of different units. Nor is there any logic in the way different units are connected. The most common imperial units we use are shown in this table.

Length	Weight	Capacity
inches	ounces	fluid ounces
1 foot = 12 inches	1 pound = 16 ounces	1 pint = 20 fluid ounces
1 yard = 3 feet	1 stone = 14 pounds	1 quart = 2 pints
1 mile = 1760 yards = 8 furlongs	1 ton = 160 stone = 2,240 pounds	1 gallon = 8 pints

You can perhaps now appreciate why the metric system became so dominant.

Relationship between metric and imperial units

In Year 6, children are introduced to the relationship between metric and imperial units. However, the only thing that children need to remember is the relationship between miles and kilometres. Thus, much of the information below is for reference only. (Note: these are all approximate equivalents.)

Length	Weight	Capacity
1 kilometre = 5/8 mile	1 ounce = 28 grams	1 pint = 568 millilitres
5 miles = 8 kilometres	**1 kilogram = 2.2 pounds**	**1 gallon = 4.5 litres**
50 miles = 80 kilometres	1 pound = 450 grams	1 litre = 1.75 pint
1 foot = 30 centimetres		
1 metre = 39 inches		

In order to anchor this conversion, it is useful to think of a running track. One lap of a running track is quarter of a mile, or 400 yards, or 440 metres. Thus, one mile is four laps of the track which equals 1,600 metres.

You will have heard of athletes running a 'four-minute mile'. The four-minute mile was thought of by many as something that was just not possible and beyond human achievement. In 1954, when British athlete Roger Bannister became the first athlete to break the four-minute mile, he was running each lap in just under a minute. This is still some feat. If you wish to appreciate just how fast athletes are, try to run one lap of the track in under one minute. If you can do this, immediately do another three laps at the same pace. When athletics went metric, the corresponding distance became 1,500 metres (the metric mile), which is $3\frac{3}{4}$ laps of the track. Children in Year 6 need to be aware that one mile is further than one kilometre.

If one mile = 1,600 metres and one kilometre = 1,000 metres, then one kilometre must be 1,000/1,600 of a mile. Simplifying this, we get:

$$\frac{1000}{1600} = \frac{10}{16} = \frac{5}{8}$$

This demonstrates why, in order to convert miles to kilometres we must multiply by $\frac{5}{8}$.

It is all about the money

Before children begin to do any number work on the topic of money, they first need to appreciate the values of different coins. Like many aspects of teaching mathematics, this is not as easy as you may think. Children can think that the bigger a coin is, the more value it has. Thus, a ten pence coin may be thought of as having more value than a twenty pence coin. In Key Stage 1, children learn about the different value coins we use and how they can be combined to represent different amounts. For example, ten pence could be made with a single coin or with two five pence coins or with five two pence coins, etc. A great deal of practical work needs to be undertaken here to make such knowledge secure. Many schools make use of plastic coins to help teach this – but it is amusing that to purchase 100 two pence coins will probably cost you more than £2.

Teaching idea

The money tin

Use a tin and a number of (real) 2p, 5p, 10p, 20p coins. We will begin with the two pence coins.

Ask the children to close their eyes and listen as you drop into the tin a sequence of two pence coins. Do this slowly and make sure each coin makes a loud noise as it is dropped. After, say, four or five coins, stop and ask the children how much is in the tin. This leads to discussion equivalent to four 2p coins is 8p, or five 2p coins is 10p. Continue adding ... how much now? Maybe then take out a couple of coins and ask the same question.

This is a great classroom activity as children love activities where they have to close their eyes and listen carefully. This activity can generate much discussion. When the children are ready, repeat with one of the other sets of coins.

This activity makes direct links between number sequences and times tables. Children are learning to count forwards and backwards in multiples of two, five and ten and as such it is useful to help children with their two, five and ten times tables.

The next barrier to consider is adding up coins that sum to more than 100p and to learn that one hundred pence is equivalent to £1. In Key Stage 1, an amount such as 135p will be expressed as £1 + 35p. It is not until Year 4 that children need to know how to write this using decimal notation – i.e. £1.35.

Operations using money are best linked to practical problems. For example, addition may be introduced by looking at the total cost of two different items, subtraction perhaps by looking at change from £1 or £5, and multiplication by perhaps looking at the cost of buying two or more of the same items.

Earlier in this book, we looked at teaching children number bonds to 10 or to 20. Children also need to know number bonds to 100. This will really help them when they move to calculating change from £1.

Teaching idea

Complement pairs

On a piece of card (or paper) write down a number and then, on a separate card, write its complement to 100. For example, 67 and 33. Repeat for more pairs and keep going until you have enough cards for your whole class.

Distribute one card to each child. They each then have to work out the complement of their number (to 100) and then find the child in the class who is their 'complement'. If you have an odd number of children, you take a card to ensure an even number of cards.

(Continued)

(Continued)

In order to inject some pace, you could use a stopwatch to time the class to complete the activity. Do not forget that answers need checking, but not by you - by the children. Perhaps you could then collect the cards in again and redistribute them to try to beat the best time.

Another way to proceed once the children have found their complement is for them to write on a whiteboard four number statements using their pair of numbers, e.g.

$$67 + 33 = 100 \qquad 33 + 67 = 100 \qquad 100 - 33 = 67 \qquad 100 - 67 = 33$$

For younger children, the pairs of numbers may all be multiples of 5 or 10.

It is then easy to extend this idea so the numbers are written as money, e.g. 66p and 33p.

For Key Stage 2 this is easily extended to look at complements of £5 or £10.

Where's my change?

At this point, you should appreciate the links here to Chapter 3, where we discussed that subtraction could be considered as either a 'take away' or a difference. Suppose you make a purchase for £7.30 and pay with a £10 note.

To work out your change you could, if you wish, do the subtraction 10 − 7.30. However, a more likely way to work out your change would be to add on to the £7.30 the amount needed to make it up to £10. For example, the shopkeeper may say, … *and 20p makes £7.50, 50p makes £8, and £2 makes £10.* Thus, the subtraction has become an addition. This is sometimes known as the **shopkeeper's method**.

When introducing money calculations to children, it is useful to go back to the empty number line to support them. The above calculation may look like:

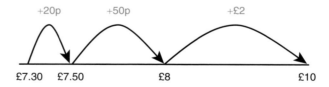

Total change = 20p + 50p + £2 = £2.70

Mastery Task

What different amounts can be made from three coins?

Children are allowed to use any coins - they can use three different coins, two the same and one different or three coins which are the same.

This activity develops a range of mathematical skills including trial and error, sequencing, and problem-solving, and also requires a deep understanding of money. However, it is also a very challenging task as there are so many different amounts that can be made. Rather than rely on the very open question above, you may prefer to scaffold it using questions such as:

- How can I use three coins to make 35 pence?
- What is the smallest/largest amount of money we can make with three coins?
- How many ways can I make 12 pence using three coins?
- Can you think of another amount of money that can be made with three coins in two different ways?
- Can you make 11 pence using three coins?
- What other amounts CANNOT be made with three coins?

Time after time

We have mentioned several times that teaching some mathematical topics is much more difficult than one may think. This also applies to the topic of **time**. Those inexperienced in teaching time often assume that this is a straightforward topic … it isn't! Many children have an awareness of time in the sense that they know there is a 'meal time', or a 'bed time' or a 'school time' – but that does not mean they have an understanding of a clock or the mathematical features of the way we measure time. Additionally, it is surprising how many children do not have daily experiences with an analogue clock. Most primary children do not wear a watch – in fact many students do not wear a watch, instead relying upon their mobile phone. This can be a problem for them when they start teaching, as timings within lessons are so important. In terms of teaching the topic of time, it is important for you to look at the objectives for each year to consider and appreciate progression.

In terms of teaching how to tell time, children are moved sequentially, from whole hour, to the half hour, to the quarter hour. This is all covered in a relatively short period, as by the end of Year 2, children should be able to tell and read time to the nearest five minutes. In Year 3, children are extended in their understanding of time when they look at a.m./p.m., 24-hour clock, analogue and digital clocks, as well as analogue clocks with Roman numerals.

Teaching idea

Sequencing time

Starting at a specific time, children either collectively or individually count forwards (and backwards) in multiples of 15 minutes.

Suppose we start at 1:00. Children would be able to say 1:15, 1:30, 1:45, 2:00, 2:15, etc.

(Continued)

(Continued)

The idea can easily be extended by:

* counting in 10-minute or 5-minute intervals

* counting in 15-minute intervals but starting at, say, 1:25

* counting in 24-hour clock.

It is useful to consider the link between decimals, fractions and time. The most obvious conceptual error that children make here is to either read the minutes as a decimal number, or read a decimal element as minutes. For example, 2 hours 30 minutes may be considered by children the same as 2.30 hours, or perhaps 1.25 hours is considered equal to 1 hour 25 minutes. This is why we have the convention of using the symbol (:) as a separator of hours and minutes. Thus, we should write 2:30 or 1:25. You will appreciate that 2 hours 30 minutes is equal to $2\frac{1}{2}$ hours (2.5 hours) and 1 hour 15 minutes is equal to $1\frac{1}{4}$ hours (1.25 hours).

Half and quarter hours are really the only practical parts of time that can be shown as decimal. In general, decimal notation of time must be discouraged.

In terms of fractions, however, much learning can be undertaken or extended by appreciating the many links to time. Many children consider that 'half past the hour' comes from the fact that the minute hand of a clock is halfway round on its journey from 12 back to 12. Similarly, at 'quarter past' the hand is at a quarter of its journey, Of course this is true, but it is also worth getting children to think of the journey of the minute hand as a fraction of 60 minutes.

There are 60 minutes in an hour and thus at 'half past' we are 'half of 60 minutes' past the hour. The time 'a quarter past/to' relates to 15 minutes past/to, as 15 is a quarter of 60. Let us extend this idea to other parts of the hour. Twenty minutes past could become $\frac{1}{3}$ 'past'. With higher ability children, you could ask them to convert times given in fractions. For example, ' $\frac{1}{3}$ to five' is the same as 4:40 or $\frac{1}{12}$ past one is the same as 1:05.

An important feature of analogue clocks should be pointed out here: at the time 'half past three', the clock's hour hand should be exactly halfway between the numbers 3 and 4. Similarly, at 5:45, the hour hand should be three-quarters of the way between 5 and 6. If your children are using cardboard clocks to help learn to tell the time, it is important that you, as the teacher, ensure that the hour hand is correctly positioned.

Teaching time, however, is not just about children being able to 'tell' the time from a clock; children need to understand the sequential nature of time. The majority of work on time is undertaken in Key Stage 1 and the topic is more or less complete by the end of Year 4. Children have to appreciate concepts such as quicker/slower and have to understand the language of time, such as first/second/third, or today/yesterday/tomorrow. They have to be able to correctly use and apply the appropriate vocabulary to describe sequences of events.

At the same time, children (in Key Stage 1) have to learn the names of the days of the week and months of the year, as well as knowing the number of minutes in an hour and the number of hours in a day. In Year 3, children are taught that there are 60 seconds in a minute and the number of days in each month, year and leap year. Conceptually, this is complicated – primarily because we are no longer working in base 10. As children move to undertaking calculations in time, one of the most common mistakes you will see relates to them using base 10 methods for addition. So, for example, 1 hour 45 minutes plus 20 minutes could be written as 1.65. Sometimes, you will see older children incorrectly applying the addition algorithm. For example, 2 hours 50 minutes plus 1 hour 50 minutes may be calculated:

$$
\begin{array}{r}
2.50 \\
+ \,_1 1.50 \\
\hline
4.00 \\
\end{array}
$$

Just as with adding or subtracting money, a deep understanding of the empty number line can be invaluable in reducing such errors. For example, in the calculation above it is useful to be able to split the 1 hour 50 minutes into 1 hour plus 10 minutes plus 40 minutes:

Task 10.5

Two boys, Howard and Peter, want to swim half a mile in a 25-metre pool.

Howard thinks he can swim this distance in 15 minutes. Peter says he can swim each length one second faster than Howard.

1. If Howard does take 15 minutes to complete the swim, how long will Peter take?

2. If Howard can swim at the same pace throughout, how fast does he swim each length?

Rounding up

In this chapter, we have considered approaches to teaching a range of topics related to measure. We hope that, by now, you have begun to appreciate the difficulties these topics can cause children and will be very thoughtful when planning lessons in measure. As in many places in this book, we again underline that much of the Primary Curriculum stands upon a foundation of number. A deep and comprehensive understanding of number and place value aids acquisition of other topics. If a child is weak in their understanding of number, they are likely to trip up very quickly when learning other areas of mathematics.

WHAT MATHS CAN **YOU** SEE?

MADE TO MEASURE

STATISTICALLY SPEAKING

- Data type
- Collecting data
- Displaying data
- Charting the right course
- Turning the tables
- Venn diagrams
- The life of pie
- Top table
- Don't be mean
- Rounding up
- What maths can you see?

Statistically speaking

This chapter looks at a variety of aspects of data handling and how to teach it. It is often the case that some children with weaker skills in number are still able to make progress in data handling. Data handling is a real opportunity for a teacher to personalise learning by linking the data to children's specific interests. However, the many links between number skills and data handling are sometimes not explored in schools as much as they might be. The principal focus for the topic of statistics in primary mathematics is collecting data, displaying this data and making some simple interpretations about what the information is telling us. There is little statistical analysis required.

Our lives are full of information – this information, or 'data', leads to decisions being made by individuals, companies, governments and even OFSTED. By collecting, displaying and analysing data, we make sense of the world around us. The handling of data is an essential life skill.

Data type

We begin by defining different types of data. When we think of data, especially in primary schools, we are often thinking about numerical data. For example, *How many of you prefer cheese 'n' onion crisps? How many brothers/sisters do you have? What is the temperature at different times of the day?* Are these all similar types of data?

To explore this further, please think carefully about the following question.

How old are you?

Most students to whom we pose this question actually hesitate. They think it is a trick question. (It sort of is!) Suppose there are two students, Tom and Jo. Tom was 19 three months ago; Jo was 19 seven months ago. Both Tom and Jo answer the question, quite correctly in their opinion, *I am 19.* We now pose the question to you, *Are both students correct?* A further question to pose at this point is, *What would you say **your** age is?*

You know that numbers in between integer values are rounded down if they are less than halfway, and round up if they are halfway or more. Do you think therefore that Jo is mathematically correct in saying her age is 19? She is nearer to 20 than 19 so her answer to the question should be 20. When considering our age, we often answer by giving the completed number of years. This is what mathematicians call the ***integral value*** – that is, the whole number ignoring any fraction. We didn't ask the question, *In terms of only completed years, how old are you?* However, we can live with others interpreting the question, *How old are you?* in this way.

This is a peculiar quirk of our number system when applied to age ... most adults round down. Many young children like to be much more accurate about their age. Children with birthdays coming up may say something akin to, *I am nearly seven* or *In one week I will be nine.* In 1982, Sue Townsend published *The Secret Diary of Adrian Mole aged 13¾.* You will find, however, that as you get older you round down more and more. Many people will round down to the nearest ten.

So, now let us return to the question, *How old are you?* How accurate is your answer? We could equally ask for your age to the nearest month, the nearest day, hour, etc. It is practically impossible to state EXACTLY how old you are; rather we give our age to a specific accuracy.

Identifying a level of accuracy applies to many elements of measure. The mass of an object could be measured to the nearest kg, g, mg, etc. The length of an object could be measured to the nearest km, m, cm, mm, etc. In short, anything that is *measured* such as time, mass, length or height can only be done so to a given ***tolerance***. Data that is 'measured' is known as ***continuous data***.

Now consider the question, *How many brothers and sisters do you have?* Here the answer must be an integer – that is, a whole number. You can count exactly the number of siblings a child has. Data that is 'counted' is known as ***discrete data***.

Although the detailed study of these classifications is beyond primary mathematics, having this knowledge will aid you as a teacher in choosing appropriate ways to display data.

Collecting data

A natural starting place for studying statistics is collecting simple data; however, children first need experience of sorting and classifying by characteristics. For example, can they sort toy cars by colour? Or could they sort shapes into those with four sides, those with more than four sides? Having put objects into categories, can they count how many objects are in each category?

Initially, children will be working with small numbers so it is easy to do this, but as numbers increase children should be introduced to the 'tally'. We have seen a number of students misinterpret the purpose of the 'tally' or 'tally charts'. Tally charts are a way to simplify the counting of a large number of objects. Tallying provides a way of keeping a simultaneous count of several categories. You are probably aware of the 'five-bar gate' where we use single lines to represent numbers 1 to 4 and strike a line through these to signify a 5. This may give us something that looks like this:

Favourite author	Tally	Frequency
J.K. Rowling	LH1 LH1	10
Roald Dahl	LH1 I	6
David Walliams	LH1 LH1 III	13
Jacqueline Wilson	IIII	4

The tally should come first. The purpose of the method here is for children to be able to ask someone who their favourite author is and record the response with a single tally, then ask the next person. When the survey is complete, the tallies are then used to calculate the frequencies for each category. Please ensure that you do not teach children that the frequencies for each category come first and from those we complete the tallies.

Displaying data

A very simple way for children to display data is using a pictogram. We begin with 'one-to-one' representation, where each picture represents a count of one, before moving on to using a single picture to represent more than one. For example:

How many sweets of each colour in a pack?		Frequency
Red	● ● ● ● ◖	19
Green	● ● ●	12
Orange	● ◖	6
Yellow	● ● ◖	10
Black	● ● ●	12

Key ● = 4 sweets

There are several things that you need to bear in mind when teaching children this topic. First, as illustrated above, when moving beyond a one-to-one representation you need to think about how you want the children to show numbers less than the value of your picture. In the example above, the scale is one picture to four sweets, so two sweets is half the picture and three sweets would be three-quarters of the picture. This can be very difficult for children to interpret.

Another consideration is what 'picture' you should use. We have observed lessons where children were required to draw dogs, cats and other animals to represent a number of pets. When teachers ask children to make up their own pictures it can lead to children spending a whole lesson drawing a single picture. Try to ensure that children use a very simple representation. An alternative approach is for you to prepare the picture yourself and then the children stick them into their table. Again, you need to think about the best use of time. Lessons such as this can be highly motivating for children, but you must remember these are mathematics lessons. The activity you choose, in any mathematics lesson, must ultimately be designed to ensure children are moving forward in their learning of mathematics.

Another error that is sometimes witnessed during lessons on pictograms is changing the size of the picture. For example, imagine a child is using this symbol to represent a house:

To represent two houses a child may draw the same shape twice as big:

This links with Chapter 10, where we discussed that similar shapes with sides in the ratio a:b have areas in the ratio $a^2:b^2$.

The error here is that the larger shape, although similar to the original, has been enlarged in both dimensions by a factor of 2, so it is actually four times the size of the original.

The media often makes this error, perhaps on purpose, as it exaggerates increases or decreases that have occurred.

Charting the right course

Consider these two charts:

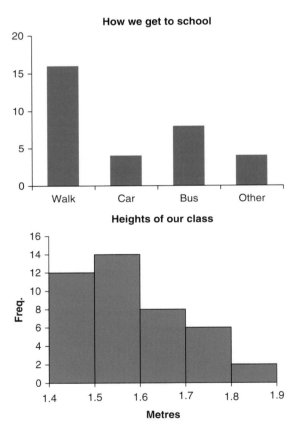

These, as we are sure you are aware, are examples of a **bar chart** and a **histogram**. Although histograms are not included in the Primary Curriculum, you need to be aware of them. It is often the case that the wrong type of chart is produced for a given data set.

The bar chart is describing categorical data. Here, the order of the bars is not important: this is discrete data. A bar chart is one way to display discrete data. You need to ensure that there is a clear space between each bar (approximately half a bar width). Histograms must only be used for continuous data, and children's heights are an example of continuous data. However, as histograms are not in the Primary Curriculum you should not be using them at all. The only type of chart you should be using to show continuous data is a line graph such as this:

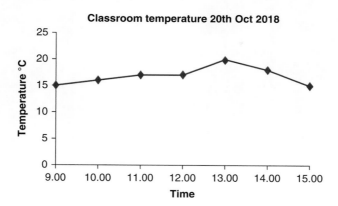

You may refer to this as a **time graph** and children should be able to produce and interpret such graphs by the end of Year 4.

Sometimes, you may see a graph such as this:

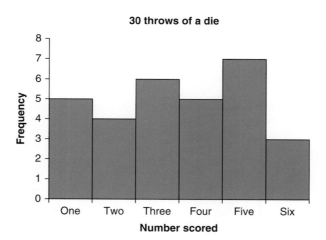

This looks like a histogram, yet the data is discrete. Therefore, this is technically an incorrect representation of the data. However, you will see such diagrams used in primary school. These are termed **block diagrams** – although to be a little pedantic, such data should really be shown as a bar chart.

This photograph below shows a student using children to form a 'live' bar chart. In the classroom, children were asked to select a picture of their favourite animal. Some chose a lion, others an elephant, etc.

In the hall, the student had set out a giant graph with the labels for each animal along the x axis and the frequencies along the y axis. Children sat in the appropriate section. From there, the student was able to ask a series of questions that really ensured the children understood the topic. As the children were actually part of the graph, there was a real sense of enjoyment, enthusiasm and high-quality learning.

Turning the tables

It is important that children can also understand data represented in tables. Although the National Curriculum does not specify exactly what this means, the following examples may be useful in giving you some ideas to use in your own teaching.

Simple table

The tally charts and pictograms mentioned above lead to simple tables. A simple table will record the frequency of a number of related categories.

Year 5 favourite pizza topping	Frequency
Plain	16
Ham & pineapple	3
Mushroom	5
Chicken	1
Other	2

Extended table

Such tables provide more than a single numerical value for each category.

Favourite pizza topping	Year 5	Year 6
Plain	16	18
Ham & pineapple	3	5
Mushroom	3	2
Chicken	1	2
Other	2	3

Carroll diagram

The extended table leads to consideration of data that is subdivided in different ways using a **Carroll diagram**. These are actually named after Lewis Carroll who, as well as writing books such as *Alice in Wonderland*, was also a very famous mathematician.

A Carroll diagram contains a wealth of information. In this example, we can see how many boys do not have pets, how many girls do have pets, how many girls are in the class, etc.

	Boys	Girls	Total
Have pets	4	8	12
Do not have pets	6	12	18
Total	**10**	**20**	**30**

A Carroll diagram does not need to just have numbers in it. This example allows children to sort themselves out according to whether they have different skills.

	Can ride a bike	Cannot ride a bike
Can swim	Vince Jim	Ron Barbara
Cannot swim	Clare Laurence Carolyn	Mary Sue

Or a Carroll diagram could be used to ask children to sort/classify themselves by other measures.

		Birthday		
		Sept - Dec	Jan - April	May - Aug
Shoe size	10	Mark	Jeanette	
	11			David Steve
	12	John		Katie
	13	Anthony	Steve	Marie

A Carroll diagram could also be used to allow children to develop their understanding of the properties of shape. For this example, the children were asked to decide which shape is in the wrong place.

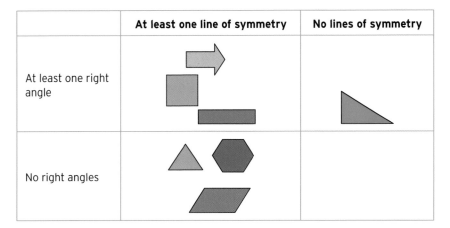

	At least one line of symmetry	No lines of symmetry
At least one right angle		
No right angles		

Venn diagrams

A ***Venn diagram*** also helps to divide sets of information into characteristics or classifications. For example, consider all of the integers from 1 to 10. We could classify these as being factors of 6, or factors of 8. Some numbers would satisfy both criteria and some numbers would satisfy neither.

This would lead to the following Venn diagram.

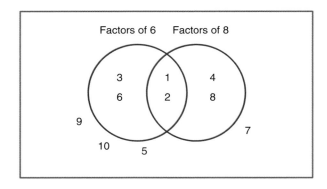

The overlap of the two circles represents the numbers that satisfy both criteria – in this case, 1 and 2 are both factors of 6 and 8.

This overlap between the circles is known as the ***intersection*** of the sets. We also have numbers that are factors of 6 but not 8 (3 and 6) and those that are factors of 8 but not 6 (4 and 8). The numbers outside the circle satisfy neither criteria.

As with Carroll diagrams, Venn diagrams can be used to look at non-numerical data. For example, in PSHE we may want children to think about what they have in common with each other and what their differences are. Venn diagrams are an excellent way to do this, as illustrated by Libby and Naomi, two children in Year 6.

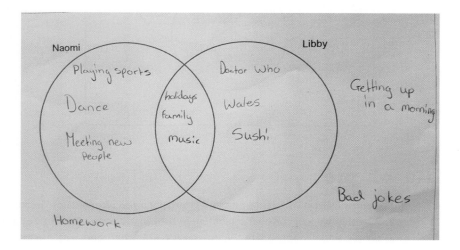

We can extend a Venn diagram to consider three different attributes of a data set. For example, suppose we wish to sort the numbers 1 to 10 using the categories, square numbers, even numbers and factors of 30.

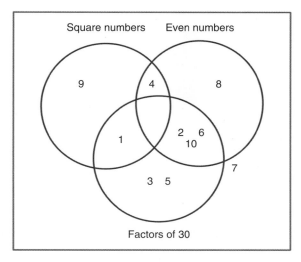

Task 11.1

Complete the Venn diagram using the numbers 1 to 20.

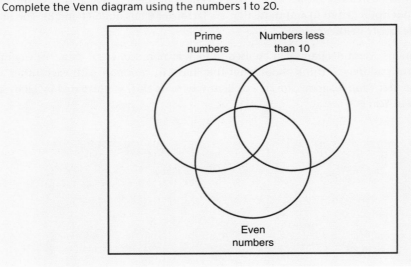

The life of pie

During Year 6, children must learn how to interpret and construct a **_pie chart_**. These incidentally are two very different skills, which we will consider separately. Whilst many people know what a pie chart is or looks like, fewer people actually appreciate the purpose of a pie chart and why it should be used instead of, say, a bar chart.

Consider the bar chart data we looked at earlier in this chapter. Let us use this data to produce a simple pie chart.

Reflection

What key differences can you see between this pie chart and the earlier bar chart?

In both charts, it is easy to identify that the category 'walk' is the largest and the category 'bus' is next largest. In the bar chart, we can use the scale along the y axis to determine the number, or frequency, for each category. We cannot tell from the pie chart how many children walk to school. However, what we can tell from the pie chart is that half of the children walk to school and approximately a quarter get the bus. In the bar chart, this fact is not obvious. (Of course, we could use the bar chart to derive this fact, but it would entail completing a number of calculations.)

Remember, the principal reason for displaying information in a chart is to allow the reader to gain an immediate sense of the information. A pie chart allows us to have an immediate sense of the **proportion** of the total for each category. Thus, children should understand that the angle of each sector represents that category as a proportion of the total of all categories.

Another way to develop understanding of pie charts is to provide additional information. For example, supposing we told you that the pie chart above represents a survey of 32 children. We can work out that 16 children must have walked to school (half of 32), but what about the other categories? For example, if the angle that represents the category 'getting the bus' was 90°, then the proportion of children catching the bus is:

$$\frac{90}{360} = \frac{1}{4}$$

Thus, the number of children getting the bus is a quarter of 32 (= 8). This work is extended in Key Stage 3 to include sectors of any angle.

If children in Year 6 are constructing a pie chart, it is essential that they are appreciative of the fact that there are 360° in a whole turn (see Chapter 8). In general, at Key Stage 2 we would expect children only to be working with simple fractions of a whole. Thus, the proportion for each sector will be in halves, quarters or thirds.

It is very easy to make errors constructing pie charts. In 2016, one regional newspaper asked its readers whether they would pay more for a pint of milk if the extra money all went to the farmers who produced the milk. The way the paper displayed the results is replicated below.

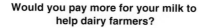

Would you pay more for your milk to help dairy farmers?

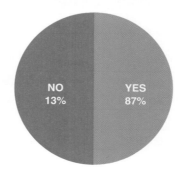

NO
13%

YES
87%

This is a picture of some Camembert cheese.

We think it is rather fitting that the French for pie chart is 'camembert'!

Top table

Take a good look around you and you will see many different uses made of tables. For example, prices for flights, train and bus timetables, online retail, hotel prices, etc. Depending upon the ability of the children in your class, you could use real data and real timetables. However, sometimes it is worth presenting children with a slightly simplified version of the real thing.

Hotel Grande		
Arrival 22nd July for 1 night 2 guests		
Room	**Includes**	**Cost**
Standard Queen	Room only	£98.20
Standard Queen	Breakfast	£115.00
Deluxe Queen	Breakfast Garden view	£130.00
Deluxe King	Breakfast Sea view	£145.00

Liverpool to Paris Charles de Gaulle					
Depart			**Return**		
Thu 10 Aug	Fri 11 Aug	Sat 12 Aug	Thu 17 Aug	Fri 18 Aug	Sat 19 Aug
Dep 15:10 Arr 17:40	Dep 15:10 Arr 17:40	Dep 12:30 Arr 14:40	Dep 18:45 Arr 19:20	Dep 18:45 Arr 19:20	Dep 15:45 Arr 16:20
Lowest Fare			Lowest Fare		
£45.99	£67.99	£53.99	£37.99	£53.99	£73.99

Train Times: Southport - Liverpool

Southport	1258	1313	1328	1343	1358
Birkdale	1302	1317	1332	1347	1402
Formby	1313	1328	1343	1358	1413
Hall Road	1320	1335	1350	1405	1420
Bootle	1330	1345	1400	1415	1430
Moorfields	1340	1355	1410	1425	1440
Liverpool Central	1344	1359	1414	1429	1444
Aigburth	1352	1407	1422	1437	1452

Using such a variety of sources allows you to bring in other aspects of mathematics such as money, time and dates, as well as allowing you to probe children's ability to undertake calculations in all of these measures.

The deep understanding that we would like children to gain in relation to data will not come from them simply being able to produce graphs, charts and tables – it comes from their ability to read, understand and interpret all types of sources. Children need to be able to extract the key informa-tion each chart or table contains. There are a wealth of questions that you could use to develop such understanding and teacher questions will begin with phrases such as, *How many ... , How much bigger ... , What fraction ... , What does this tell you?* etc. Thus, there is a great deal of oral work that can be undertaken here to cement such understanding. However, planning such questions is essen-tial in order to ensure their effectiveness.

Don't be mean

The only formal statistical analysis that is taught in primary school relates to calculation of the **mean**. 'The mean' is a measure of average.

There are three different measures of average: the mean itself (the value when all of the numbers are summed up and divided by the quantity of numbers); the mode (the most common number); and the median (the central value after numbers are arranged in ascending/descending order).

You may recall these three measures of average from your own schooling. Up until the Primary Curriculum changed in 2014, children were expected to know and use all three measure of average. However, we are now only concerned with the mean. In our opinion this is a pity, as calculating a mean is a rather uninteresting task. If we have ten numbers, we add them up and divide by 10; if we have eight numbers we divide by 8. It can become quite a 'closed' task. Studying all three measures of average allows us to consider why there are three different measures and can lead to discussion about which measure is the most appropriate.

Task 11.2

Missing data

Twenty-three children take a mathematics examination. The teacher marks all the papers and calculates that the mean mark for the class is 72%.

Two children, Matt and Tierney, were absent for the examination which they sit when they return to school. Matt scores 54% and Tierney gets 84%.

What is the new mean mark for the whole class including Matt and Tierney?

Kenneth Baker, when he was Secretary of State for Education, famously stated that he wanted all children to be above average. Similar quotes have since been attributed to a number of other politicians. Statisticians are always very amused when such comments are made, as it evidences a clear misunderstanding of what a 'mean' actually is.

An average can never be used as a target, because as data changes the average moves at the same time. To help explain this, imagine you have a number of sunflowers. You measure each one and calculate the mean height. Some of the sunflowers will be above that height and some will be below. Now let us assume that every flower grows by exactly 8 cm and you now calculate the new mean. This value will be exactly 8 cm above the original mean because each flower grew by the same amount. However, the number of flowers either above or below that mean value will be exactly the same as before. For any statistic, the mean value can increase, but half the values will still be above that mean and half will be below. **It is simply not possible to have everything above average.**

If a parent ever comes up to you and says, *My child is below average*, your informed reply should be, *So is half the population*. In any attribute, whether it is height or mathematics marks, an individual person is either above average or below average. However, the wonderful thing about children is that for everything they are 'below average' at, there is something they will be 'above average' at. Your job as a teacher is to help find those things in each member of your class.

Rounding up

The National Curriculum uses the term 'statistics' as the collective name for all elements covered in this chapter. However, we feel that perhaps that word limits our appreciation of everything that needs to be covered in this section of the curriculum.

In this chapter, we have shown you that statistics is not just about drawing graphs. Understanding data in all of its forms requires the ability to collect information, to display information, to interpret information and to summarise information. The ability to handle data is an essential life skill.

You can choose examples of data and statistics that link to children's individual interests and, thus, they will be able to appreciate the relevance of what you are teaching much more easily than some other topics, where application can occasionally become contrived.

Most important of all, deep understanding of statistics comes from not simply 'doing', but by rich conversation and discussion arising from the data, chart or table being considered – although by now, we hope that you appreciate this is true in every topic.

WHAT MATHS CAN YOU SEE?

Favourites

Participant Details ⊗

Simon Neave Rogers

Masses

Gender: **M** | BIB: **26635** | Nationality: **GBR**

Last Crossed: **40K**

Splits	Time (hh:mm:ss)	Time of Day (hh:mm:ss)	Pace (min/km)
Start	00:00	10:00:12	NA
5K	20:18	10:20:29	4.06
10K	41:11	10:41:22	4.12
15K	01:02:32	11:02:43	4.17
20K	01:24:05	11:24:16	4.20
Half	01:28:49	11:29:00	4.21
25K	01:45:34	11:45:45	4.22
30K	02:07:13	12:07:24	4.24
35K	02:29:42	12:29:53	4.28
40K	02:52:38	12:52:49	4.32
Finish	03:02:06	13:02:17	4.32

Powered by **TATA** CONSULTANCY SERVICES

STATISTICALLY SPEAKING

MOVING ON

- **Multiplication of two decimal numbers**
- **Division by decimal numbers**
- **Dividing a fraction by a fraction**
- **Why does the rule for division of fractions always work?**
- **Feeling negative?**
- **Segatnecrep sdrawkcab**
- **Further grid method**
- **The power of negatives**
- **Setting the standard**
- **Deriving the nth term**
- **Other sequences**
- **Pascal's Triangle**
- **Pythagoras' Theorem**
- **Rounding up**
- **What maths can you see?**

Moving on

In this final chapter, we want you to begin thinking about the transition into Key Stage 3. The Primary Curriculum is clear in not wanting children to be moved on to this next level while they are still in primary school. Rather, primary aged children need to demonstrate a deep understanding of the Key Stage 2 curriculum to become 'secondary ready'.

This chapter takes some of the topics we have covered in our book and shows you how they are built upon during Key Stage 3. This chapter is not intended to cover the entire Key Stage 3 mathematics syllabus, but rather to point you towards some key topics where the Key Stage 2 curriculum is developed.

Unlike the primary mathematics curriculum, content in Key Stage 3 is not organised by year or age group.

> (In Key Stage 3) ... pupils should build on Key Stage 2 and connections across mathematical ideas to develop fluency, mathematical reasoning and competence in solving increasingly sophisticated problems. ... Decisions about progression should be based on the security of pupils' understanding and their readiness to progress to the next stage.

Mathematics Programmes of Study: Key Stage 3 National Curriculum in England

It is useful for you to look at the Key Stage 3 Programme of Study to see how it builds upon the work children have covered in Key Stages 1 and 2. However, to get you thinking about Key Stage 3 we begin with a problem.

The size of any TV monitor is the diagonal distance from one corner of the screen to another. This diagram represents a 55-inch rectangular TV monitor of width 48 inches. Calculate the height of the screen. (You may use a calculator to work this out.)

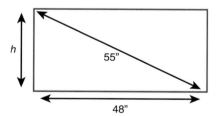

As you will no doubt be aware, this problem can be solved using Pythagoras' Theorem – it is a real-life application of mathematics. It is also worth recognising that even in the twenty-first century, we still use inches to measure televisions, so this is also an everyday use of imperial units of measure. (Mind you, if we did use centimetres, this would be a 140 cm TV screen, which sounds a great deal bigger!)

Reflection

After answering this question, list every mathematical skill that a child needs to have and every concept they need to understand, in order to successfully complete the task.

Look very closely at the list of mathematical skills you have produced. Before you go any further, have a think about where in a child's mathematical education you think each of these skills are first introduced to children.

Let us now look at how a child in Year 8 or Year 9 is expected to calculate the answer to this question. A model answer may look something like this:

$$a^2 + b^2 = c^2$$
$$48^2 + h^2 = 55^2$$
$$2{,}304 + h^2 = 3{,}025$$
$$h^2 = 3{,}025 - 2{,}304$$
$$h^2 = 721$$
$$h = \sqrt{721}$$
$$h = 26.85 \text{ inches}$$

We list now, in no particular order, some of the skills that you will have needed to employ in finding the above solution. Compare these with the list you made.

- Addition, subtraction and multiplication.
- Interpreting a word problem.
- Recognising a right-angled triangle.
- Substituting into simple formula.
- Inverse operations.
- Units of measure.
- Squaring numbers.
- Finding square roots of numbers.
- Using a simple mathematical diagram to represent a mathematical problem.
- Rounding of numbers.

Apart from the actual Pythagoras Theorem itself, every other element and skill is something that a child would first encounter in their primary school. As a primary teacher, you are an important element in the mathematical development of all children entering secondary school. If children are taught effectively in Key Stage 2, the progression into Key Stage 3 is much more comfortable for them. This is what we mean by 'secondary ready'.

We feel it is important for you as a primary school teacher to know about some of the work children will cover in secondary school, so you will have a better appreciation of what the term 'secondary ready' really means and how you can contribute to children reaching this milestone.

Multiplication of two decimal numbers

Consider a calculation such as 0.2×0.3. Many children, and some students, knowing that the product of 2 and 3 is 6, and knowing that there must be a decimal point in there somewhere, will write the answer as 0.6. However, being the type of student you are, you will know that the correct answer is 0.06. So why is this the correct answer?

One way of looking at this is to say that we know 0.2 (or $\frac{1}{5}$) is smaller than 1, so our product must get smaller; we are in effect finding $\frac{1}{5}$ of 0.3 (or finding $\frac{3}{10}$ of 0.2). Therefore, 0.6 cannot be the answer as that is bigger than either number. However, an easy way to explain what is happening here is to do the same calculation with fractions:

$$0.2 \times 0.3 = \frac{2}{10} \times \frac{3}{10} = \frac{6}{100} = 0.06$$

Similarly:
$$0.25 \times 0.03 = \frac{25}{100} \times \frac{3}{100} = \frac{75}{10000} = 0.0075$$

You can see that for every decimal place in the two numbers being multiplied together, there is an equivalent number of decimal places in the answer. This is why some teachers give children the rule, *ignore the decimal point, count the number of decimal places, do a long multiplication and then stick the point in*. We think teaching by just giving such a rule is insufficient to develop deep understanding in children.

Division by decimal numbers

Consider $24 \div 1.2$. In the same way that you now know you can write $3 \div 4$ as $\frac{3}{4}$, we would like you to consider this as a fraction.

$$24 \div 1.2 = \frac{24}{1.2}$$

This is an 'awkward' fraction as it has decimals in it. However, you are now skilled in 'cancelling down' and 'cancelling up'. In this case, let us 'cancel up' by multiplying both numerator and denominator by 10.

$$\frac{24}{1.2} = \frac{240}{12} = 20$$

Note that once we have converted the fraction so that it has a non-decimal denominator, the division (which was a Key Stage 3 level question) becomes a Key Stage 2 level question.

Another example is 2.6 ÷ 0.5. Expressing this as a fraction and multiplying by $\frac{10}{10}$ gives:

$$\frac{2.6}{0.5} = \frac{26}{5}$$

For this, we can now use the Key Stage 2 method described in Chapter 6 when we changed fractions to decimals.

$$5\overline{)26.^10}\,\,^{5.2}$$

Again, we have changed a Key Stage 3 level question into a Key Stage 2 task.

Multiplying by $\frac{10}{10}$ will work for any decimal divisor that has a single decimal place. If the divisor has two decimal places, multiply numerator and denominator by 100. For example, 7.5 ÷ 0.25:

$$7.5 \div 0.25 = \frac{7.5}{0.25}$$

$$= \frac{7.5}{0.25} \times \frac{100}{100}$$

$$= \frac{750}{25}$$

Note: to simplify $\frac{750}{25}$ we would suggest you cancel down rather than jump to a long division algorithm.

$$= \frac{750}{25} = \frac{150}{5} = \frac{30}{1} = 30$$

At this point, children sometimes feel the need to reintroduce the decimal point by dividing by 10 or 100. **This is incorrect**. We know that $\frac{3}{3}$ or $\frac{4}{4}$ or $\frac{13}{13}$ or $\frac{10}{10}$ are all equal to 1. So when we multiply a fraction by $\frac{10}{10}$ or $\frac{100}{100}$ we are actually only multiplying by 1, and when we multiply any number by 1, it stays the same.

Dividing a fraction by a fraction

Consider $\frac{1}{2} \div \frac{1}{8}$. It can be quite difficult to think about this calculation in terms of apples or pieces of cake. However, first think of half a whole.

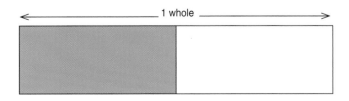

Now think of $\frac{1}{8}$ of the same whole.

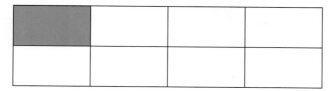

The question can be thought of as, *How many of the red pieces will fit into the purple piece?*

Our answer is four parts will fit, thus $\frac{1}{2} \div \frac{1}{8} = 4$.

Another way to consider the same question is to use a fraction wall.

1 whole							
$\frac{1}{2}$				$\frac{1}{2}$			
$\frac{1}{8}$	$\frac{1}{8}$	$\frac{1}{8}$	$\frac{1}{8}$	$\frac{1}{8}$	$\frac{1}{8}$	$\frac{1}{8}$	$\frac{1}{8}$

Thus, there are **four** eighths in a half.

Can you see how this links to multiplying by the reciprocal of the divisor?

$$\frac{1}{2} \div \frac{1}{8} = \frac{1}{2} \times \frac{8}{1}$$
$$= \frac{8}{2}$$
$$= 4$$

We know that this is a point where many children can stumble. Another way of inspiring confidence in their own answers is to link back to our inverse laws for multiplication and division.

If we are not sure that $36 \div 9 = 4$, we can check by multiplying 4 by 9 to see if we get 36. Similarly, if we are not sure that $\frac{1}{2} \div \frac{1}{8} = 4$, we can check by multiplying 4 by $\frac{1}{8}$, which pleasingly gives us $\frac{4}{8}$ or $\frac{1}{2}$.

Why does the rule for division of fractions always work?

The method you are likely to be familiar with for division of fractions comes from the fact that any fraction multiplied by its inverse gives us 1.

For example:
$$\frac{2}{3} \times \frac{3}{2} = \frac{6}{6} = 1$$

$$\frac{3}{5} \times \frac{5}{3} = \frac{15}{15} = 1$$

$$\frac{9}{10} \times \frac{10}{9} = \frac{90}{90} = 1$$

As you now know, any division can be represented as a fraction, for example $3 \div 7$ can be written as $\frac{3}{7}$.

Let us consider $\frac{2}{3} \div \frac{5}{6}$. We will write this as a fraction, to give us:

$$\frac{\frac{2}{3}}{\frac{5}{6}}$$

Now we will multiply the numerator and the denominator by the reciprocal of the divisor $\left(\frac{6}{5}\right)$.

Remember $\frac{\frac{6}{5}}{\frac{6}{5}} = 1$. This looks much more complicated than it really is.

$$\frac{\frac{2}{3}}{\frac{5}{6}} = \frac{\frac{2}{3} \times \frac{6}{5}}{\frac{5}{6} \times \frac{6}{5}} = \frac{\frac{12}{15}}{\frac{30}{30}} = \frac{\frac{12}{15}}{1} = \frac{12}{15} = \frac{4}{5}$$

By multiplying both parts of the fraction by the reciprocal of the divisor, the new denominator will always be 1. It is relatively easy to explain why it works, but in our experience most teachers of mathematics don't!

Mastery Task

Use the idea above to see if you can prove the general law for division of algebra by looking at:

$$\frac{a}{b} \div \frac{c}{d}$$

Feeling negative?

Perhaps one property of number that many remember from their school days is the rule 'two minuses make a plus' (*sic*). This is a poor shorthand for what is really happening and if it is taught using these words, it can lead to considerable confusion. Even if children remember that rule, their ability to apply it is decidedly mixed and the understanding of why this rule works appears to be a huge secret ... nobody knows! What the phrase is really about is subtracting negative numbers.

We would like to begin to explain this property of number by thinking about grammar. You may have heard that a sentence can contain a ***double negative***. Some examples are:

- *I never did nothing.*

- *I never said nothing.*

- *I never saw no one.*

Each sentence is intended to state a negative, but the second negative word within it cancels the intended meaning. If somebody never did 'nothing' then they must have done 'something'. Some students find this quite a difficult concept to appreciate. In order to be grammatically correct the sentences should be:

- *I never did anything* or *I did nothing*

- *I never said anything* or *I said nothing*

- *I never saw anyone* or *I saw no one*

We have heard a child use the phrase, *I never said nothing to no one*. This of course contains three negatives, so it actually means what it was meant to mean.

A useful way to demonstrate the mathematical effect of subtracting negative numbers is to use a series of numbered cards. Imagine we have six cards; each of them has a number written on it. For example:

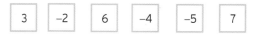

Add up these numbers. It is actually quite a nice activity to ask children how they would add up these six numbers. Some may start by looking at just the positive numbers $3 + 6 + 7 = 16$, and then the negative numbers -2, -4 and $-5 = -11$. Thus, the total of these six numbers is $16 - 11 = 5$. There are many other variations on how to sum these six numbers, all of which can provide stimulating class discussion. Nevertheless, whichever way you do it, **these six numbers together will always give you a total of 5.**

Put these six cards in a single envelope. This envelope now represents the number 5 because the numbers on the card sum to 5. Now, you are going to take out just one card from the envelope. Can you predict what the remaining numbers left in the envelope will add up to?

Suppose you take out the card with 3 on it. In the envelope, we would be left with:

This adds up to 2. So subtracting 3 from the total that was 5 gives us 2. We could write the number sentence **5 – 3 = 2, which seems very logical**.

Let us return to our envelope with all six numbers in it. Now suppose you take out the card with –4 on it. In the envelope, we would be left with:

This adds up to 9. By subtracting the –4 card from our total (which was 5) our total is now 9.

Subtracting a negative four has the effect of increasing the total by four.

We could write this in a number sentence as **5 – (–4) = 9**. As we have said in other places throughout the book, this is not mathematical proof, but rather it is a demonstration of the fact that *subtracting a negative number has led to the numerical value increasing.*

Segatnecrep sdrawkcab

This section will consider circumstances where a percentage increase or decrease has already been applied to a value and we need to find the original number before that change was made.

Task 12.1

Imagine that in a sale, a coat that did cost £140 is reduced by 15%. After some time, the sale comes to an end and the price of the coat is now raised by 15%.

Is the price of the coat now more than, or less than, the original price of £140?

This task is useful to show that reducing a number by a given percentage and then raising it by the same percentage does not return us to our original amount. Let us now consider a similar problem, but without knowing the original price.

In a shop sale there is 10% off all TVs. If the sale price of a TV is £756, what was the original price?

Many children would try to solve this by finding 10% of £756 and adding it on, getting an answer of £831.60 (£756 + £75.60). However, having completed Task 12.1 you know this is not the correct answer. If it was, you could calculate 10% of £831.60, subtract this from £831.60 and it would give us the sale price. If you are not sure at this point … try it!

Start at the beginning. We do not know what the original price of the TV was. However, we DO know that because we got 10% discount in the sale, what we have actually paid for the TV is 90% of its original price. There are two slightly different ways of proceeding from this point. The first of these uses a proportion method.

Method 1

If 90% of the original price is £756

Then 10% of the original price is £756/9 = £84

Thus, 100% of the original price is £84 × 10 = £840

Method 2

The second method is almost an algebraic approach.

90% of the original price is £756

We know that 90% = 0.9 and let us use the ? symbol to represent the original price. Therefore: $0.9 \times ? = 756$

Now using inverse operations: $? = 756 \div 0.9 = £840$

The first method works quite nicely where we are dealing with simple percentages but can lead to some difficult calculations for others. The second method always works for any percentage reductions and also for percentage increases.

Example 1

A woman has a discount voucher for a 35% discount on her online shopping bill. If her bill after the discount is £69.16, how much would she have had to pay if she didn't have the voucher?

£69.16 represents 65% of the original amount

Therefore 65% of ? = £69.16

$0.65 \times ? = £69.16$

Which means $? = £69.16 \div 0.65$

$? = £106.40$

The original bill before the discount was **£106.40**.

Example 2

A bill for a car repair is £462 and includes VAT of 20%. What was the bill without the VAT?

VAT of 20% has been added onto an original amount. Thus, the bill we have to pay represents 120% of that original amount. The original bill (100%) plus the VAT (20%). We can write this as:

120% of ? = £462

i.e. $1.20 \times ? = 462$

Which means ? = $462 \div 1.20$

? = £385

The original bill before VAT was added was **£385**.

Further grid method

In Chapter 5, we looked at the grid method as an aid to multiplication. In Key Stage 3, this can be used as a useful bridge to introducing algebraic multiplication of brackets.

Consider a square of side x. The area of the square is x^2. We now extend one of the sides by three. (Note: for this task, the units are not important provided they are all the same.)

Now the sides are x and $x + 3$. The area can be found by multiplying these terms together. This is easily understood with the following diagram.

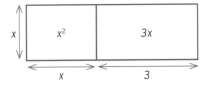

$$\text{Hence } A = x\,(x + 3)$$
$$= x^2 + 3x$$

We can use a similar grid to demonstrate a multiplication such as $(x + 5)\,(x + 3)$

	x	5
x	x^2	$5x$
3	$3x$	15

$$\text{Hence } (x + 5)\,(x + 3) = x^2 + 5x + 3x + 15$$
$$= x^2 + 8x + 15$$

Mastery Task

Think how you could use the grid method to model the following:

1. $(x - 1)(x + 4)$

2. $(x - 2)(x + 2)$

The power of negatives

Here we want to explore a little further how the topic of **indices** is developed in Key Stages 3 and 4. We will begin with multiplication of powers. As with many topics in this book, we begin with a demonstration of the method using numbers, before generalising it.

By the end of Key Stage 2, children will know (or perhaps we should say, they should know, or perhaps even more precisely, they have been taught) what a square and a cubic number is. So, now consider how to calculate $4^2 \times 4^3$. An obvious method is to work out each term and then multiply. Thus:

$$4^2 = 4 \times 4 = 16 \text{ and } 4^3 = 4 \times 4 \times 4 = 64$$

So:

$$4^2 \times 4^3 = 16 \times 64 = 1{,}024$$

Another way to think of this is $4^2 \times 4^3 = (4 \times 4) \times (4 \times 4 \times 4) = 4^5$. (Note: we can leave the answer in **index form**.) Provided the numbers being raised to any power are the same, we can extend this to any multiplication of indices.

$$3^4 \times 3^5 = 3^9$$

$$6^6 \times 6^2 = 6^8$$

Applying the similar logic to division we get:

$$2^5 \div 2^3 = (2 \times 2 \times 2 \times 2 \times 2) \div (2 \times 2 \times 2)$$

$$= 32 \div 8 = 4 \text{ (which is the same as } 2^2)$$

In terms of explaining this, we can see that there is a 2^3 in both of the numbers being divided, which cancel out the effect of each other. Sometimes, this is better understood as a division:

$$2^5 \div 2^3 = \frac{2 \times 2 \times 2 \times 2 \times 2}{2 \times 2 \times 2} = \frac{2 \times 2}{1} = 2^2$$

This works with any number and so we can generalise these techniques using the symbol a or x to represent that general number:

$$a^3 \times a^4 = (a \times a \times a) \times (a \times a \times a \times a) = a^7$$

$$x^5 \div x^3 = \frac{x \times x \times x \times x \times x}{x \times x \times x} = x^2$$

This then leads to the general rules that you may recall from secondary school:

$$a^m \times a^n = a^{m+n}$$

$$a^m \div a^n = a^{m-n}$$

Sometimes teachers may state, *We add to times powers and subtract to divide powers*. Such a statement requires caution as it can lead to conceptual errors if it is not qualified. For example, a common error children make here is to apply this to questions where numbers are not the same, such as writing $2^4 \times 3^5 = 6^9$.

Now consider $4^3 \div 4^3$.

This is the same as $64 \div 64 = 1$.

In fact, we know from Key Stage 1 that dividing any number by itself will give 1. Therefore we do not need to convert the power to a number to perform the calculation. Thus:

$$4^{10} \div 4^{10} = 1$$

$$10^6 \div 10^6 = 1$$

$$x^5 \div x^5 = 1$$

However, if we apply the law of indices introduced above, we can subtract the powers as follows:

$$4^{10} \div 4^{10} = 4^0$$

$$10^6 \div 10^6 = 10^0$$

$$x^5 \div x^5 = x^0$$

We know that each of these answers is 1. Thus, **any number to the power of 0 must equal 1.** We can generalise this as **$a^0 = 1$**.

Let us now extend this to examples where we are dividing by a larger number.

$$2^4 \div 2^6 = \frac{2 \times 2 \times 2 \times 2}{2 \times 2 \times 2 \times 2 \times 2 \times 2} = \frac{1}{2 \times 2} = \frac{1}{2^2}$$

However, using our method for dividing indices by subtracting powers, we would get $2^4 \div 2^6 = 2^{-2}$.

Thus $2^{-2} = \frac{1}{2^2}$.

It can be demonstrated, using the expanded division method above, that this works using any number or letter.

For example, using the method for division of indices:

$$a^3 \div a^7 = a^{-4}$$

Or by expanded division:

$$a^3 \div a^7 \frac{a \times a \times a}{a \times a \times a \times a \times a \times a \times a} = \frac{1}{a^4}$$

Therefore:

$$a^{-4} = \frac{1}{a^4}$$

Any number raised to a negative power is equal to the reciprocal of the number to the positive power. We generalise this as $\mathbf{a^{-n} = \dfrac{1}{a^n}}$

Setting the standard

In Chapter 4 we talked about big numbers such as the population of the world is £7.3 billion or UK spending on education is £102 billion. As soon as we begin writing numbers that contain more than, say, six digits, it can become difficult to read them or to get a sense of their size.

Standard index form allows us to write any number using our knowledge of powers of 10. From our work on indices in this book, we know:

$$1,000 = 10^3$$
$$100 = 10^2$$
$$10 = 10^1$$
$$1 = 10^0$$
$$1/10 = 0.1 = 10^{-1}$$
$$1/100 = 0.01 = 10^{-2}$$
$$1/1000 = 0.001 = 10^{-3}$$

Similarly, from our discussion in Chapter 4, we know that one million is 10^6 and one billion is 10^9. It is important here to appreciate the symmetry of large and small powers of 10.

one hundred = 10^2 one hundredth = 10^{-2}

one million = 10^6 one millionth = 10^{-6}

one billion = 10^9 one billionth = 10^{-9}

This means we can write any number in standard index form. A number in standard form is defined as *the product of a number between 1 and 10 and a power of 10.*

For example, consider the number 7.3 billion:

$$7.3 \text{ billion} = 7.3 \times 1,000,000,000$$

$$= 7.3 \times 10^9$$

Part of the problem with the teaching of standard form in Key Stage 3 is that children are often asked to convert numbers to standard form that do not require being in standard form, such as 3,500, so they do not see its usefulness.

Similarly, we use standard form to represent very small numbers. For example, the diameter of the eye of a fly is approximately two ten-millionths of a metre:

$$2 / 10,000,000 = 0.0000002$$

$$= 2 \times 10^{-7}$$

The real power of standard form is seen in science, where we are dealing with very large numbers in areas such as astronomy, and very small numbers in areas such as nuclear physics.

Deriving the nth term

This section links to substituting into simple formulae, which we covered in Chapter 7. The key fact that we want children to notice is that the number of 'ns' in the formula (which we call the **coefficient of n**) determines the increase (or decrease) between consecutive terms.

For example, 3n, 3n + 5, 3n + 9, 3n – 2 are different sequences that will all begin at different values, but will all increase in threes from their starting point as the coefficient of n is 3.

nth term	1st term	2nd term	3rd term	4th term	5th term
3n	3	6	9	12	15
3n + 5	8	11	14	17	20
3n + 9	12	15	18	21	24
3n – 2	1	4	7	10	13

Similarly, 2n, 2n + 5, 2n + 18, 2n – 1 will all go up in twos as the coefficient of n is 2.

nth term	1st term	2nd term	3rd term	4th term	5th term
2n	2	4	6	8	10
2n + 5	7	9	11	13	15
2n + 18	20	22	24	26	28
2n – 1	1	3	5	7	9

However, for 28 − 5n, 21 − 5n, 7 − 5n **the coefficient of n is −5**. Thus, each sequence will **go down by 5** from its starting value.

nth term	1st term	2nd term	3rd term	4th term	5th term
28 − 5n	23	18	13	8	3
21 − 5n	16	11	6	1	−4
7 − 5n	2	−3	−8	−13	−18

This means that for any linear sequence we can identify the main part of the nth term (the coefficient of n) by considering the common difference. This is then adjusted by inspection to match perfectly with our given sequence.

Now let us try to find the formula for some of the sequences we looked at in Chapter 7.

Sequence	Common difference	Part of formula		nth term
1, 3, 5, 7	going UP in twos	2n	However, a formula of 2n would give us the sequence 2, 4, 6, 8 … Our sequence is one less than this so we need to subtract 1.	2n − 1
20, 18, 16, 14	going DOWN in twos	−2n	However, a formula of −2n would give us the sequence −2, −4, −6, −8 … Our sequence needs to be increased by 22.	22 − 2n
42, 52, 62, 72	going UP in tens	10n	However, a formula of 10n would give us the sequence 10, 20, 30, 40 … Our sequence needs to be increased by 32	10n + 32
13, 18, 23, 28	going UP in fives	5n	However, a formula of 5n would give us the sequence 5, 10, 15, 20 … Our sequence needs to be increased by 8.	5n + 8

Other sequences

Many patterns can generate sequences that instead of having a common difference, the differences between consecutive numbers change. Consider:

$$3, 8, 15, 24, 35 \dots$$

Here, the differences are 5, 7, 9, 11, etc. – the differences themselves form a linear sequence. Such sequences come from a quadratic expression that can be derived from many sources. Finding the algebraic expressions to generate such sequences is how the topic is developed in Key Stage 3.

For the above sequence the nth term is $n(n+2)$.

Thus, we get:

	Value of n	Calculation	Output
1st term	1	$1 \times (1+2) = 1 \times 3$	3
2nd term	2	$2 \times (2+2) = 2 \times 4$	8
3rd term	3	$3 \times (3+2) = 3 \times 5$	15
4th term	4	$4 \times (4+2) = 4 \times 6$	24
5th term	5	$5 \times (5+2) = 5 \times 7$	35

Task 12.2

Consider the sequences generated by the following formulae. Find the first six terms of each.

$$\frac{1}{2}n\,(n+2)$$
$$2n\,(n+1)$$
$$(n-1)\,(n+1)$$
$$n\,(n+1)\,(n+2)$$

Pascal's Triangle

Blaise Pascal was a seventeenth-century French mathematician. One of his most famous contributions to mathematics has become known as **Pascal's Triangle**, although as with some other aspects of mathematics, the person whose name we associate with the topic didn't discover it; the number sequence had been known about for hundreds of years in other countries, including India and China.

For each row, each number is generated by summing the two numbers directly above it. We begin with a 1. This element is our 'zero row'. Thus, the first row added is 1, 1, the second row added is 1, 2, 1, etc.

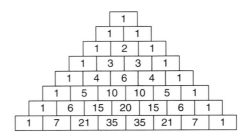

In Chapter 3 we discussed powers of 11. We can know that any number to the power of zero gives 1. What do you notice?

$$11^0 = 1$$

$$11^2 = 121$$

$$11^3 = 1,331$$

$$11^4 = 14,641$$

Task 12.3

Work out 11^5 and 11^6. Does this fit in with Pascal's Triangle? Can you explain what is happening?

Another interesting fact about Pascal's Triangle is that the sum of each row of numbers gives us all the powers of 2.

Row	Sum of row	Equivalent to
0	1	2^0
1	$1 + 1 = 2$	2^1
2	$1 + 2 + 1 = 4$	2^2
3	$1 + 3 + 3 + 1 = 8$	2^3
4	$1 + 4 + 6 + 4 + 1 = 16$	2^4
5	$1 + 5 + 10 + 10 + 5 + 1 = 32$	2^5

The numbers generated in Pascal's Triangle have an enormous number of applications. For example, in algebra, each row provides the coefficients for the expansion of $(a + b)^n$. Thus:

$(a + b)^0 =$ 1 coefficient is 1

$(a + b)^1 =$ $a + b$ coefficients are 1, 1

$(a + b)^2 =$ $a^2 + 2ab + b^2$ coefficients are 1, 2, 1

$(a + b)^3 =$ $a^3 + 3a^2b + 3ab^2 + b^3$ coefficients are 1, 3, 3, 1

These *coefficients* are also linked to probability theory. If, for example, you throw a coin a given number of times, Pascal's Triangle can predict the number of heads you will get and thus we can calculate the probability of obtaining any given number of heads.

If you throw a coin three times you could get anything between zero and three heads. Pascal's coefficients for n = 3 are 1, 3, 3 and 1, which sum up to 8. This leads to:

Number of heads (h)	Pascal's coefficients For n = 3	Probability P(h)
0	1	1/8
1	3	2/8
2	3	2/8
3	1	1/8
Total =	8	1

If we throw the coin four times, we can get up to four heads. This would give:

Number of heads (h)	Pascal's coefficients For n = 4	Probability P(h)
0	1	1/16
1	4	4/16
2	6	6/16
3	4	4/16
4	1	1/16
Total =	16	1

At Key Stage 3, these probabilities could be confirmed by children constructing the **sample space**. That is, systematically listing all possible combinations of outcomes.

Another interesting fact about Pascal's Triangle is the many number sequences it contains.

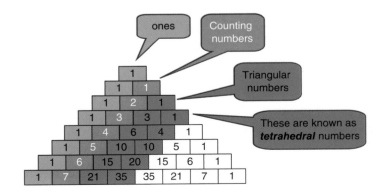

Finally, for us (although there is much more) if we align each row to the left, we would get the following:

1								
1	1							
1	2	1						
1	3	3	1					
1	4	6	4	1				
1	5	10	10	5	1			
1	6	15	20	15	6	1		
1	7	21	35	35	21	7	1	

↑

Now the counting numbers are in the second column. If we take any of these numbers, looking at the number immediately to the right and adding it to the number below that, amazingly, gives us the square of the number.

1								
1	1							
1	2	1						
1	3	3	1					
1	4	6	4	1				
1	5	10	10	5	1			
1	6	15	20	15	6	1		
1	7	21	35	35	21	7	1	

$$2^2 = 1 + 3$$
$$3^2 = 3 + 6$$
$$4^2 = 6 + 10$$
$$5^2 = 10 + 15$$
$$6^2 = 15 + 21$$
$$6^2 = 15 + 21$$

Using the same diagram, starting at 1 on the left-hand side, sum the numbers diagonally upwards. The first two are uninteresting as there is just a 1 in each.

1								
1	1							
1	2	1						
1	3	3	1					
1	4	6	4	1				
1	5	10	10	5	1			
1	6	15	20	15	6	1		
1	7	21	35	35	21	7	1	

If we start on the third row and sum the upward diagonal (which is pink), we get $1 + 1 = 2$. If we start on the fourth row and sum the upward diagonal (blue), we get $1 + 2 = 3$. Then on the fifth row, the upward diagonal (pink) gives $1 + 3 + 1 = 5$. The sixth diagonal gives $1 + 4 + 3 = 8$, etc. From the work we did in Chapter 3, you will recognise these as Fibonacci numbers.

Pythagoras' Theorem

We started this chapter by looking at a problem that required the use of Pythagoras' Theorem to solve. It would therefore be an apt way to conclude this chapter by looking at why Pythagoras' Theorem works. Incidentally, Pythagoras did not invent Pythagoras' Theorem; it was known about by many other civilisations before the Greeks. However, the Greeks were great recorders of mathematics, so he has his name on the theory (just like Pascal and Fibonacci).

There are many different ways to prove the theorem and to demonstrate why it works. However, we will look at just one way, which is based upon area of triangles and squares.

We begin by taking a square which has sides 7 cm, in which we construct another square of side **c** cm with each vertex 4/7 along the side.

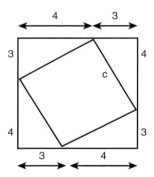

Area large square = Area each triangle plus area small square:

$$7^2 = 4 \times \tfrac{1}{2} (3 \times 4) + c^2$$

$$49 = 24 + ^2$$

$$\mathbf{25 = c^2}$$

Thus: $c = 5$ cm

If c must be 5 cm, we have shown that the hypotenuse in one of the right-angled triangles is 5 cm and the dimensions of that triangle satisfy $3^2 + 4^2 = 5^2$. This is the most famous of the **Pythagorean triplets**. Multiples of these numbers also work such as $6^2 + 8^2 = 10^2$ or $15^2 + 20^2 = 25^2$.

The other famous Pythagorean triplet is 5, 12, 13.

We can now generalise this method by taking a square which has sides $(\mathbf{a} + \mathbf{b})$ in which we again construct another square of side **c** cm.

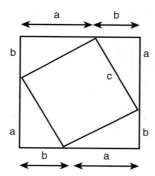

Area large square = Area each triangle plus area small square:

$$(a + b)^2 = 4 \times (\tfrac{1}{2}a \times b) + c^2$$

$$a^2 + 2ab + b^2 = 2ab + c^2$$

Subtracting 2ab from each side gives: $\mathbf{a^2 + b^2 = c^2}$

Provided we are working with right-angled triangles, this is always true.

Rounding up

As primary teachers, you will not be teaching the topics featured in this chapter. However, to be a high-quality teacher of primary mathematics, you need to have a good understanding of where children have come from and where they are going. Without understanding the next stage of a child's mathematical education, how can you be sure you have prepared them adequately?

You will plan every lesson you teach, only after considering what children already know and what they now need to know in order to build upon this existing knowledge, in order to progress.

A Key Stage 1 teacher needs to know about the mathematics children learn in the Foundation Stage as well as what they will be learning in Year 3. Teaching in upper Key Stage 2 requires deep understanding of the mathematics taught in lower Key Stage 2, as well as knowing about the mathematics children will be taught in Key Stage 3. Without knowing this, you cannot ensure that children will be 'secondary ready'.

We have not attempted to cover the whole of the Key Stage 3 curriculum in this chapter, but hopefully we have identified a wide range of topics where secondary teachers are clearly building upon the foundations you will have laid in primary school. We hope you can recognise these links and that having thought about them, you will feel more confident in ensuring each child you teach is ready to progress to secondary school.

WHAT MATHS CAN YOU SEE?

APPENDICES

1. What maths can you see?
2. Task answers
3. Mathematics National Curriculum by topic
4. Roman numerals 1–1,000

Appendix 1 What maths can you see?

Maths mastery

1 Masters of the classroom

This picture was taken in Palm Springs in California. We think this a great photograph to begin getting children to think about size and proportion. Can you estimate the height of the statue? We need to make some assumptions about the height of the people we can see in the picture and then scale up. How easy is this?

Like any of these ideas, it is not important to get a unique correct answer. Rather the picture is a springboard for class discussion of ideas and thinking. What else could you ask?

Number

2 Not as easy as 1, 2, 3

We saw this in a bistro; the staff used these buckets to assign numbers to food orders. We thought it would be a wonderful display for a classroom that could be used in so many ways to develop number. For Early Years classes a teacher could remove one or two buckets and the children could identify which is missing. Or the buckets could be arranged in a different order to allow children to think about sequences. Some of the buckets had cutlery in them. If a teacher put, say, two forks in each – or perhaps three spoons in each – we have immediate links to repeated addition and to times tables.

3 A ray of sunshine

This picture of a local building is a great example of how you can see opportunities for maths every-where. It would be useful for reinforcing arrays. We can clearly see the possibilities to help count in threes, sevens and nines. Just looking at the top block of windows we can explore: 5×3, 5×6 and 5×9. Vertically, blocks of 3×7 but also 6×7 and 9×7.

Buildings are a good way to help develop subitising skills; each group of three and nine are patterns which can be recognised without having to count every window.

4 Maths is mental

This map appears at Liverpool Central Station. In addition to showing the order of stations (which is topological, similar to the London tube map) this chart gives the time in minutes to each station from Liverpool Central.

This could be used in the same way as a number line. Some simple questions could be, *How long does it take to get from Hall Road to Southport or to get from Moorfields to Old Roan?* This equates to doing subtraction by finding differences of numbers.

A much more sophisticated question could be, *How long does it take to get from Southport to Hunts Cross or to get from Cressington to Bank Hall?* Here, the student has to appreciate that Central is a kind of zero so Liverpool Central to Cressington is 11 minutes and Central to Bank Hall is 8 minutes; this total time is 19 minutes. (Note: there are no changes on the Southport to Hunts Cross line.)

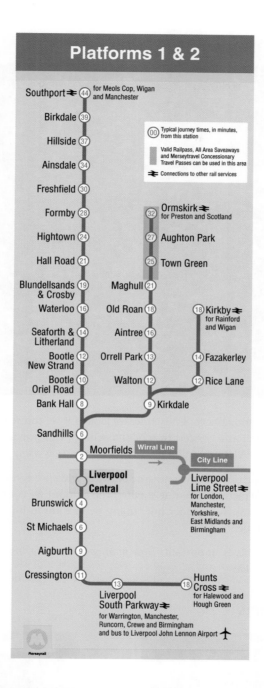

We can go further by asking children how long it would take to get from, say, Crosby to Old Roan. What assumptions do they need to make regarding connecting trains? There really is a wealth of number work within this picture.

5 Making sum sense

What a colourful and interesting photo. Every time we look at it we can see something different about it. Any crowd scene, whether at a concert or school assembly, can provide opportunities to develop estimation skills. The most obvious question we can ask here is, *How many people are there in the picture?*

Taking a small part of the picture by imagining or drawing grids, we can estimate how many people there are. Say we divide the picture into nine squares; the amount we count in each square can then be multiplied by 9. We can then consider how many people are in blue waterproofs by assessing how much of each grid is blue.

Developing observation skills is important: *How many people are facing the camera? How many are sitting on someone else's shoulders?*

6 Recurring problems

Both of these sets of photographs were taken on cycle ways.

On the left-hand side path, all distances on the signposts are in miles, and parts of miles are given as fractions. The other pathway has signposts displayed in kilometres, and parts of kilometres are given either in decimal or in metres.

In each case we can ask similar questions about how far apart these places are. This then leads to a real-life application of subtraction of fractions or decimals. The signs in metric units require an understanding of not only decimals, but conversions from kilometres to metres.

You could ask children to create a number line that shows each place mentioned on the sign. This could be done as a scale drawing – alternatively, it just may indicate how far apart each of the places are away from each other.

7 The joy of *x*

How many melons are there? In 2016 this question went viral on Facebook, Instagram and Twitter with fierce arguments about the answer. Many people said there are none, as the picture has only parts of melons, not a single whole melon.

A different strategy is to think about joining the pieces together. We have four halves which can make two whole melons. Now we can cut one of the remaining pieces into three quarter pieces – putting these with the remaining three shapes gives us another three whole melons. This method gives us five melons.

Many people said that it is impossible to recreate this picture with five melons. Yes, the four halves can be made from two melons but a $\frac{3}{4}$ piece of melon can only be made from a whole melon. Thus, there must have been six melons to make the picture. What do you think?

You may wish to use this as a link to algebra. For example:

- Suppose m is the number of melons bought. Then the total number of melons in the picture could be expressed as:

$$T = \frac{3}{4}m + \frac{3}{4}m + \frac{3}{4}m + \frac{3}{4}m + \frac{1}{2}m + \frac{1}{2}m + \frac{1}{2}m + \frac{1}{2}m$$

  or

  $$T = 0.75\,m + 0.75\,m + 0.75\,m + 0.75\,m + 0.5\,m + 0.5\,m + 0.5\,m + 0.5\,m$$

- Suppose m is the cost of a single melon. Then the total cost (C) could be expressed as:

  $$C = \frac{3}{4}m + \frac{3}{4}m + \frac{3}{4}m + \frac{3}{4}m + \frac{1}{2}m + \frac{1}{2}m + \frac{1}{2}m + \frac{1}{2}m$$

- Suppose m represents the weight of a melon. Then the total weight (W) of the melons in the picture could be written:

  $$W = \frac{3}{4}m + \frac{3}{4}m + \frac{3}{4}m + \frac{3}{4}m + \frac{1}{2}m + \frac{1}{2}m + \frac{1}{2}m + \frac{1}{2}m$$

What if the total weight of these melons is 12 kg. Can we use algebra to work out the weight of one melon?

Geometry

8 The shape of things to come

This picture was taken on a clear summer day over St Helens when four aeroplanes passed by, almost simultaneously, creating a beautiful image. The key question here is, *What do you see?* Some will only see what appears to be an isosceles triangle. *Is it isosceles? Is it right-angled? How can we tell for certain?*

However, others may see two parallel lines that are intersected by two other lines. What size are the angles? How could we measure these angles? How could you recreate this picture?

9 Losing the plot

Perhaps the maths in this picture is more obvious than some of our photographs, but that doesn't mean it is of less value. This was taken on the Ring of Kerry near Killarney in Ireland. The clear, still water creates a perfect symmetrical reflection of the rock and its vegetation. There is also a symmetry of colour, which is sometimes neglected when teaching this topic. Rotate the photograph 90 degrees. You now have an abstract replication of symmetry. This would also be a useful link to some artwork where the theme of symmetry could be explored further.

Measurement

10 Made to measure

While planning our book we went to the pub. Each of us ordered half a pint of beer. However, as we ordered different types of beer, they came in different types of glasses. This set us talking for some time about the size of each glass and whether one glass contained more beer. Eventually we asked for two of a third type of half pint glass and poured each beer into the new glass. We discovered … there was exactly the same amount of beer in each!

In your ITT course you may study the work of Piaget. He talked about children acquiring the concept of *conservation*. This is about the knowledge that redistribution of a material will not affect its weight or length or mass or volume. This photograph (or perhaps a similar one without beer) could introduce a lesson that will allow children to explore such ideas of conservation.

Statistics

11 Statistically speaking

This is real data from a runner competing in the 2017 London Marathon. Like other tables that are discussed in Chapter 11, there is a wealth of questions that could be asked here relating to time and distance.

It may be useful to explore average pace per km. *Which was the fastest or slowest 5 km? What could the time for each km be if the average pace for 5 km is 4 mins 20 secs? Does the runner get quicker or slower? What was his time at the halfway point? How long did it take him to run the second half of the marathon?*

You could recreate this table for a different athlete giving the children the time of day at each 5 km and getting them to work out how long each 5 km took. Alternatively, give them the time he has taken to run each 5 km and ask them to work out the time of day at each split. Another idea would be to get the children to convert the table to miles.

Actually, as good as these times were, Simon was a little disappointed that he didn't break the 3-hour mark. He was 2 minutes and 6 seconds over. What would he have to do to break 3 hours? Where could he make up that amount of time?

Transition

12 Moving on

We thought we would conclude the book with some lovely flowers. The Fibonacci sequence is a beautiful pattern in itself, but has so many applications in nature. Many flowers have petals which correspond to terms in the sequence. You can encourage children to count petals and leaves. Plants don't study maths, they just grow in the most efficient manner which links directly to our sequence.

If you cut a banana along its length you will see three sections. If you do so with an apple you will see five sections. You can also see Fibonacci patterns in shells, sunflowers – and even in the shapes of galaxies.

If you divide each number in the Fibonacci sequence by the number immediately before it, something strange happens as the ratio approaches a constant we call the 'golden ratio'. This links directly to art.

For much more on this, look at **http://jwilson.coe.uga.edu/emat6680/parveen/fib_nature.htm**.

Appendix 2 Task answers

1 Masters of the classroom

Task 1.1

3, 7.5, 12, 16.5   Linear sequence with common difference of 4.5

3, 6, 12, 24   Each term is doubled to get the next one

3, 9, 12, 13.5   Each difference is halved

3, 9, 12, 21   Each term is generated by adding the two previous numbers

3, –6, 12, –24   Each term is multiplied by negative 2

Other sequences can be generated by consideration of patterns rather than using any operations:

3, 3, 12, 12   or   3, –3, 12, –12 etc.

Task 1.2

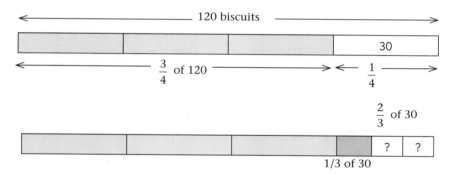

Colette kept $\frac{2}{3}$ of 30 = **20 biscuits**

2 Not as easy as 1, 2, 3

Task 2.1

1. The child may:

   - Count quicker than the speed of moving the fingers.

   - Move fingers quicker than the speed they count.

   - Count a number twice as they move to the next hand.

2. When children count as part of a group in a classroom setting the counting can become quite robotic. The child is counting one, two, three, four, five, six, se-ven, eight, nine. Seven is the only number which has two syllables and can therefore sometimes be assigned two counts.

Task 2.2

- $31 + 5 = 40$

- $45 + 23 = 102$

- $122 + 42 = 204$

- $43 - 4 = 35$

- $53 - 22 = 22$

- $215 - 142 = 33$

3 A ray of sunshine

Task 3.1

Counting forward from –10 to 6 (either in one go or in two jumps) gives 16.

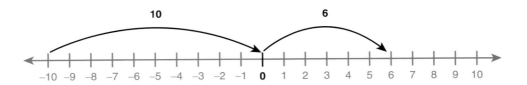

Half of 16 is 8. So, we can either count forwards 8 from –10, or count backwards from 8 to 6.

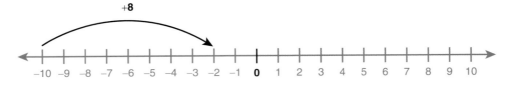

Gives us the mid-point of –2.

Task 3.2

$81 = 3 \times 3 \times 3 \times 3$

$15 = 3 \times 5$

$45 = 3, 3, 5$

$$49 = 7 \times 7$$

$$82 = 2 \times 41$$

$$77 = 7 \times 11$$

$$42 = 2 \times 3 \times 7$$

$$56 = 2 \times 2 \times 2 \times 7$$

Task 3.3

57,902; 6,347; 4,453

If we start with any number and multiply it by 5 the answer will always end in 5 or zero. Therefore when 1 is added the final number will end in 6 or 1.

4 Maths is mental

Task 4.1

Here we will not insult you by giving you each answer, as we are sure you can derive the correct answer for each yourself. For each question, we want you to use some of the different methods discussed in the chapter, including using the number line in a variety of ways and thinking about which, for you, is the most efficient. While you are doing this, you should be thinking about how you would explain this to a whole class. It is worth pointing out that sometimes the language we use when addressing a whole class is different to when working one-to-one. So, you should be thinking about the types of questions you would ask in each case.

Task 4.2

1. 16

2. 4

3. −4

4. 14

5 Making sum sense

Tasks 5.1 and 5.2

You will have a variety of different responses here depending on the methods you have used.

For each of the methods used, check you have the same solution and that you are secure with each stage of the calculation. Keep practising them to develop improved fluency, especially with those methods you are less secure in carrying out.

Task 5.3

There are many possible solutions. Here are the most common you should be using:

Add	Subtract	Multiply	Divide
add	minus	product	share
plus	take away	times	group
totalling	subtract	double	halve
sum	difference	groups of	
counting on	counting down	lots of	
increase	decrease		

6 Recurring problems

Task 6.1

$$\frac{7}{8} = 7 \div 8$$

$$\begin{array}{r} 0.875 \\ 8\overline{\smash{\big)}7.^{7}0^{6}0^{4}0} \end{array}$$

Task 6.2

1. Ratio b:g = 20:15 = 4:3

2. $\frac{2}{5}$ are strawberry. There are 12 strawberry sweets.

3. (a) 3:1 (b) 15 (c) 36

7 The joy of χ

Task 7.1

 = 7   = 5   △ = 3

Task 7.2

As we have two different symbols, we are looking for any two numbers that make this balance. There are many solutions. For example, if the number on the left was a 2, then the number on the right must be a 4. Although at first children may seek random numbers that balance the equation, you should be encouraging them to adopt a systematic approach, by perhaps listing possible solutions.

$$4 + 0 = 10 - 6$$
$$4 + 1 = 10 - 5$$
$$4 + 2 = 10 - 4$$

Even though we have two different symbols, it may be that each symbol represents the same number, so we could have:

$$4 + 3 = 10 - 3$$

Do not forget that each number may also be a decimal or fraction. For example:

$$4 + 3.7 = 10 - 2.3$$

In a formal algebraic equation, if the same symbol is repeated, it must represent the same value. So, if instead of the given equation, we had:

$$4 + \boxed{} = 10 - \boxed{}$$

The missing number on both sides must now be the same, thus there is only one single correct answer, which is 3.

8 The shape of things to come

Task 8.1

A – square

B – pentagon

C – parallelogram

D – rectangle

E – isosceles triangle

F – hexagon

G – right-angled scalene triangle

H – trapezium

I – equilateral triangle

J – rhombus

K – heptagon

L – trapezium

M – octagon

Task 8.2

A – cylinder

B – cuboid or square based prism

C – cube

D – triangular based pyramid

E – triangular based prism

F – square based pyramid

G – cone

H – sphere

I – hexagonal based prism

J – hexagonal based pyramid

Task 8.3

Net B

Task 8.4

93°

135°

53°

115°, 65°, 115°

9 Losing the plot

Task 9.1

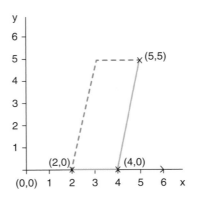

The missing coordinate is (3,5).

Task 9.2

The answer is NOT a rectangle.

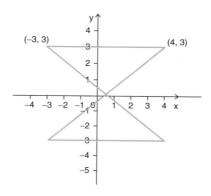

Task 9.3

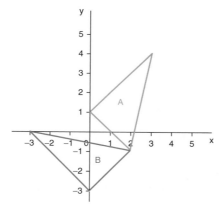

10 Made to measure

Task 10.1

This is a really lovely task that takes some thinking about. It is much more difficult without a cube so asking you (or asking children) to work this out without such a concrete resource is really testing your (and their) ability to visualise images.

3 faces painted yellow = 8 cubes (each of the vertices)

2 faces painted yellow = 12 cubes (the middle one along each edge)

1 face painted yellow = 6 cubes (the central one on each face)

0 faces painted yellow = 1 cube (the only one you cannot see)

Task 10.2

1. 30 cm × 18 cm, 1:9

2. Base 6 cm height 9 cm

Task 10.3

1. 12 km

2. 1:166,000

Task 10.4

1. A 330, B 375, C 405

2. A –0.8, B –0.2, C 0.3

3. A 30.5, B 34, C 38.5

Task 10.5

1. Peter swims each length one second faster than Howard so his total time will be 32 seconds faster than 15 mins = 8 minutes, 28 seconds.

2. To complete this task, we need to convert $\frac{1}{2}$ mile to metres. As one mile is 1,600 metres, $\frac{1}{2}$ mile is 800 metres.

   Each length is 25 metres. No. of lengths to swim = 800 ÷ 25 = 32.

   Thus, the boys need to swim 32 lengths to complete this distance.

   Calculations with time are difficult as time is not base 10.

   The best way to proceed is to work in seconds.

   $$15 \text{ minutes} = 15 \times 60 = 900 \text{ seconds}$$

   Each length needs to be 900 ÷ 32 = **28.125 seconds**

Task 11.1

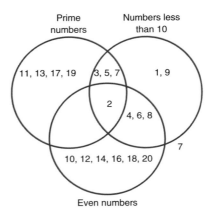

Task 11.2

The most common wrong answer for this type of question is 70%, as children will add the mean mark to the new marks and divide by 3.

However, the two new marks need to be added to the total marks of the 23 children who sat the test. This isn't given, but can be calculated.

If 23 children have a mean of 72 then the total of all their marks must be:

$$23 \times 72 = 1,656$$

Add the new scores:

$$1,656 + 54 + 84 = 1,794$$

New mean = 1,794 / 25 (as there are now 25 children in total) = **71.76**

12 Moving on

Task 12.1

We can reduce £140 by 15% in two ways.

1. We can find 15% and subtract 15% of £140 = 0.15 × 140 = £21

    £140 − £21 = £119

2. We can find 85% of £140

    85% of £140 = 0.85 × 140 = £119

    We now raise £119 by 15%

    15% of £119 = £17.85

If we increase £119 by £17.85 we get £136.85.

Answer: it is **LESS** than the original price.

Task 12.2

	term					
	1	2	3	4	5	6
$\frac{1}{2}n(n+2)$	1.5	4	7.5	12	17.5	24
$2n(n+1)$	6	16	30	48	70	96
$(n-1)(n+1)$	0	3	8	15	24	35
$n(n+1)(n+2)$	6	24	60	120	210	336

Task 12.3

Pascal's Triangle

$11^4 = 14{,}641$ which perfectly fits the fourth row of Pascal's Triangle. However, at first it seems that Pascal's Triangle doesn't predict for higher powers of 11.

For example: $11^5 = 161{,}051$

It actually **does** work if you avoid double digits in each space and instead 'carry' as in column addition.

4th row is		1	4	6	4	1	
Adding from right hand side	1	6	1	0	5	1	
		1	1+4+1=6	4+6+1=11 / 1 down carry 1	6+4=10 / 0 down carry 1	4+1	1

It works again for 11^6 as there are no two-digit numbers generated when adding.

Appendix 3 Mathematics National Curriculum by topic

Number – number and place value	
Y1	count to and across 100, forwards and backwards, beginning with 0 or 1, or from any given number
	count, read and write numbers to 100 in numerals; count in multiples of twos, fives and tens
	given a number, identify one more and one less
	identify and represent numbers using objects and pictorial representations including the number line, and use the language of: equal to, more than, less than (fewer), most, least
	read and write numbers from 1 to 20 in numerals and words.
Y2	count in steps of 2, 3 and 5 from 0, and in tens from any number, forwards and backwards
	recognise the place value of each digit in a two-digit number (tens, ones)
	identify, represent and estimate numbers using different representations, including the number line
	compare and order numbers from 0 up to 100; use <, > and = signs
	read and write numbers to at least 100 in numerals and in words
	use place value and number facts to solve problems.
Y3	count from 0 in multiples of 4, 8, 50 and 100; find 10 or 100 more or less than a given number
	recognise the place value of each digit in a three-digit number (hundreds, tens, ones)
	compare and order numbers up to 1,000
	identify, represent and estimate numbers using different representations
	read and write numbers up to 1,000 in numerals and in words
	solve number problems and practical problems involving these ideas.
Y4	count in multiples of 6, 7, 9, 25 and 1,000
	find 1,000 more or less than a given number
	count backwards through zero to include negative numbers
	recognise the place value of each digit in a four-digit number (thousands, hundreds, tens and ones)
	order and compare numbers beyond 1,000

(Continued)

(Continued)

	identify, represent and estimate numbers using different representations
	round any number to the nearest 10, 100 or 1,000
	solve number and practical problems that involve all of the above and with increasingly large positive numbers
	read Roman numerals to 100 (I to C) and know that over time, the numeral system changed to include the concept of zero and place value.
Y5	read, write, order and compare numbers to at least 1,000,000 and determine the value of each digit
	count forwards or backwards in steps of powers of 10 for any given number up to 1,000,000
	interpret negative numbers in context, count forwards and backwards with positive and negative whole numbers, including through zero
	round any number up to 1,000,000 to the nearest 10, 100, 1,000, 10,000 and 100,000
	solve number problems and practical problems that involve all of the above
	read Roman numerals to 1,000 (M) and recognise years written in Roman numerals.
Y6	read, write, order and compare numbers up to 10,000,000 and determine the value of each digit
	round any whole number to a required degree of accuracy
	use negative numbers in context, and calculate intervals across zero
	solve number and practical problems that involve all of the above.

Number – addition and subtraction	
Y1	read, write and interpret mathematical statements involving addition (+), subtraction (−) and equals (=) signs
	represent and use number bonds and related subtraction facts within 20
	add and subtract one-digit and two-digit numbers to 20, including zero
	solve one-step problems that involve addition and subtraction, using concrete objects and pictorial representations, and missing number problems such as 7 = ☐ − 9.
Y2	solve problems with addition and subtraction: • using concrete objects and pictorial representations, including those involving numbers, quantities and measures • applying their increasing knowledge of mental and written methods
	recall and use addition and subtraction facts to 20 fluently, and derive and use related facts up to 100

	add and subtract numbers using concrete objects, pictorial representations, and mentally, including:
	• a two-digit number and ones
	• a two-digit number and tens
	• two two-digit numbers
	• adding three one-digit numbers
	show that addition of two numbers can be done in any order (commutative) and subtraction of one number from another cannot
	recognise and use the inverse relationship between addition and subtraction and use this to check calculations and solve missing number problems.
Y3	add and subtract numbers mentally, including:
	• a three-digit number and ones
	• a three-digit number and tens
	• a three-digit number and hundreds
	add and subtract numbers with up to three digits, using formal written methods of columnar addition and subtraction
	estimate the answer to a calculation and use inverse operations to check answers
	solve problems, including missing number problems, using number facts, place value, and more complex addition and subtraction.
Y4	add and subtract numbers with up to four digits using the formal written methods of columnar addition and subtraction where appropriate
	estimate and use inverse operations to check answers to a calculation
	solve addition and subtraction two-step problems in contexts, deciding which operations and methods to use and why.
Y5	add and subtract whole numbers with more than four digits, including using formal written methods (columnar addition and subtraction)
	add and subtract numbers mentally with increasingly large numbers
	use rounding to check answers to calculations and determine, in the context of a problem, levels of accuracy
	solve addition and subtraction multi-step problems in contexts, deciding which operations and methods to use and why.
Y6	See multiplication and division.
Number – multiplication and division	
Y1	solve one-step problems involving multiplication and division, by calculating the answer using concrete objects, pictorial representations and arrays with the support of the teacher.

(Continued)

(Continued)

Y2	recall and use multiplication and division facts for the 2, 5 and 10 multiplication tables, including recognising odd and even numbers
	calculate mathematical statements for multiplication and division within the multiplication tables and write them using the multiplication ($\times$), division ($\div$) and equals ($=$) signs
	show that multiplication of two numbers can be done in any order (commutative) and division of one number by another cannot
	solve problems involving multiplication and division, using materials, arrays, repeated addition, mental methods, and multiplication and division facts, including problems in contexts.
Y3	recall and use multiplication and division facts for the 3, 4 and 8 multiplication tables
	write and calculate mathematical statements for multiplication and division using the multiplication tables that they know, including for two-digit numbers times one-digit numbers, using mental and progressing to formal written methods
	solve problems, including missing number problems, involving multiplication and division, including positive integer scaling problems and correspondence problems in which n objects are connected to m objects.
Y4	recall multiplication and division facts for multiplication tables up to 12×12
	use place value, known and derived facts to multiply and divide mentally, including: multiplying by 0 and 1; dividing by 1; multiplying together three numbers
	recognise and use factor pairs and commutativity in mental calculations
	multiply two-digit and three-digit numbers by a one-digit number using formal written layout
	solve problems involving multiplying and adding, including using the distributive law to multiply two digit numbers by one digit, integer scaling problems and harder correspondence problems such as n objects are connected to m objects.
Y5	identify multiples and factors, including finding all factor pairs of a number, and common factors of two numbers
	know and use the vocabulary of prime numbers, prime factors and composite (non-prime) numbers
	establish whether a number up to 100 is prime and recall prime numbers up to 19
	multiply numbers up to four digits by a one- or two-digit number using a formal written method, including long multiplication for two-digit numbers
	multiply and divide numbers mentally drawing upon known facts
	divide numbers up to four digits by a one-digit number using the formal written method of short division and interpret remainders appropriately for the context
	multiply and divide whole numbers and those involving decimals by 10, 100 and 1,000
	recognise and use square numbers and cube numbers, and the notation for squared and cubed

	solve problems involving multiplication and division including using their knowledge of factors and multiples, squares and cubes
	solve problems involving addition, subtraction, multiplication and division and a combination of these, including understanding the meaning of the equals sign
	solve problems involving multiplication and division, including scaling by simple fractions and problems involving simple rates.
Y6	multiply multi-digit numbers up to four digits by a two-digit whole number using the formal written method of long multiplication
	divide numbers up to four digits by a two-digit whole number using the formal written method of long division, and interpret remainders as whole number remainders, fractions, or by rounding, as appropriate for the context
	divide numbers up to four digits by a two-digit number using the formal written method of short division where appropriate, interpreting remainders according to the context
	perform mental calculations, including with mixed operations and large numbers
	identify common factors, common multiples and prime numbers
	use their knowledge of the order of operations to carry out calculations involving the four operations
	solve addition and subtraction multi-step problems in contexts, deciding which operations and methods to use and why
	solve problems involving addition, subtraction, multiplication and division
	use estimation to check answers to calculations and determine, in the context of a problem, an appropriate degree of accuracy.

Number - fractions	
Y1	recognise, find and name a half as one of two equal parts of an object, shape or quantity
	recognise, find and name a quarter as one of four equal parts of an object, shape or quantity.
Y2	recognise, find, name and write fractions a third, a quarter, two quarters and three quarters of a length, shape, set of objects or quantity
	write simple fractions, for example a half of 6 = 3, and recognise the equivalence of two quarters and a half.
Y3	count up and down in tenths; recognise that tenths arise from dividing an object into 10 equal parts and in dividing one-digit numbers or quantities by 10
	recognise, find and write fractions of a discrete set of objects: unit fractions and non-unit fractions with small denominators

(Continued)

(Continued)

	recognise and use fractions as numbers: unit fractions and non-unit fractions with small denominators
	recognise and show, using diagrams, equivalent fractions with small denominators
	add and subtract fractions with the same denominator within one whole
	compare and order unit fractions, and fractions with the same denominators
	solve problems that involve all of the above.

Number – fractions (including decimals)

Y4	recognise and show, using diagrams, families of common equivalent fractions
	count up and down in hundredths; recognise that hundredths arise when dividing an object by one hundred and dividing tenths by ten
	solve problems involving increasingly harder fractions to calculate quantities, and fractions to divide quantities, including non-unit fractions where the answer is a whole number
	add and subtract fractions with the same denominator
	recognise and write decimal equivalents of any number of tenths or hundredths
	recognise and write decimal equivalents to a quarter, half and three quarters
	find the effect of dividing a one- or two-digit number by 10 and 100, identifying the value of the digits in the answer as ones, tenths and hundredths
	round decimals with one decimal place to the nearest whole number
	compare numbers with the same number of decimal places up to two decimal places
	solve simple measure and money problems involving fractions and decimals to two decimal places – *used to be with a calculator.*

Number – fractions (including decimals and percentages)

Y5	compare and order fractions whose denominators are all multiples of the same number
	identify, name and write equivalent fractions of a given fraction, represented visually, including tenths and hundredths
	recognise mixed numbers and improper fractions and convert from one form to the other and write mathematical statements > 1 as a mixed number
	add and subtract fractions with the same denominator and denominators that are multiples of the same number
	multiply proper fractions and mixed numbers by whole numbers, supported by materials and diagrams
	read and write decimal numbers as fractions

	recognise and use thousandths and relate them to tenths, hundredths and decimal equivalents
	round decimals with two decimal places to the nearest whole number and to one decimal place
	read, write, order and compare numbers with up to three decimal places
	solve problems involving number up to three decimal places
	recognise the per cent symbol (%) and understand that per cent relates to 'number of parts per hundred', and write percentages as a fraction with denominator 100, and as a decimal
	solve problems which require knowing percentage and decimal equivalents of 1/2, 1/4, 1/5, 2/5, 4/5 and those fractions with a denominator of a multiple of 10 or 25.
Y6	use common factors to simplify fractions; use common multiples to express fractions in the same denomination
	compare and order fractions, including fractions > 1
	add and subtract fractions with different denominators and mixed numbers, using the concept of equivalent fractions
	multiply simple pairs of proper fractions, writing the answer in its simplest form
	divide proper fractions by whole numbers
	associate a fraction with division and calculate decimal fraction equivalents [for example, 0.375] for a simple fraction
	identify the value of each digit in numbers given to three decimal places and multiply and divide numbers by 10, 100 and 1,000 giving answers up to three decimal places
	multiply one-digit numbers with up to two decimal places by whole numbers
	use written division methods in cases where the answer has up to two decimal places
	solve problems which require answers to be rounded to specified degrees of accuracy
	recall and use equivalences between simple fractions, decimals and percentages, including in different contexts.

Ratio and proportion

Y6	solve problems involving the relative sizes of two quantities where missing values can be found by using integer multiplication and division facts
	solve problems involving the calculation of percentages [for example, of measures, and such as 15% of 360] and the use of percentages for comparison
	solve problems involving similar shapes where the scale factor is known or can be found
	solve problems involving unequal sharing and grouping using knowledge of fractions and multiples.

(Continued)

(Continued)

Algebra	
Y6	use simple formulae
	generate and describe linear number sequences
	express missing number problems algebraically
	find pairs of numbers that satisfy an equation with two unknowns
	enumerate possibilities of combinations of two variables.

Measurement	
Y1	compare, describe and solve practical problems for: • lengths and heights [for example, long/short, longer/shorter, tall/short, double/half] • mass/weight [for example, heavy/light, heavier than, lighter than] • capacity and volume [for example, full/empty, more than, less than, half, half full, quarter] • time [for example, quicker, slower, earlier, later]
	measure and begin to record the following: • lengths and heights • mass/weight • capacity and volume • time (hours, minutes, seconds)
	recognise and know the value of different denominations of coins and notes
	sequence events in chronological order using language [for example, before and after, next, first, today, yesterday, tomorrow, morning, afternoon and evening]
	recognise and use language relating to dates, including days of the week, weeks, months and years
	tell the time to the hour and half past the hour and draw the hands on a clock face to show these times.
Y2	choose and use appropriate standard units to estimate and measure length/height in any direction (m/cm); mass (kg/g); temperature (°C); capacity (litres/ml) to the nearest appropriate unit, using rulers, scales, thermometers and measuring vessels
	compare and order lengths, mass, volume/capacity and record the results using $>$, $<$ and $=$
	recognise and use symbols for pounds (£) and pence (p); combine amounts to make a particular value
	find different combinations of coins that equal the same amounts of money

	solve simple problems in a practical context involving addition and subtraction of money of the same unit, including giving change
	compare and sequence intervals of time
	tell and write the time to five minutes, including quarter past/to the hour and draw the hands on a clock face to show these times
	know the number of minutes in an hour and the number of hours in a day.
Y3	measure, compare, add and subtract: lengths (m/cm/mm); mass (kg/g); volume/capacity (l/ml)
	measure the perimeter of simple 2D shapes
	add and subtract amounts of money to give change, using both £ and p in practical contexts
	tell and write the time from an analogue clock, including using Roman numerals from I to XII, and 12-hour and 24-hour clocks
	estimate and read time with increasing accuracy to the nearest minute; record and compare time in terms of seconds, minutes and hours; use vocabulary such as o'clock, a.m./p.m., morning, afternoon, noon and midnight
	know the number of seconds in a minute and the number of days in each month, year and leap year
	compare durations of events [for example to calculate the time taken by particular events or tasks].
Y4	convert between different units of measure [for example, kilometre to metre; hour to minute]
	measure and calculate the perimeter of a rectilinear figure (including squares) in centimetres and metres
	find the area of rectilinear shapes by counting squares
	estimate, compare and calculate different measures, including money in pounds and pence.
Y5	convert between different units of metric measure (for example, kilometre and metre; centimetre and metre; centimetre and millimetre; gram and kilogram; litre and millilitre)
	understand and use approximate equivalences between metric units and common imperial units such as inches, pounds and pints
	measure and calculate the perimeter of composite rectilinear shapes in centimetres and metres (and representing algebraically)
	calculate and compare the area of rectangles (including squares), and including using standard units, square centimetres (cm^2) and square metres (m^2) and estimate the area of irregular shapes
	estimate volume [for example, using 1 cm^3 blocks to build cuboids (including cubes)] and capacity [for example, using water]
	solve problems involving converting between units of time
	use all four operations to solve problems involving measure [for example, length, mass, volume, money] using decimal notation, including scaling.

(Continued)

(Continued)

Y6	solve problems involving the calculation and conversion of units of measure, using decimal notation up to three decimal places where appropriate
	use, read, write and convert between standard units, converting measurements of length, mass, volume and time from a smaller unit of measure to a larger unit, and vice versa, using decimal notation to up to three decimal places
	convert between miles and kilometres
	recognise that shapes with the same areas can have different perimeters and vice versa
	recognise when it is possible to use formulae for area and volume of shapes
	calculate the area of parallelograms and triangles
	calculate, estimate and compare volume of cubes and cuboids using standard units, including cubic centimetres (cm^3) and cubic metres (m^3), and extending to other units [for example, mm^3 and km^3].

Geometry – properties of shapes	
Y1	recognise and name common 2D and 3D shapes, including: • 2D shapes [for example, rectangles (including squares), circles and triangles] • 3D shapes [for example, cuboids (including cubes), pyramids and spheres].
Y2	identify and describe the properties of 2D shapes, including the number of sides and line symmetry in a vertical line
	identify and describe the properties of 3D shapes, including the number of edges, vertices and faces
	identify 2D shapes on the surface of 3D shapes [for example, a circle on a cylinder and a triangle on a pyramid]
	compare and sort common 2D and 3D shapes and everyday objects.
Y3	draw 2D shapes and make 3D shapes using modelling materials; recognise 3D shapes in different orientations and describe them
	recognise angles as a property of shape or a description of a turn
	identify right angles, recognise that two right angles make a half-turn, three make three quarters of a turn and four a complete turn; identify whether angles are greater than or less than a right angle
	identify horizontal and vertical lines and pairs of perpendicular and parallel lines.
Y4	compare and classify geometric shapes, including quadrilaterals and triangles, based on their properties and sizes
	identify acute and obtuse angles and compare and order angles up to two right angles by size
	identify lines of symmetry in 2D shapes presented in different orientations
	complete a simple symmetric figure with respect to a specific line of symmetry.

Y5	identify 3D shapes, including cubes and other cuboids, from 2D representations
	know angles are measured in degrees: estimate and compare acute, obtuse and reflex angles
	draw given angles, and measure them in degrees
	identify: • angles at a point and one whole turn (total 360°) • angles at a point on a straight line and half a turn (total 180°) • other multiples of 90°
	use the properties of rectangles to deduce related facts and find missing lengths and angles
	distinguish between regular and irregular polygons based on reasoning about equal sides and angles.
Y6	draw 2D shapes using given dimensions and angles
	recognise, describe and build simple 3D shapes, including making nets
	compare and classify geometric shapes based on their properties and sizes and find unknown angles in any triangles, quadrilaterals and regular polygons
	illustrate and name parts of circles, including radius, diameter and circumference and know that the diameter is twice the radius
	recognise angles where they meet at a point, are on a straight line, or are vertically opposite, and find missing angles.

Geometry – position and direction	
Y1	describe position, direction and movement, including whole, half, quarter and three-quarter turns.
Y2	order and arrange combinations of mathematical objects in patterns and sequences
	use mathematical vocabulary to describe position, direction and movement, including movement in a straight line and distinguishing between rotation as a turn and in terms of right angles for quarter, half and three-quarter turns (clockwise and anti-clockwise).
Y3	**No content**
Y4	describe positions on a 2D grid as coordinates in the first quadrant
	describe movements between positions as translations of a given unit to the left/right and up/down
	plot specified points and draw sides to complete a given polygon.
Y5	identify, describe and represent the position of a shape following a reflection or translation, using the appropriate language, and know that the shape has not changed.
Y6	describe positions on the full coordinate grid (all four quadrants)
	draw and translate simple shapes on the coordinate plane, and reflect them in the axes.

Statistics	
Y2	interpret and construct simple pictograms, tally charts, block diagrams and simple tables
	ask and answer simple questions by counting the number of objects in each category and sorting the categories by quantity
	ask and answer questions about totalling and comparing categorical data.
Y3	interpret and present data using bar charts, pictograms and tables
	solve one-step and two-step questions [for example, 'How many more?' and 'How many fewer?'] using information presented in scaled bar charts and pictograms and tables.
Y4	interpret and present discrete and continuous data using appropriate graphical methods, including bar charts and time graphs
	solve comparison, sum and difference problems using information presented in bar charts, pictograms, tables and other graphs.
Y5	solve comparison, sum and difference problems using information presented in a line graph
	complete, read and interpret information in tables, including timetables.
Y6	interpret and construct pie charts and line graphs and use these to solve problems
	calculate and interpret the mean as an average.

Appendix 4 Roman numerals 1–1,000

1-20		21-40		41-60		61-80		81-100		101-120		121-140		141-160		161-180		181-200	
1	I	21	XXI	41	XLI	61	LXI	81	LXXXI	101	CI	121	CXXI	141	CXLI	161	CLXI	181	CLXXXI
2	II	22	XXII	42	XLII	62	LXII	82	LXXXII	102	CII	122	CXXII	142	CXLII	162	CLXII	182	CLXXXII
3	III	23	XXIII	43	XLIII	63	LXIII	83	LXXXIII	103	CIII	123	CXXIII	143	CXLIII	163	CLXIII	183	CLXXXIII
4	IV	24	XXIV	44	XLIV	64	LXIV	84	LXXXIV	104	CIV	124	CXXIV	144	CXLIV	164	CLXIV	184	CLXXXIV
5	V	25	XXV	45	XLV	65	LXV	85	LXXXV	105	CV	125	CXXV	145	CXLV	165	CLXV	185	CLXXXV
6	VI	26	XXVI	46	XLVI	66	LXVI	86	LXXXVI	106	CVI	126	CXXVI	146	CXLVI	166	CLXVI	186	CLXXXVI
7	VII	27	XXVII	47	XLVII	67	LXVII	87	LXXXVII	107	CVII	127	CXXVII	147	CXLVII	167	CLXVII	187	CLXXXVII
8	VIII	28	XXVIII	48	XLVIII	68	LXVIII	88	LXXXVIII	108	CVIII	128	CXXVIII	148	CXLVIII	168	CLXVIII	188	CLXXXVIII
9	IX	29	XXIX	49	XLIX	69	LXIX	89	LXXXIX	109	CIX	129	CXXIX	149	CXLIX	169	CLXIX	189	CLXXXIX
10	X	30	XXX	50	L	70	LXX	90	XC	110	CX	130	CXXX	150	CL	170	CLXX	190	CXC
11	XI	31	XXXI	51	LI	71	LXXI	91	XCI	111	CXI	131	CXXXI	151	CLI	171	CLXXI	191	CXCI
12	XII	32	XXXII	52	LII	72	LXXII	92	XCII	112	CXII	132	CXXXII	152	CLII	172	CLXXII	192	CXCII
13	XIII	33	XXXIII	53	LIII	73	LXXIII	93	XCIII	113	CXIII	133	CXXXIII	153	CLIII	173	CLXXIII	193	CXCIII
14	XIV	34	XXXIV	54	LIV	74	LXXIV	94	XCIV	114	CXIV	134	CXXXIV	154	CLIV	174	CLXXIV	194	CXCIV
15	XV	35	XXXV	55	LV	75	LXXV	95	XCV	115	CXV	135	CXXXV	155	CLV	175	CLXXV	195	CXCV
16	XVI	36	XXXVI	56	LVI	76	LXXVI	96	XCVI	116	CXVI	136	CXXXVI	156	CLVI	176	CLXXVI	196	CXCVI
17	XVII	37	XXXVII	57	LVII	77	LXXVII	97	XCVII	117	CXVII	137	CXXXVII	157	CLVII	177	CLXXVII	197	CXCVII
18	XVIII	38	XXXVIII	58	LVIII	78	LXXVIII	98	XCVIII	118	CXVIII	138	CXXXVIII	158	CLVIII	178	CLXXVIII	198	CXCVIII
19	XIX	39	XXXIX	59	LIX	79	LXXIX	99	XCIX	119	CXIX	139	CXXXIX	159	CLIX	179	CLXXIX	199	CXCIX
20	XX	40	XL	60	LX	80	LXXX	100	C	120	CXX	140	CXL	160	CLX	180	CLXXX	200	CC

201-220		221-240		241-260		261-280		281-300		301-320		321-340		341-360		361-380		381-400	
201	CCI	221	CCXXI	241	CCXLI	261	CCLXI	281	CCLXXXI	301	CCCI	321	CCCXXI	341	CCCXLI	361	CCCLXI	381	CCCLXXXI
202	CCII	222	CCXXII	242	CCXLII	262	CCLXII	282	CCLXXXII	302	CCCII	322	CCCXXII	342	CCCXLII	362	CCCLXII	382	CCCLXXXII
203	CCIII	223	CCXXIII	243	CCXLIII	263	CCLXIII	283	CCLXXXIII	303	CCCIII	323	CCCXXIII	343	CCCXLIII	363	CCCLXIII	383	CCCLXXXIII
204	CCIV	224	CCXXIV	244	CCXLIV	264	CCLXIV	284	CCLXXXIV	304	CCCIV	324	CCCXXIV	344	CCCXLIV	364	CCCLXIV	384	CCCLXXXIV
205	CCV	225	CCXXV	245	CCXLV	265	CCLXV	285	CCLXXXV	305	CCCV	325	CCCXXV	345	CCCXLV	365	CCCLXV	385	CCCLXXXV
206	CCVI	226	CCXXVI	246	CCXLVI	266	CCLXVI	286	CCLXXXVI	306	CCCVI	326	CCCXXVI	346	CCCXLVI	366	CCCLXVI	386	CCCLXXXVI
207	CCVII	227	CCXXVII	247	CCXLVII	267	CCLXVII	287	CCLXXXVII	307	CCCVII	327	CCCXXVII	347	CCCXLVII	367	CCCLXVII	387	CCCLXXXVII
208	CCVIII	228	CCXXVIII	248	CCXLVIII	268	CCLXVIII	288	CCLXXXVIII	308	CCCVIII	328	CCCXXVIII	348	CCCXLVIII	368	CCCLXVIII	388	CCCLXXXVIII
209	CCIX	229	CCXXIX	249	CCXLIX	269	CCLXIX	289	CCLXXXIX	309	CCCIX	329	CCCXXIX	349	CCCXLIX	369	CCCLXIX	389	CCCLXXXIX
210	CCX	230	CCXXX	250	CCL	270	CCLXX	290	CCXC	310	CCCX	330	CCCXXX	350	CCCL	370	CCCLXX	390	CCCXC
211	CCXI	231	CCXXXI	251	CCLI	271	CCLXXI	291	CCXCI	311	CCCXI	331	CCCXXXI	351	CCCLI	371	CCCLXXI	391	CCCXCI
212	CCXII	232	CCXXXII	252	CCLII	272	CCLXXII	292	CCXCII	312	CCCXII	332	CCCXXXII	352	CCCLII	372	CCCLXXII	392	CCCXCII
213	CCXIII	233	CCXXXIII	253	CCLIII	273	CCLXXIII	293	CCXCIII	313	CCCXIII	333	CCCXXXIII	353	CCCLIII	373	CCCLXXIII	393	CCCXCIII
214	CCXIV	234	CCXXXIV	254	CCLIV	274	CCLXXIV	294	CCXCIV	314	CCCXIV	334	CCCXXXIV	354	CCCLIV	374	CCCLXXIV	394	CCCXCIV
215	CCXV	235	CCXXXV	255	CCLV	275	CCLXXV	295	CCXCV	315	CCCXV	335	CCCXXXV	355	CCCLV	375	CCCLXXV	395	CCCXCV
216	CCXVI	236	CCXXXVI	256	CCLVI	276	CCLXXVI	296	CCXCVI	316	CCCXVI	336	CCCXXXVI	356	CCCLVI	376	CCCLXXVI	396	CCCXCVI
217	CCXVII	237	CCXXXVII	257	CCLVII	277	CCLXXVII	297	CCXCVII	317	CCCXVII	337	CCCXXXVII	357	CCCLVII	377	CCCLXXVII	397	CCCXCVII
218	CCXVIII	238	CCXXXVIII	258	CCLVIII	278	CCLXXIII	298	CCXCVIII	318	CCCXVIII	338	CCCXXXVIII	358	CCCLVIII	378	CCCLXXVIII	398	CCCVCVIII
219	CCXIX	239	CCXXXIX	259	CCLVIX	279	CCLXXIX	299	CCXCIX	319	CCCXIX	339	CCCXXXIX	359	CCCLIX	379	CCCLXXIX	399	CCCXCIX
220	CCXX	240	CCXL	260	CCLX	280	CCLXXX	300	CCC	320	CCCXX	340	CCCXL	360	CCCLX	380	CCCLXXX	400	CD

401-420		421-440		441-460		461-480		481-500		501-520		521-540		541-560		561-580		581-600	
401	CDI	421	CDXXI	441	CDXLI	461	CDLXI	481	CDLXXXI	501	DI	521	DXXI	541	DXLI	561	DLXI	581	DLXXXI
402	CDII	422	CDXXII	442	CDXLII	462	CDLXII	482	CDDLXXXII	502	DII	522	DXXII	542	DXLII	562	DLXII	582	DLXXXII
403	CDIII	423	CDXXIII	443	CDXLIII	463	CDLXIII	483	CDLXXXIII	503	DIII	523	DXXIII	543	DXLIII	563	DLXIII	583	DLXXXIII
404	CDIV	424	CDXXIV	444	CDXLIV	464	CDLXIV	484	CDLXXXIV	504	DIV	524	DXXIV	544	DXLIV	564	DLXIV	584	DLXXXIV
405	CDV	425	CDXXV	445	CDXLV	465	CDLXV	485	CDLXXXV	505	DV	525	DXXV	545	DXLV	565	DLXV	585	DLXXXV
406	CDVI	426	CDXXVI	446	CDXLVI	466	CDLXVI	486	CDLXXXVI	506	DVI	526	DXXVI	546	DXLVI	566	DLXVI	586	DLXXXVI
407	CDVII	427	CDXXVII	447	CDXLVII	467	CDLXVII	487	CDLXXXVII	507	DVII	527	DXXVII	547	DXLVII	567	DLXVII	587	DLXXXVII
408	CDVIII	428	CDXXVIII	448	CDXLVIII	468	CDLXVIII	488	CDLXXXVIII	508	DVIII	528	DXXVIII	548	DXLVIII	568	DLXVIII	588	DLXXXVIII
409	CDIX	429	CDXXIX	449	CDXLIX	469	CDLXIX	489	CDLXXXIX	509	DIX	529	DXXIX	549	DXLIX	569	DLXIX	589	DLXXXIX
410	CDX	430	CDXXX	450	CDL	470	CDLXX	490	CDXC	510	DX	530	DXXX	550	DL	570	DLXX	590	DXC
411	CDXI	431	CDXXXI	451	CDLI	471	CDLXXI	491	CDXCI	511	DXI	531	DXXXI	551	DLI	571	DLXXI	591	DXCI
412	CDXII	432	CDXXXII	452	CDLII	472	CDLXXII	492	CDXCII	512	DXII	532	DXXXII	552	DLII	572	DLXXII	592	DXCII
413	CDXIII	433	CDXXXIII	453	CDLIII	473	CDLXXIII	493	CDXCIII	513	DXIII	533	DXXXIII	553	DLIII	573	DLXXIII	593	DXCIII
414	CDXIV	434	CDXXXIV	454	CDLIV	474	CDLXXIV	494	CDXCIV	514	DXIV	534	DXXXIV	554	DLIV	574	DLXXIV	594	DXCIV
415	CDXV	435	CDXXXV	455	CDLV	475	CDLXXV	495	CDXCV	515	DXV	535	DXXXV	555	DLV	575	DLXXV	595	DXCV
416	CDXVI	436	CDXXXVI	456	CDLVI	476	CDLXXVI	496	CDXCVI	516	DXVI	536	DXXXVI	556	DLVI	576	DLXXVI	596	DXCVI
417	CDXVII	437	CDXXXVII	457	CDLVII	477	CDLXXVII	497	CDXCVII	517	DXVII	537	DXXXVII	557	DLVII	577	DLXXVII	597	DXCVII
418	CDXVIII	438	CDXXXVIII	458	CDLVIII	478	CDLXXVIII	498	CDXCVIII	518	DXVIII	538	DXXXVIII	558	DLVIII	578	DLXXVIII	598	DXCVIII
419	CDXIX	439	CDXXXIX	459	CDLIX	479	CDLXXIX	499	CDXCIX	519	DXIX	539	DXXXIX	559	DLIX	579	DLXXIX	599	DXCIX
420	CDXX	440	CDXL	460	CDLX	480	CDLXXX	500	D	520	DXX	540	DXL	560	DLX	580	DLXXX	600	DC

601-620		621-640		641-660		661-680		681-700		701-720		721-740		741-760		761-780		781-800	
601	DCI	621	DCXXI	641	DCXLI	661	DCLXI	681	DCLXXXI	701	DCCI	721	DCCXXI	741	DCCXLI	761	DCCLXI	781	DCCLXXXI
602	DCII	622	DCXXII	642	DCXLII	662	DCLXII	682	DCLXXXII	702	DCCII	722	DCCXXII	742	DCCXLII	762	DCCLXII	782	DCCLXXXII
603	DCIII	623	DCXXIII	643	DCXLIII	663	DCLXIII	683	DCLXXXIII	703	DCCIII	723	DCCXXIII	743	DCCXLIII	763	DCCLXIII	783	DCCLXXXIII
604	DCIV	624	DCXXIV	644	DCXLIV	664	DCLXIV	684	DCLXXXIV	704	DCCIV	724	DCCXXIV	744	DCCXLIV	764	DCCLXIV	784	DCCLXXXIV
605	DCV	625	DCXXV	645	DCXLV	665	DCLXV	685	DCLXXXV	705	DCCV	725	DCCXXV	745	DCCXLV	765	DCCLXV	785	DCCLXXXV
606	DCVI	626	DCXXVI	646	DCXLVI	666	DCLXVI	686	DCLXXXVI	706	DCCVI	726	DCCXXVI	746	DCCXLVI	766	DCCLXVI	786	DCCLXXXVI
607	DCVII	627	DCXXVII	647	DCXLVII	667	DCLXVII	687	DCLXXXVII	707	DCCVII	727	DCCXXVII	747	DCCXLVII	767	DCCLXVII	787	DCCLXXXVII
608	DCVIII	628	DCXXVIII	648	DCXLVIII	668	DCLXVIII	688	DCLXXXVIII	708	DCCVIII	728	DCCXXVIII	748	DCCXLVIII	768	DCCLXVIII	788	DCCLXXXVIII
609	DCIX	629	DCXXIX	649	DCXLIX	669	DCLXIX	689	DCLXXXIX	709	DCCIX	729	DCCXXIX	749	DCCXLIX	769	DCCLXIX	789	DCCLXXXIX
610	DCX	630	DCXXX	650	DCL	670	DCLXX	690	DCXC	710	DCCX	730	DCCXXX	750	DCCL	770	DCCLXX	790	DCCXC
611	DCXI	631	DCXXXI	651	DCLI	671	DCLXXI	691	DCXCI	711	DCCXI	731	DCCXXXI	751	DCCLI	771	DCCLXXI	791	DCCXCI
612	DCXII	632	DCXXXII	652	DCLII	672	DCLXXII	692	DCXCII	712	DCCXII	732	DCCXXXII	752	DCCLII	772	DCCLXXII	792	DCCXCII
613	DCXIII	633	DCXXXIII	653	DCLIII	673	DCLXXIII	693	DCXCIII	713	DCCXIII	733	DCCXXXIII	753	DCCLIII	773	DCCLXXIII	793	DCCXCIII
614	DCXIV	634	DCXXXIV	654	DCLIV	674	DCLXXIV	694	DCXCIV	714	DCCXIV	734	DCCXXXIV	754	DCCLIV	774	DCCLXXIV	794	DCCXCIV
615	DCXV	635	DCXXXV	655	DCLV	675	DCLXXV	695	DCXCV	715	DCCXV	735	DCCXXXV	755	DCCLV	775	DCCLXXV	795	DCCXCV
616	DCXVI	636	DCXXXVI	656	DCLVI	676	DCLXXVI	696	DCXCVI	716	DCCXVI	736	DCCXXXVI	756	DCCLVI	776	DCCLXXVI	796	DCCXCVI
617	DCXVII	637	DCXXXVII	657	DCLVII	677	DCLXXVII	697	DCXCVII	717	DCCXVII	737	DCCXXXVII	757	DCCLVII	777	DCCLXXVII	797	DCCXCVII
618	DCXVIII	638	DCXXXVIII	658	DCLVIII	678	DCLXXVIII	698	DCXCVIII	718	DCCXVIII	738	DCCXXXVIII	758	DCCLVIII	778	DCCLXXVIII	798	DCCXCVIII
619	DCXIX	639	DCXXXIX	659	DCLIX	679	DCLXXIX	699	DCXCIX	719	DCCXIX	739	DCCXXXIX	759	DCCLIX	779	DCCLXXIX	799	DCCXCIX
620	DCXX	640	DCXL	660	DCLX	680	DCLXXX	700	DCC	720	DCCXX	740	DCCXL	760	DCCLX	780	DCCLXXX	800	DCCC

801-820		821-840		841-860		861-880		881-900		901-920		921-940		941-960		961-980		981-1,000	
801	DCCCI	821	DCCCXXI	841	DCCCXLI	861	DCCCLXI	881	DCCCLXXXI	901	CMI	921	CMXXI	941	CMXLI	961	CMLXI	981	CMLXXXI
802	DCCCII	822	DCCCXXII	842	DCCCXLII	862	DCCCLXII	882	DCCCLXXXII	902	CMII	922	CMXXII	942	CMXLII	962	CMLXII	982	CMLXXXII
803	DCCCIII	823	DCCCXXIII	843	DCCCXLIII	863	DCCCLXIII	883	DCCCLXXXIII	903	CMIII	923	CMXXIII	943	CMXLIII	963	CMLXIII	983	CMLXXXIII
804	DCCCIV	824	DCCCXXIV	844	DCCCXLIV	864	DCCCLXIV	884	DCCCLXXXIV	904	CMIV	924	CMXXIV	944	CMXLIV	964	CMLXIV	984	CMLXXXIV
805	DCCCV	825	DCCCXXV	845	DCCCXLV	865	DCCCLXV	885	DCCCLXXXV	905	CMV	925	CMXXV	945	CMXLV	965	CMLXV	985	CMLXXXV
806	DCCCVI	826	DCCCXXVI	846	DCCCXLVI	866	DCCCLXVI	886	DCCCLXXXVI	906	CMVI	926	CMXXVI	946	CMXLVI	966	CMLXVI	986	CMLXXXVI
807	DCCCVII	827	DCCCXXVII	847	DCCCXLVII	867	DCCCLXVII	887	DCCCLXXXVII	907	CMVII	927	CMXXVII	947	CMXLVII	967	CMLXVII	987	CMLXXXVII
808	DCCCVIII	828	DCCCXXVIII	848	DCCCXLVIII	868	DCCCLXVIII	888	DCCCLXXXVIII	908	CMVIII	928	CMXXVIII	948	CMXLVIII	968	CMLXVIII	988	CMLXXXVIII
809	DCCCIX	829	DCCCXXIX	849	DCCCXLIX	869	DCCCLXIX	889	DCCCLXXXIX	909	CMIX	929	CMXXIX	949	CMXLIX	969	CMLXIX	989	CMLXXXIX
810	DCCCX	930	DCCCXXX	850	DCCCL	870	DCCCLXX	890	DCCCXC	910	CMX	930	CMXXX	950	CML	970	CMLXX	990	CMXC
811	DCCCXI	831	DCCCXXXI	851	DCCCLI	871	DCCCLXXI	891	DCCCXCI	911	CMXI	931	CMXXXI	951	CMLI	971	CMLXXI	991	CMXCI
812	DCCCXII	832	DCCCXXXII	852	DCCCLII	872	DCCCLXXII	892	DCCCXCII	912	CMXII	932	CMXXXII	952	CMLII	972	CMLXXII	992	CMXCII
813	DCCCXIII	833	DCCCXXXIII	853	DCCCLIII	873	DCCCLXXIII	893	DCCCXCIII	913	CMXIII	933	CMXXXIII	953	CMLIII	973	CMLXXIII	993	CMXCIII
814	DCCCXIV	834	DCCCXXXIV	854	DCCCLIV	874	DCCCLXXIV	894	DCCCXCIV	914	CMXIV	934	CMXXXIV	954	CMLIV	974	CMLXXIV	994	CMXCIV
815	DCCCXV	835	DCCCXXXV	855	DCCCLV	875	DCCCLXXV	895	DCCCXCV	915	CMXV	935	CMXXXV	955	CMLV	975	CMLXXV	995	CMXCV
816	DCCCXVI	836	DCCCXXXVI	856	DCCCLVI	876	DCCCLXXVI	896	DCCCXCVI	916	CMXVI	936	CMXXXVI	956	CMLVI	976	CMLXXVI	996	CMXCVI
817	DCCCXVII	837	DCCCXXXVII	857	DCCCLVII	877	DCCCLXXVII	897	DCCCXCVII	917	CMXVII	937	CMXXXVII	957	CMLVII	977	CMLXXVII	997	CMXCVII
818	DCCCXVIII	838	DCCCXXXVIII	858	DCCCLVIII	878	DCCCLXXVIII	898	DCCCXCVIII	918	CMXVIII	938	CMXXXVIII	958	CMLVIII	978	CMLXXVIII	998	CMXCVIII
819	DCCCXIX	839	DCCCXXXIX	859	DCCCLIX	879	DCCCLXXIX	899	DCCCXCIX	919	CMXIX	939	CMXXXIX	959	CMLIX	979	CMLXXIX	999	CMXCIX
820	DCCCXX	840	DCCCXL	860	DCCCLX	880	DCCCLXXX	900	CM	920	CMXX	940	CMXL	960	CMLX	980	CMLXXX	1000	M

Index

Index

Index